The Cupboard Under the Stairs

Paul Mason is a writer. He also delivers victim-focused training and inspirational talks to professionals and support agencies working in the field of child sexual abuse. He has helped influence service standards for male victims of abuse. As part of his voluntary work, he created and subsidised the influential Systematic Abuse of Males (SAM) programme, for which he won the Una Padel Outstanding Individual of the Year award for 2009, presented by the Centre for Crime and Justice Studies. He now lives on an island with his three dogs.

PAUL MASON

The Cupboard Under the Stairs

A Boy Trapped in Hell . . .

MAINSTREAM
PUBLISHING

EDINBURGH AND LONDON

First published in Great Britain in 2013 by
MAINSTREAM PUBLISHING COMPANY
(EDINBURGH) LTD
7 Albany Street
Edinburgh EH1 3UG

ISBN 9781845967895

This book is a work of non-fiction based on the life, experiences and
recollections of the author. In some limited cases names of people have been
changed to protect the privacy of others. The author has stated to the
publishers that, except in such minor respects not affecting the substantial
accuracy of the work, the contents of this book are true

A catalogue record for this book is available
from the British Library

Printed in Great Britain by
CPI Group (UK) Ltd, Croydon, CR0 4YY

1 3 5 7 9 10 8 6 4 2

Enjoy life, but be attentive. Don't think there are no beasts just because the forest is silent.

Acknowledgements

This has been a difficult book to write, not only because it contains my innermost thoughts and details of what happened to me throughout my life but also because it primarily concerns my blood-relative family. Although he is no longer with us, I love my brother as much as any brother could. Likewise, even though as a child I did not understand her behaviour, my mother will remain someone whom I love and for whom I have much sympathy. Like many others, she was a victim of a monster who called himself a father.

I know that there will be some who read this book and condemn it as a breach of privacy and perhaps trust, a story that should never have been shared or put into print. While I can understand that some people would prefer that this difficult subject was not openly discussed, the truth of the matter is that if we are to save children from suffering or help victims to recover, then there is a need to know and understand as much as we can about paedophiles and child sex offenders and the true legacy of their vile actions. I have not sensationalised my life or the incidents that fill it, and nor have I ever wanted to. What you read here is the product of a lifetime's experience; it is the grim reality of a nightmarish existence. I feel certain that similar abuse is happening to other children right now.

The vast majority of people who have endured child sexual abuse have no objection to being called 'victims'. It is a popular misconception, created by those working in the support network field, that instead we like to be categorised as 'survivors'. It's absolute nonsense and political correctness gone wild. As far as I am aware, the last thing any abused person concerns themselves with is what they are classed as, a victim or a survivor. Ultimately, we are all human beings. No one, especially an innocent child, deserves to be manipulated, imprisoned and abused by a parent, guardian or any adult. I use the term 'victim' frequently in this book, not because I am seeking sympathy or because it's an emotive term, but because that is what anyone who suffers unwarranted abuse or harm is: a victim.

I have written several books on various subjects, and ordinarily I can produce pages of people who merit thanks for their positive part in the creation of the work; in this instance, writing the acknowledgements is a far more difficult exercise. Some people, for obvious reasons, I prefer not to name, so that their privacy is maintained. I have deliberately kept many of the people mentioned in these pages as anonymous as is possible. That is my wish, not anyone else's, and I do it out of respect for them and their families.

My two wonderful children have been there beside me for every step of this difficult journey. A thank you is not enough. The greatest accolade I can give is that I trust you and I will always love you. I want to thank Detective Sergeant Chris Churchman of the Metropolitan Police. If a man could ever be described as an angel, then it is he. My mistrust of the police and the prosecutorial legal system they operate within (not the judiciary) is not without reason. It is not the result of bitterness, paranoia or animosity. For more than three decades, I was a serving police officer and during that time I witnessed all kinds of corruption, unlawful activities and deliberate incompetence, all supposedly in the name of the law. Chris Churchman, however, is the consummate professional. If any police force should ever wish to seek guidance on how to treat and properly deal with a victim of child sexual abuse, then I would beg them to seek out Chris. Throughout the police investigation, he was a beacon shining brightly above the sea of investigative bureaucracy and legal jargon that often defies logic. Of one thing I am certain: if more police officers adopted his approach, more victims would come forward and speak out and more sexually motivated crime would be solved. Had it not been for Chris, I might well have given up on pursuing my case.

I also want to mention (not thank or praise) the Crown Prosecution Service (CPS). Their crass and inept attitude and lack of understanding was unbelievable, a great example of how lopsided the English legal system is, falling on the side of the paedophile because the case was historical and therefore some witnesses were ill or dead. They failed me by allowing my father to walk away free. Even the police were alarmed by their decision not to prosecute.

Looking back over my life, I see that there have been several positive influences that have kept me focused on everyday living, not least the actor Adam West, who is best known for his portrayal of the Caped Crusader, Batman. For me, there is no other actor who portrayed Batman and the fight between good and evil as accurately as he did. Had Bob Kane and Bill Finger never initially created Batman, the likelihood is I would not be writing these words. It was Batman who helped me survive my childhood, so I place on record my appreciation to those three individuals and pledge my lifelong allegiance to Batman.

As I grew out of childhood, I found new heroes, those representing Leeds United football club. Despite having had a professional association (books and various writings) with what was at the time my local team (Carlisle FC), my real passion has always been Leeds United. Elland Road became my surrogate home, a place where I felt part of a unique family, where no one judged or ostracised me, a place where I could scream with joy and elation, or, in more recent times, frustration. The late Bill Shankly was right when he said football was much more than a game; for me, it provided a life. I am proud to wear the mark of Leeds United permanently, in the shape of a tattoo on my left arm. Leeds is a city where I once lived and served in the police force, the place where my daughter was born and which my son visits every other week of the football season. It's the greatest city in the world and, for me, that stems from its football team: marching on together.

I want to say a big thank you to Bill Campbell and his excellent team at Mainstream, who have provided support throughout the work and kept me focused on the task. Your efforts are greatly appreciated.

Finally, I hope this book provides hope and inspiration for the many thousands of victims of child sexual abuse across the world. It's a harrowing and often arduous journey we make, with more dead ends than open highways. Despite everything (and in my case that includes the obvious failures of the English legal system in the form of the CPS), we must keep travelling the route, always looking forward and never behind, never standing still until we know we are safe. Sometimes we may feel as though the light at the end of the tunnel is nothing more than another steam train thundering towards us, ready to plough into us and take us back to a place we no longer choose to be. But that's what is important. We *do* have freedom of choice. We can achieve, and no, we aren't different; it's society that has the problem, not us. If we don't stand tall and proud, express our concerns and tell our stories, no matter how unpalatable they may be to others, the world will never know. Together, we can do it.

Paul Mason
April 2013

Contents

Introduction

'Please, Dad, please, please let me out. I don't like it. I'm frightened. I'm scared. Please, Dad, please let me out.' My frantic pleas went unheeded. No matter how much I sobbed and begged to be let out, every scream, cry and noise I made was totally ignored. As a three-year-old child, an innocent little boy, my crime had been to live, to be born to a vile and disgusting man who portrayed himself as a paragon of virtue, a father and a highly respected serving police officer.

This was the first time I had been put in the cupboard under the stairs. It was a place I feared; for me, it had the reputation and appearance of a dark and dingy hole. My father would constantly remind me and my older brother, John, that it was the entrance to hell. 'That's the place where naughty boys are put. At the very back lives the Devil. He drags naughty little boys from there down into the ground and into hell.' You can imagine the fear that the mere mention of that place induced. He would regularly use it as a frightener, staring at us with mean intent, then glancing towards the crooked door that was the entrance to the cupboard under the stairs.

What an absolutely vile thing for a father to tell his sons. No normal parent would consider tormenting the minds of young, innocent children so peculiarly. But my father was no ordinary person; he was evil personified, an absolute bastard of a man. I will no longer refer to him in this work as 'dad' or 'father'. In real life, my brother and I called him 'it' or 'Jack', so, from here, I will refer to that person as 'Jack'.

On that day, I had been sitting in the living room and, as had become normal practice, I tried to remain invisible to him, since even at that tender age I knew that he didn't like me or want me around him. Jack made it clear to me that I was anything but wanted. He would constantly remind me that 'little boys should be seen and not heard'.

This time, I had been ordered to sit on the floor in front of him, close to a roaring coal fire. I was stripped naked and had no idea of what was to come. He sat close to me, almost crouching over me. I can vividly remember the sickly smell of stale cigarette smoke that seemed to be a part of him and oozed from his skin and mouth, caused by a lifetime of relentless smoking, 50 or 60 a day. More importantly for me, I recall every word he uttered to me that day and I can still see the hatred he held for me in his cold, black-looking eyes as he began his personal crusade for complete control of a small child, his own son.

'Do you know how much you get on my tits? You are a real pain in the arse. You're the little boy who isn't wanted. You shouldn't be here. You shouldn't exist,' he told me. Although I was a young child, I was able to understand the meaning of those words. They served their purpose. Each time he reminded me of these facts, I became more subservient to him, feeling I should be grateful to him for giving me life. I was scared because, naively, I thought he was going to send me back to the place where he had first found me, the shop or wherever it might have been that he had got me from. Worse still, maybe he would send me to meet the Devil in the cupboard under the stairs. That cupboard – its contents and all it stood for – still terrifies me to this day. The fear of incarceration in a dark, confined space has ruled much of my life. I'm not ashamed to say that I am scared of the dark and all the shadowy secrets it holds.

The absence of paternal love and affection in the three short years of my existence had caused me to believe that I was nothing more than a toy to him, not even human, let alone a little boy with a child's needs, feelings and emotions. My role in life was to be an object of derision and a whipping-boy he could shout at or slap, punch or kick whenever he was angry or upset about something, which seemed to be much of the time. It didn't necessarily have to be me who caused him pain or grief; I was simply the punchbag on which he could vent his aggression.

On the occasion in question, I innocently asked him why, if he didn't want me, had he got me. I didn't like the way he made me feel and desperately wanted to stop doing whatever it was that made him despise me so much. All I really wanted was for him to pick me up and give me a caring cuddle, to make me feel loved and wanted and a part of the family, rather than something to be ignored. 'Get you?' he roared back at me. 'I didn't get you. I wouldn't want something as pathetic as you. We didn't get you. You were presented to us. You came from here.' He was pointing at his trousers.

I had done it again, agitated and upset him. He rose to his feet, fumbling at the fly of his trousers, before pulling out his penis. 'You came out of here. That's the end of my cock. Like wee, you were pissed out.' He made me stand up. 'Kiss my cock. Kiss the end of my cock, you little bastard. See what it tastes like. This is where you came from. This is part of you.'

Without warning, he grabbed hold of my head with both of his hands and pulled my face towards his penis. 'Kiss it, I said,' he yelled. I didn't want to go anywhere near the thing, yet I knew it was something I had to do. I had seen my mother and my brother kissing it, my mother when they were in bed and Jack had asked me to get in beside them, and my brother in the bathroom, so I accepted that it was part of my life, something we all had to do to him. I moved forward and quickly kissed its end and instantly pulled my head away. The smell of stale wee and cigarettes was sickening.

'Do it again. This time, put it in your mouth or I'll have to force it in there.' Again, he yanked my head towards him. With one hand, he was stroking it up and down, and I remember thinking how ugly it looked. I hoped my own would never look or smell so awful. I became anxious and began to cry. I begged him to let me go, but he had his other hand clamped firmly round the back of my neck and lower head. 'Put the fucking thing in your mouth,' he demanded. Something inside told me that if I did this, my life would never be the same, yet I had no alternative. I closed my eyes, opened my mouth and felt it go inside. He jerked it forward and shouted at me, 'Suck it, suck it.' It was horrible. It tasted salty and he had shoved it so far into my throat that it made me gag.

Instinctively, I pulled away and dropped to the safety of the floor, pleading with him to leave me alone. Looking up, I saw him stroking it with faster and more vigorous movements. His facial expression changed from one of anger and hatred to one of pleasure. Before I knew it, he ejaculated all over my naked body. I moved to get out of its way and some fell onto the fireside rug where I lay.

'You stupid little boy, why did you move?' he said, wiping the end of his penis with a handkerchief, which he immediately put back into his trouser pocket. He was panting like a dog as he crouched over me. 'Look at me and listen. I didn't want you, nor did your mother, nor does anyone else. You are here because no one else wanted you, so you have to do everything I say. You are mine, do you understand that? You are a replacement child.'

I felt scared and confused. I didn't understand what he meant, so I asked him. 'You are nothing more than a replacement for my little boy who is no longer with us. He was my little boy. His name was Robert. If he had been here, you wouldn't exist. The only reason you are here is because the doctor told me to have another child. You were never wanted or needed. Do you understand? You are a replacement child. Remember that for the rest of your life. You are the little boy who nobody wanted. No one will ever take any notice of you or believe anything you say. You will always be second best.'

I still wasn't certain what he meant by all of this. However, I wanted to know more about Robert and where he was now, so again I asked. 'How dare you mention a thing like that to me? Robert was my son. He is nothing to do with you. I don't ever want to hear you mention his name again. You won't speak of him again, do you understand? You are nothing to this family, so don't ever talk of him again.'

In my innocence, I had expected Jack to say something along the lines of Robert had moved away or he was in heaven; instead, I received more threats. Again, I asked where Robert was and why he was no longer here. That was it, without warning, Jack picked up a metal ruler, which he often used for drawings of electrical diagrams, from a nearby table. He raised it in the air above my head and smacked it down onto my scalp. He held it side-on to inflict the maximum pain and damage. I felt the edge slice open my scalp and screamed out as blood instantly began to run down my face and into my eyes. I couldn't see and my head felt like it had been ripped wide open. I was inconsolable and yelling out in agony; it was the worst pain imaginable.

The Cupboard Under the Stairs

My crying and screaming were my downfall. He lifted me from the floor and put me under his arm. 'I told you not to mention his name again. Robert is dead. Now that's it. You know where you're going now, don't you? You're going to meet the Devil. Unless you shut up, he'll come and get you. Now be quiet.' In one movement, he pulled open the door and threw me into the place I so feared: the cupboard under the stairs. I had barely landed on the concrete floor when the door slammed shut behind me and the bolt slid across to prevent my escape.

It was pitch black in there and I was petrified. It was as cold, dark and inhospitable as I had imagined it to be. My cries went unheeded. I felt suffocated by the gloom of that rotten place. The blood continued to drip down my face and, with no clothes to wipe it away with, I was forced to use my arms and hands to clear it. My vision was impaired by blood, tears and above all darkness. I was shaking with fear and sobbing uncontrollably. Then I heard a scratching noise and a guttural groaning sound that seemed to come from the very back of the cupboard. I thought it was the Devil rising from hell and coming to get me, so I kept quiet and remained motionless. My heart was beating rapidly and I could hear it thumping in my chest. I sat as still as I could for what seemed like an eternity. I was terrified by everything in this dank and pitch-black hellhole.

Later, I could hear noises from the living room. It was Jack laughing and talking to himself as he watched the television. He had already forgotten I was there. He was right: I meant nothing to him or anyone else. Tears began to roll down my face and I felt scared and very much alone.

The legacy of the tiny cupboard under the stairs has lived with me ever since, 50 years so far. I can vividly recall every detail about it. Over a period of several years,

I was to get to know the feel and shape of every brick, and the perfectly formed underside of the wooden steps that ranged from the drop of step one at the back of the cupboard, its lowest point, to step six at its highest. Every part of the rough concrete floor would at one time or another slice open the skin of my legs or knees as I scrambled about in the darkness, desperately looking for a place of comfort. It was tiny, and in all I would estimate that there was sufficient room for an old-style stand-up Hoover, a few small boxes of household clutter and very little else. This most certainly was not a place for a small child.

With one of the cupboard walls being the exterior wall of the house, it was always a cold place, an ideal home and breeding ground for creepy insects such as spiders, woodlice and earwigs, and, of course, for evil monsters. The top edge of the wooden door ran parallel with the slope of the staircase, so that it was higher at one side than at the other. The space behind the door was the forgotten and unfriendly place that, I think, every house has, a place where no one truly likes to spend time. In many houses, it is the loft or attic space, but it can be anywhere that is dark and unwelcoming, that warrants no cleaning or decoration simply because it's not at all pleasant. I suspect that if people were asked to describe such places they would say there was something unsettling about them, even that they were haunted. These are places that make the hairs on the back of the neck stand upright and send shivers down the spine.

That's precisely how the cupboard under the stairs remains to me. It was to become my prison and a place I feared beyond every other horror in the entire world, a living hell created in a tiny house in Cumbria. A house or home should be a sanctuary, a place of safety for a small child. Instead, my family home was a shell that I still refer to as 'the place where I lived'. It was never a home to me, or to my mother or brother. It was made into a hell to satiate the deviant desires of the man who had the audacity to call himself my father, a man I feared until the day he died.

Chapter 1

The family

I was born at the Cumberland Infirmary, Carlisle, in 1959. For all too long a period of my life, it was not something I was glad of. Had I known of the absolutely hellish childhood that was to be forced on me, and the impact it would have on the rest of my life, then I probably would have chosen not to make any kind of entrance into this world.

My earliest recollections are of when I was probably about two years old, certainly no older. (Many of the incidents as they occurred were so traumatic as to remain with me throughout my childhood and adult life, and others have come back to me through therapy.) They are of seeing Jack beat my mother and, when he stepped in to stop the abuse, my brother (eight years older) was beaten too, though 'battered' seems a more appropriate word to describe the punishment Jack dished out. When I say beaten, I don't mean the odd slap or push. The attacks were violent and accompanied by loud verbal abuse; blood was almost always drawn as a result of punches or kicks.

I quickly learned from those early experiences that if you were a child or a woman, Jack was not a person to mess with. He liked to rule the roost, his home, by fear and control, nothing else. However, he wouldn't ever consider confronting another man, and I can recall not one occasion throughout my life when he was aggressive or abusive towards a man, or any adult outside the family.

I have no memory of what precisely it was that had caused him to explode into a frenzy of rage. Sadly, I do know that such scenes happened with great frequency. It seemed that there was some sort of disharmony between him and my mam every couple of days. This would be followed by a brief period of intense love and passion between them. It was confusing to us as children, as all the bad stuff that had gone before and which we had seen or heard seemed to be instantly forgotten.

On this occasion, John and I had been playing in the back garden when we heard my mother screaming and Jack shouting abusive names at her. I think John's reaction was the reason this incident stuck in my memory. He knew I was frightened and took hold of me and gave me a comforting cuddle; he led me to the back of the garden, behind an apple tree and well away from the house. I was told to stay there until he came out to get me. John disappeared into the house, and I felt alone and not a little scared. This was my first encounter with fear and there was nowhere to run. I waited for several minutes, then decided to go into the house after him.

As I walked into the living room, I saw Jack strike my mam in the face with the back of his right hand. It made a sickening noise and my mam was knocked to the floor by the force of the blow. It was then that John jumped between them and told him to stop it. Jack lunged at him, slapping him hard around the face with his left hand, and I saw blood spurt out of John's mouth as he too dropped to the floor. It was a scene that caused my blood to run cold, and when Jack turned and glared at me, I ran out of the house and back into the garden, where John had left me. I stood there motionless for a long time. I closed my eyes tightly, blocking out the world and believing that by doing so I would become invisible to Jack and he could not hurt me.

After a while, the shouting stopped, and a little later my mam came out to me. She seemed angry and sternly told me to get back in the house and go straight to bed. I was confused by the whole episode: the violence, my mam and John being hurt by Jack, and now my mam being angry with me and telling me to go to bed. It was still daylight and nowhere near bedtime. However, I knew not to question my mam when she was clearly so upset, so I ran as fast as I could through the living room and up the stairs into the bedroom I shared with John, slamming the door closed behind me.

John was already in bed. He was sobbing and had a handkerchief in his mouth to stem the bleeding. The blow to the head that Jack had dealt him had caused him to bite into his tongue; he had bitten a hole right through it. He told me to be quiet, to get undressed and into bed as quickly as I could and to go to sleep, as I would then be free and safe. Sleep wasn't an option. My mind was in turmoil about all that I had seen. Jack was a monster. Poor John. He quietly cried and neither Mam nor Jack came to see that he was all right. We could still hear the deep tones of Jack's voice drifting up through the floorboards. I couldn't understand what was being said properly, but John could and he told me that Jack was still saying horrid things to Mam, calling her names, and she was crying and begging him to stop. I was worried that he might still be hurting her and wanted to go and check to see she was OK. John told me to stay where I was and not to worry; she would be OK and I had to go to sleep.

The following morning, nothing was said about the incidents of the day before. Mam acted as though nothing had happened and John reminded me not to ask or say a word about it. It was as if I had imagined it all, except there were bruises on Mam's face and John's. So far as first memories go, that one is pretty abhorrent. Seeing Jack act like that towards Mam and John made me wary of him and reluctant to approach him about anything.

The house where we lived was a two-bedroom terraced house on a housing estate directly outside the main entrance to RAF Carlisle, known within the Ministry of Defence (MoD) as RAF 14MU (maintenance unit). The estate itself was called Crindledyke Estate. It consisted of just 30 houses, all pink-brick terraced properties, some with two bedrooms and some with three. The houses had been built in three separate rows. These were referred to by residents of the estate as 'the front row', 'the middle row' and 'the back row'. We lived in the back row, furthest away from the main road that ran directly in front of the estate, the A6. The back row consisted of four houses.

The estate still exists to this day and sits three miles north of Carlisle town centre. It was, in the 1960s, a beautiful environment, entirely rural. Crindledyke was surrounded by country lanes, fields and rolling hills; there were cows, sheep, trees, fresh air and very little else. The nearest shop was two miles away, and to do anything as a family, a car was needed; buses were infrequent, and while there was a station nearby, the train to Carlisle was expensive and took a long time, as it stopped at every station en route. We were the only family on the estate who had no car. Instead, Jack had a Vespa scooter and that was it. Therefore, much to his satisfaction, my mother, my brother and myself were virtually trapped on the estate.

Back in the early 1960s, every house on that estate was occupied by a male police officer and his family, all different ranks and age groups. Not one policewoman lived there. Jack was a policeman, a man who upheld the law, protected the vulnerable, defended the weak and removed the liberty of those who caused harm to others. Sounds very impressive when you say it like that, doesn't it? The reality is, Jack was an utter bastard to his family. Yet, outside the family home, he was apparently respected by his peers and regarded as someone who could turn his hand to most things and do a good job. In his spare time, he repaired televisions, radios and occasionally watches, the last being something he'd learned from his own father.

I can remember fortnightly visits to see Jack's parents, my grandparents, who lived in a suburb of Carlisle called Stanwix. It was always a Sunday when we visited. Jack would make us walk two miles from Crindledyke to their bungalow in Briar Bank. My granny, as I was to call her, clearly had no time for me. Nor did my grandad, although, when he wasn't drunk, he would allow me to sit with him while he repaired watches. More often than not, I was ignored. I would be given an old tennis ball and sent out in all weathers to play on an area of grass that lay behind their home. John would be allowed to remain in the bungalow and given biscuits and cake. He would sneak some of the biscuits out and give them to me during the walk home. Naturally, I didn't like visiting them at all.

My grandad had at one time been a police officer. Later, he turned to watch repairs and, from what I have heard, spent a great deal of time in the bookmaker's. He and Jack looked very alike: gnarled and bitter and twisted faces and an arrogant air. They were cold and calculating individuals, without a care for anyone or anything but themselves.

As far as I can recall, my granny originally hailed from Edinburgh and had been a nurse of some kind. By the time I was a child, she did nothing but sit looking into the coal fire in the tiny living room of their bungalow. I am saddened to say that I have no fond memories of these people. They didn't seem like family at all, and I recall that at Easter and Christmas and on birthdays they never sent cards or presents. It's a sad indictment of our relationship that when they passed away I felt no great emotion, and nor did John. I have never visited or felt the urge to visit either's grave.

My mother, Mary, worked part time on a fruit and vegetable stall in Carlisle market. She would catch a bus to get to and from town. Jack didn't like this, as he had no control over her when she was at work, and there were many arguments between them about it. One such disagreement came about when Jack told my mam she had to resign because the family who owned the fruit and vegetable stall were a bad influence on her. At the time, I had no idea what this meant; now, looking back, I can understand that they could see how unhappy she was in her marriage and tried to suggest options for her. The family who owned the stall were always friendly to me and John, and later in life I was to learn from them that they saw Jack for what he was: a bully and a bastard to his wife and family. So much influence did Jack hold and so manipulative was he that he managed to get Mam a job at RAF 14MU as a packer, basically packing RAF equipment into containers to be shipped around the world. I remember she worked in 'A' Shed. These sheds were huge aircraft-hangar-type buildings.

My mother's side of the family were much more normal and nicer, and I know I had proper grandparents who genuinely cared, and aunties and uncles and cousins who were loyal and open. On my mother's side, there was no pretence, no falsehoods or airs and graces, just honest family.

I called my grandparents on my mam's side Nanna and Grandad. They lived in Sheehan Crescent, Raffles, a rough, tough housing estate in Carlisle that had been forgotten by the local council and authorities. It wasn't a picturesque sort of place; instead of flowers, many front gardens were filled with washing machines, spin dryers, car parts and detritus of all types, yet despite this, or what anyone in authority might say, the people of Raffles were devoutly loyal to their own. Sure, there were bad sorts, mainly drunken fighters, and therefore the residents of the area were often regarded as the hardest in Carlisle. The Sheehan Crescent I knew as a child no longer exists in its original form; the houses are long gone, demolished by the council.

My memories of Raffles are good. When I was taken there as a child, my nanna and grandad always made us feel very welcome. The other families and children who lived in Sheehan Crescent and in nearby Dobinson Road were always pleasant to me and John, recognising us as members of a local family. Our visits were all the more pleasurable because more often than not Jack wouldn't go to Raffles. I think he found it intimidating – it was full of 'criminals and crap', he would say – so it was generally my mam who took us there. We would have to catch one bus to get us from Crindledyke into Carlisle town centre, then another out to Orton Road, Raffles, so it was always something of an adventure. Nanna would be waiting for us and welcome us with a big hug and kiss before sitting me, as the smallest child, on her knee and regaling me with stories about her own life and my mother.

One detail came to the fore in many of her stories: her strong dislike of Jack. She would repeat her mantra that he was 'a shit of a man' and tell John and me how she had never wanted our mam to marry him. One story she would tell us was about one of his rare visits to Raffles and how she threw him out of the house because of his horrible behaviour. Apparently he had given John a good hiding, causing my grandad to pin him up against the wall and threaten to batter him if he touched a child like that again. Typically, Jack didn't fight back against a man. Instead, when he was shown the door, he stood outside at a safe distance and threatened to get the police round because my nanna and grandad had assaulted him! He shouted that if my mother wanted to remain married to him and see the children again, she would have to leave with him. My nanna would say that my mam had no choice; the threat of losing her home and her children was too strong, so she went with him.

There were times when my mother's family didn't get to see my mam, John or me, all because Jack wouldn't allow contact of any sort. In the end, my uncle sorted things out and some reconciliation was achieved, but it was never completely resolved. Nanna would get very upset and cry when she told us these stories. The intense hatred she felt for Jack is something that will live with me for ever. It wasn't helped by the fact that he had said to her that he despised children because they were a drain on time, energy and resources. Children were hugely important to her. I loved Nanna. She would tell me to forgive my mam for not being able to give us enough attention, that it was because she was scared of Jack and he demanded too much.

Grandad was a builder's labourer, but I remember him for the fantastic things he would create from a solitary piece of wood: toy ships and boats, and even a lorry. It was amazing to watch him whittle away at a wooden clothes-peg and transform it into a submarine or a Grenadier Guard-style soldier.

I loved being around Nanna and Grandad, and I learned more about proper family life from them than I ever did from Jack. Their home was a sanctuary from the outside world. I always felt safe there. In their house, there was no hidden agenda; they said it as it was.

The family

When they passed away, I still wasn't very old; their deaths were traumatic experiences and left me feeling that something important was missing from my life. After my nanna died, there was some kind of family issue that resulted in Jack refusing to allow my mam to attend her own mother's funeral. Instead, she had to stand some distance away and observe from afar. He forbade her to grieve with her own family. The long-term outcome of this was that various elements of my mam's side of the family were never close to us again – a situation that no doubt pleased Jack, since it helped him to dominate my mam and control every aspect of her life.

John, my brother, was born in 1951, and while there were eight years between us, he was always there looking out for me, as far back as I can remember. In hindsight, we didn't share a typical brotherly relationship. I think we were both too damaged for that. However, he was very protective of me and would always put himself in the firing line if it would prevent me from being hurt. I suspect he did likewise for Robert when he was alive. As I grew older, I realised that John had a hatred of confrontation; he would sooner run from a fight than get involved. Yet I have so many recollections of him, throughout my childhood, voluntarily taking beatings and various forms of punishment from Jack in order to defend me or our mam.

John first mentioned Robert's death to me when I was about three or four. From the first time Jack ever said Robert's name to me, and that I was a replacement, I was curious to know more. I wanted to understand why God would take a child. Much of my early knowledge of the Mason family history was gleaned from secret bedtime discussions with John, whispers in the night that conjured all kinds of horrific images. I couldn't know that nothing my childish imagination could create would be worse than the reality of what was to come in future years.

Robert was born in 1955. At this time, the family lived in Cliff Road, Sandysike, near Longtown, a place that's closer to the Scottish Borders than to Carlisle. As on Crindledyke Estate, all the properties here were police houses, occupied by policemen and their families. Having visited Sandysike and the row of houses that remains, the main thing that strikes me about the place is its remoteness. It's simply two blocks of terraced houses that, to all intents and purposes, have been dropped in the middle of nowhere. Local history records that they were connected with the War Office and the long-defunct RAF Longtown, an airfield that came into being in 1941 and ceased to be used after the end of the Second World War.

Cliff Road was a turning directly off the main A7 trunk road, although in more recent times it has been bypassed by a newer section of the A7, which must have made the houses seem even more remote. Cliff Road itself is quiet – it doesn't lead to anywhere in particular – and back in the 1950s one imagines there was very little traffic. It was there that my parents lived with John and Robert. John always told me that it was a scary place to live and how he dreaded the night. The two rows of houses were lit by a few streetlights, but the surrounding area was bleak and very dark.

I know relatively little of the life they led there, but John would tell me that shouting and beatings were very much part of the existence that Jack forced upon his family. He was selfish and uncaring, and it was all about him being the master, the sole voice of any importance. John explained to me that Robert was very frightened of Jack and said he didn't like it when he was taken into Jack's bedroom on his own.

Nanna often mentioned Robert. She described Robert as being like a little angel, a smiling happy little boy, until

Jack's influence took hold. Then he became quiet and tearful. She would tell me that she wanted to take John and him away from Jack, to live with them in Raffles, where they could be safe and happy. She said that when my mam brought John and Robert round to visit, they would often sit on her knee and cry and say they didn't want to go home. I always felt the same when visiting her.

At the time Robert died, Jack had effectively ostracised my mother from everyone. Cliff Road was not the sort of place that was easily accessible. The family had no telephone and the only person who maintained regular contact with the world beyond Sandysike was Jack.

The story of Robert's death remains as sad to me now as it was back when I first heard it as a small child. I have managed to piece the tale together, mainly through listening to my mother and John. Jack never said much to me about it; he just used to issue threats such as: 'If you don't do as I tell you, you will end up dead like Robert.' I know he spoke to John about it, though.

It seems that on 20 September 1958 Robert was out playing in a field in front of the house, across Cliff Road and perhaps 60 yards from the house. He was apparently playing with some teenagers. I have never found out who these people were. John could not remember Robert playing in the field and said it was more normal for them to be playing in the back garden of the house.

Whatever the circumstances, the group were playing and Robert was somehow involved. An object had been thrown or kicked into a static water tank in the same field. This was MoD property and must have been ineffectively fenced off, since Robert was able to gain access to it. It was the sort of tank that one often sees elevated above buildings on government bases. It was made up of different bolted-together sections and panels and was about five feet tall, twenty feet long and eight feet wide.

For some unknown reason, Robert went to retrieve the object. None of the group playing thought anything of it, apparently, and let him, a three-year-old child, climb into the tank to recover it. Now, the dangers and difficulties facing a small child trying to retrieve an object from deep water should be obvious to anyone, even a group of teenagers.

According to Jack's version of events, relayed to me by John, one of the group came running to the house and told him Robert had fallen into the tank. Jack apparently got him out and gave him the kiss of life. The doctor had been called, and when he arrived and saw Jack giving the kiss of life to Robert, he placed his hand on Jack's shoulder and said, 'Jack, he is gone. Get Mary pregnant again as soon as you can, so you can replace Robert.' I am that replacement child.

In recent years, I have tried to find out more about Robert's death, but without much success. I have obtained a copy of his death certificate. It clearly states on the document that no post-mortem was carried out. Officials I have spoken to say this is strange, since the death wasn't the result of natural causes. A coroner can order a post-mortem when death has been the result of an accident or unusual circumstance, yet on this occasion, none was held. The death certificate merely states, 'Accidental death through drowning.' Despite my best efforts, I have been unable to locate a police report or a record of an inquest.

Chapter 2

Welcome to hell

Life at Crindledyke Estate was anything but harmonious. Looking back, it was chaotic. There always seemed to be some kind of crisis or fall-out that had to be dealt with. I quickly learned during my early years that Jack's mantra, 'Little boys should be seen and not heard', was advice that needed to be adhered to in his presence, especially when I was alone with him. As a policeman, he worked shifts, and it didn't take me long to work out when he was and wasn't going to be around. When he wasn't there, it was like a great cloud of gloom, doom and depression had been lifted from the house. The fear his very presence created evaporated and the atmosphere was totally different.

It's difficult to describe how one person can control the emotions of an entire family and influence the others' every thought, every waking moment. That was what Jack was excellent at. None of us ever knew where we stood with him. His mood swings were incredible. One moment he seemed OK, the next he was stomping around the house, swearing and lashing out at us.

Our next-door neighbours were a couple called Mollie and Eddie. Their children had grown up and moved away. They always seemed like a friendly couple, and when I used to play out in the garden, Mollie would ask how we all were and if I was OK. She had a pet budgerigar and would often lift me over the wire fence that separated the two gardens so that I could go in and see it. I remember how warm and cosy Mollie's house was compared with ours. They were identical in layout and size, yet their house just seemed much less intimidating than ours.

On one occasion, when I was about three, Jack, on learning from my mother that Mollie had taken me to see her budgerigar, came round to her house, grabbed hold of me and apologised to Mollie for my being such a nuisance and so demanding. I remember him telling Mollie, 'He's a horrible child. I don't know where he has come from sometimes, but if he doesn't behave, he'll be going back.' Mollie volunteered that it was she who had invited me in. Her words, to this day, remain prominent in my mind: 'He's a lovely little boy. He's no bother at all, Jack.'

Her kind words might have meant something to me, but they made no impact on Jack, who took hold of me and yanked me out of Mollie's house and back to our own, where my trousers were pulled down and I was laid across his knee. Marking each syllable with a slap to my bottom, he told me, 'You are a naughty boy. You will not annoy our neighbours. Little boys should be seen and not heard.' The slaps seemed to grow in ferocity, and my screams of pain and cries for mercy went unheeded, as always. Once the punishment was delivered, I was thrown to the floor and ordered to remain there until I was told I could move. With little or no understanding of what he was doing, I saw him pull down his own trousers, brown corduroys, and his string underpants and begin to stroke his hand up and down his penis. It was so wrong and I couldn't understand why he wasn't at all bothered about me lying there in tears. I felt ill, so I closed my eyes and didn't open them for a few moments. Then he told me to get up and go to my bed.

I can't recall where my mam was when this happened. She had been in the house but had disappeared when Jack dragged me in from Mollie's. Later in life, I was told by Mollie that my mam would frequently go round to speak to her when Jack was on the rampage or, as she put it, 'when he was in one of his moods'. This went some way to explaining where my mam was during some of Jack's attacks on us children. Her tendency to disappear meant that we often had to face Jack very much on our own. She was frequently absent at the worst times, but John and I never discussed this fact or even mentioned it.

Mollie's husband, Eddie, rarely said a word or paid any attention to us. He seemed to be one of those people who just get on with their lives, people who don't want to know about let alone get involved in other people's problems. There certainly wasn't any kind of friendship between him and Jack. The odd nod of acknowledgement was as far as it went between the pair.

On the other side, there lived the Smith family. They were kind, considerate and had their own children, both of whom were older than me. The Smiths moved to the Highlands of Scotland for a while, before returning several years later. Mr Smith once came round during a heated argument and asked Jack if there was some kind of problem. He asked to speak with my mam. John and I were listening from our bedroom and could hear Mam begging Mr Smith to leave it be and go back to his home, telling him it was just an argument and no one was being hurt. I often wonder how different our lives might have been had people like Mr Smith acted on their perceptions. He clearly knew violence was occurring, but without real evidence he could do nothing to prevent it.

When I was a little older than three, I ran away from home. It was shortly after my birthday, which was the first major disappointment of my life. In the build-up to the day, my mam had made a big thing about good boys getting what they wanted at Christmas and especially on their birthdays. I was asked what my favourite toy was. Living near an RAF base did have its merits for a small child; every day, dozens of lorries of all sizes and types would enter the base through its main gate, which was about 100 yards from our house. I would gaze in wonderment at multi-wheeled monsters as they transported RAF and Ministry of Defence property to and from the base. So it was that I told my mam that I'd like a little lorry to play with. I knew the very sort I wanted; I had seen one of the other children on the estate playing with one. It was a model Seddon about a foot long. It looked fantastic to me, every bit as good as the real thing.

The night before the big day, Jack, in his inimitable style, asked if I was excited about my birthday and receiving presents. He reminded me that only good little boys got the presents they wanted and asked if I thought I had been good. I told him yes, I thought I had been a good boy. That was the moment he first told me of a thing he said he had watching me day and night. He called it 'Brookie'. It wasn't so much the name as the tone of his voice when he said it that scared me. My imagination ran riot, conjuring terrifying images. Brookie instantly became symbolic of everything I was afraid of. It was my every fear and worst nightmare all rolled into one.

Jack looked at me in a suspicious way, his eyes like slits and his brow furrowed. 'Brookie tells me that you haven't been a good boy, that you have been a horrid little boy who deserves to be smacked and given no presents at all.' I didn't respond because I was so frightened that this thing was close by and watching me. I felt that it knew what I was thinking.

I asked to go to bed. My mam intervened and told me

that I should, and to wash my hands and face before doing so. She said she would be up shortly to put my light out. This reassured me a bit, but I didn't feel safe. The bedroom I shared with John was at the back of the house. It was always very dark, even in the summer, especially so with the thick curtain we had permanently hanging in the window.

I went to bed feeling more than a little scared. In every dark corner, I imagined Brookie watching me. After a few hours, I heard John come in. He'd been out playing with his friends. He didn't hang about downstairs and came straight to bed. Not wishing to disturb me, he didn't put the light on. He shuffled about in the darkness, fumbling his way round the bedroom. 'Are you awake?' I heard him whisper. I told him I was and immediately explained that Brookie was in the room and to be careful because he reported everything back to Jack. He must have been able to tell by my voice how frightened I was, but for some reason he seemed loath to discuss it, advising me to forget it and go to sleep. I tried, but it didn't happen, and soon John and I were chatting away in whispers.

He told me that Jack had told him about Brookie too but had added something altogether more frightening to his tale. He said that Jack had explained that deep inside the mattresses of our beds were creatures called 'ghoulash'. These things lay in hiding and when roused would eat the flesh of naughty little boys. I began to cry, but John quickly calmed me down by saying that he had killed all the ghoulash in our room, so there was nothing for me to worry about.

We were forced into silence when we heard Jack climb the stairs and begin to get ready for work on the night shift. Even though it was night-time and we probably wouldn't have seen anything of him, we were glad to hear him leaving. It was always a relief when he was going to be out of the house, as it meant he wasn't about to hit us or tell us off simply for being there. Within a few minutes, we heard the front door close and, for eight hours at least, he was gone from our lives.

We must have fallen asleep, because the next thing I knew, John was standing on his bed screaming and pointing at the wall. His eyes were bulging and he was as white as a sheet. He was shouting, 'Brookie, Brookie!' I began to scream too. Having heard our terror-filled voices, Mam burst into the room and switched on the light. For a split second, I thought I saw a tall, well-built, dark, hooded figure standing where my brother pointed. It didn't look like a shadow. It seemed three-dimensional and very real. It looked like a man with a face that was gnarled and tired; it looked weary. In the blink of an eye, it was gone. John collapsed on the bed, crying and repeating out loud that Brookie was in our room.

My mam gave us a reassuring cuddle before putting us both back into bed and telling us to go back to sleep. John wouldn't be pacified and couldn't stop crying. 'Mam, Mam, Brookie is here. I saw him stood there. He had a hood on like a monk and he was angry.' Again, he pointed to the very spot where I too had seen the hooded figure. My mam asked me if I had seen anything. I was so worried by Brookie that I couldn't speak, so I nodded my head to let her know I had. I hadn't described what I had seen to anyone, so I felt sure John must have seen the same hooded figure as I had. To a child, this could mean only one thing: Brookie was real – he existed!

What my mother told us then was one of the most disturbing things anyone had ever said to me. Sitting at the end of my bed, she told us the following story: 'Many years ago, when your father used to work near Longtown, he would go to work on a police bicycle. His patrol area often took him through woodland and quiet country lanes and tracks. He had to carry out his patrols throughout the night, checking the security of houses, buildings and other sensitive areas before cycling to a police call box and phoning in to report "all correct" and state the location he had checked.

'One night shift, he was out patrolling on his bicycle. It was the dead of night and there was no light anywhere. He heard a growling voice repeatedly calling out his name, so he stopped and listened. He heard the voice again, calling out his name over and over. Then, in the distance, he saw something; it was a hooded figure, like a monk. It raised its arm and beckoned him to come over, so he did. As he neared it, he saw its face. He said it was the Devil. It had a long pointed face, pointed ears, a large hooked nose, two bright-red eyes, a forked tongue and two horns coming out of the top of its head.

'The creature grabbed hold of his hand and told him that he should not be frightened, that he was not alone and to call out if he ever needed its help. It told him that every man has good and bad in him, and it's easy to be confused by the two because each man has his own needs and desires. The creature told him he could fulfil his needs, but there would be sacrifices he had to make to achieve what he wanted. All he had to do was shake hands with the creature and it would look after him. He shook the creature's hand before cycling straight back to Cliff Road and calling in to the station to report sick. He was ill for a few days and wouldn't speak again about the encounter. Your father has been haunted by this creature, the Devil or whatever you want to call it, ever since that night.'

I was stunned and completely traumatised by the tale. My mam wasn't the sort of person to want to deliberately frighten us and part of me still thinks that she told us the story because she herself was frightened. I imagine Jack told her the story in an attempt to control her through fear, or to somehow justify his abusive behaviour by telling her he was 'special' or 'chosen'. I don't know if she believed in the literal truth of it or not. I think, in her own way, she may have been trying to warn us that Jack was a bad man. Whatever her reasons, it definitely wasn't the right thing to tell two children, one aged ten and one aged nearly three. When she left our bedroom, John and I were plunged back into darkness and decided that it would be safer to sleep in the same bed, so I climbed in beside him.

The following morning, it was my birthday, and the terrors of the night before were quickly forgotten as I skipped down the stairs, excited at the thought of this being my special day. I pushed open the door at the foot of the stairs, which opened directly onto the living room. I was greeted by the stark reality that there were no presents on view. There was no sign of a toy lorry or anything else, no special greeting or celebrations. To all intents and purposes, it was just another day. I was disappointed and wanted to cry.

I was too scared to ask if I had any presents. Jack hadn't yet gone to bed and was loitering downstairs. He had got home late from his night shift and wanted a cooked breakfast. My mam was faffing about after him, making his breakfast, attempting to keep him happy. He sat in his usual armchair, looking thoroughly miserable and completely pissed off at my appearance. 'Paul,' he called to me, 'come here, right now.' I knew from the tone of his voice that this was not a happy Jack, so without delay I did as I was asked. I stood in front of him, his skinny frame draped in the armchair. 'Go fetch my slippers from upstairs, now.' I ran up the stairs and went into his bedroom, grabbed his slippers and came back down. I was like a puppy dog eager to please its master. I bent down and placed them on his feet.

Meanwhile, my mother was serving up his cooked breakfast. John and I had our usual bowl of cereal in the kitchen, while Mam and Jack ate their food off trays in the living room. John was looking anxious about something, intense and almost frightened. He was pushing his cereal around the bowl and hardly ate any of it. He leaned across the table towards me and whispered that he had some sweets for me in the bedroom. They were his birthday present to me and he would give them to me later. It felt good that someone had remembered and cared.

As was usual, John and I had to wait until we were called through from the kitchen. This was one of Jack's rules; my mother rarely enforced it when she was alone with us. In fact, when it was just the three of us, we usually ate together. After what seemed like an eternity, Jack called me through to the living room. He hadn't moved from the armchair. 'Remember what I said,' he told me. 'Naughty boys don't get presents. Brookie came to see me last night. He said he had come to see you as well and that you have been a very bad boy, Paul. But you have got a present.' He reached down beside his chair and produced a small, scratched and well-used multicoloured ball. 'Here you are. Happy birthday. Now go and play in the garden with it, but watch the plants.'

I was elated. I had got a birthday present. Sure, it wasn't a lorry or anything like that, but what I had was just as significant: a second-hand ball meant that someone cared. I thanked him and my mam and rushed outside.

John wasn't allowed out to play with me. When I went inside to find him, Mam said he had been taken upstairs by Jack and that I wasn't to go upstairs or I might disturb them and make Jack angry. I wondered what was happening and whether it was something to do with seeing Brookie the night before. It seemed like John was being treated specially. For a moment, I felt jealous; it was my birthday, not his, yet he was getting additional attention. It didn't seem fair at all.

I returned to the garden and tossed the ball in the air, kicked it, rolled it, threw it, bounced it. There's only so much a small child can do to keep himself amused with a ball, especially when he is playing alone. I stopped when I heard a tiny scream. It sounded like John. I stood still and listened. John was crying. It wasn't a sobbing cry but more of a pain-induced outburst. He was being hurt by something or someone.

I ran back into the house. My mam was standing at the kitchen sink washing the dishes. She was singing and seemed oblivious to the world around her. I pulled at her pinny to get her attention. I told her that I could hear John crying upstairs, that the noises were coming from their bedroom window, which was open. I asked her if John was all right, because I was scared Brookie might be hurting him.

The look on her face was one of absolute panic; her eyes widened and her jaw dropped. Her response wasn't at all what I expected. She told me, 'Go back outside and play with your ball, there's a good boy. John is with your father. Just ignore the noises. I'm sure he'll be down to play ball with you very soon.' The significance of Brookie seemed lost on her. I was worried that this thing, this entity, might have got both John and Jack (although my only real concern was for my brother). Mam didn't seem to think that Brookie posed a threat, however, so I was forced to trust her judgement and went back outside.

In the garden, I could still hear the crying and sobbing noises coming from the upstairs bedroom. John seemed to be very upset, but there wasn't any shouting or screaming, so I believed that Jack wasn't hurting him. In fact, I heard Jack's dull tones telling John to be quiet and reassuring him that everything would be all right. The next thing, a hand appeared under the net curtain and pulled the window shut.

I was bored playing with a ball on my own, but I made happy and excited noises in the faint hope that John would hear, believe that I was having great fun and that he was missing out on something and therefore come downstairs and join me. It didn't happen. I was out there on my own for most of the morning.

I needed the toilet, so I ran back into the house to find Mam. She wasn't in the kitchen or the living room. I decided to go to the bathroom by myself and clambered up the stairs. It is something that I now greatly regret doing, for what I saw was not only confusing but made me physically sick. Jack was standing absolutely naked in the centre of the bathroom. On his knees in front of him was John. He was naked too. Neither of them saw me. Jack had his hands around his penis. I heard John say, 'No more, Dad, please no more. I don't want it in my mouth any more. I'm going to be sick.' Then I saw Jack pull back before covering John's face and body with wee. My brother's tearful eyes were filled with sadness and horror, and he was clearly being forced to do something he found wrong. I could see on his body red marks where he had been slapped and hit. It was devastating, witnessing my brother being humiliated like that. I ran back downstairs to find my mam to tell her what Jack was doing to John.

I looked everywhere, but she wasn't to be found. My need for the toilet was getting all the more urgent, so I went out into the back garden. There was no way I was going upstairs to the bathroom again, so I peed into a drain next to the back door. 'Paul Mason, what are you doing?' I heard a voice call out. When I looked up, Mollie and my mam were standing on the neighbours' side of the garden fence. They had caught me in the act. Mollie was laughing and asked me why I didn't use the bathroom. Behind her, my mam stared at me with a pleading and sorrowful look that melted me; there was no way that I would ever defy her or deliberately get her into any trouble. I didn't reply to Mollie's question. Instead, I ran to show her the ball I had got for my birthday. My indiscretion was pretty much forgotten there and then.

My mam saw the anguished look on my face and bent over the fence to lift me onto Mollie's side. I was again taken to see her budgerigar and was given half a Bounty bar as a treat for my birthday. We stayed at Mollie's for what felt like a long time before my mam made a move to go home. As soon as we got into the house, she went into a state of panic. She told me to stay downstairs. She rushed up to the bedroom she shared with Jack, firmly closing the door behind her as she entered. I could hear the muffled sound of a discussion between them.

I waited, but no one came downstairs, so I wandered up to my bedroom, where I found John sitting on the end of his bed. He looked very sad and very lost. I sat down next to him and gave him a big hug. He said he didn't want to talk to anyone, but he gave me a brief cuddle in return and told me that once he was old enough he was going to leave home. This statement worried me, because I didn't know how old you had to be to leave home and whether in John's case it was imminent. 'I really hate him, Paul. I hate him. He is a cruel, evil bastard,' he blurted out, before bursting into tears. I told him to talk quietly because Brookie or Jack might hear him. I gave him the biggest hug I could in the hope that I could squeeze the sadness and pain from him. I hated to see John upset and hurting so much. That was the first time I remember feeling emotional loyalty for anyone. I desperately wanted to make him feel better.

The moment didn't last long. My heart missed a beat when I heard a noise by the bedroom door. I looked up to see Jack standing with his arms by his sides in an aggressive pose, although the overall brutish image was somewhat diminished as he was dressed in nothing more than a pair of string underpants. His face was distorted and he looked angry. He yelled out, 'Evil! Fucking evil, am I? I'll show you what fucking evil is, you little sod.'

He lunged at John and grabbed him by the face, yanking him off the bed before punching him in the stomach. I was sent flying off the bed and the force of the punch caused John to vomit on the bedroom floor. Jack dropped him to the ground, gave him a slight kick on the leg and stood looking down at us both. I could see that he was trembling with anger as he pointed at the stream of sick on the bedroom carpet. I was crying. I could hear myself sobbing and pleading with him to stop hurting John and to get out and leave us alone. He snapped back at me, 'I'll hurt who I want. You'll be next if you don't shut your mouth. Now stop snivelling and clean that fucking mess up right now.' He stomped out of the bedroom in military goose-step fashion, his scrawny legs seemingly having a life of their own. He slammed the door closed behind him. For now, it was over and we were safe.

This was bad. I knew it was bad because John didn't move. He lay there looking broken and beaten. This wasn't at all how I imagined a birthday should be. In fact, if this was how they were always going to be, then I didn't ever want another birthday. I desperately wanted someone to save us, to get us out of the house and to make it all better. I wanted Jack gone; I wanted him dead.

It was as though, to Jack, John and I were the enemy; we were hated in the house where we lived. I wasn't sure how the situation could ever be improved. At the tender age of three, I recognised that any kind of relationship with Jack would be difficult and would have to be on his terms alone. I lost something of immense importance that day. Something deep inside my soul fractured and fell into emotional oblivion. I have wondered ever since what it might have been; perhaps it was something as fundamentally important as respect or trust. Something has been noticeably absent in my life ever since. People with whom I have had relationships have referred to things like my emotional aloofness or the invisible barriers I erect to prevent anything or anyone getting close to me. Jack ripped something out of me and destroyed it that day, and after that I felt emotionally separate from everyone except my brother and mother.

For now, though, life had to go on and we tried to keep things on an even keel – a difficult task in the insane world we lived in. Ridiculously, we, the children, had to take steps to manage the adults, making sure we were all but invisible to Jack in particular and being careful not to do anything that could remotely upset him. Our lives weren't our own. We couldn't develop, play and laugh like others did; we couldn't love; we had to stay silently hidden from view, speaking when spoken to and not before.

We were forced to do the most disgusting things, such as collecting the bits of toenail Jack picked from his claw-like, deformed feet and discarded on the carpet. If he later found a piece of toenail, he would explode into a frenzy of abuse and violence. This all seemed strange to me. It was him who was tossing them onto the carpet in the first place, yet we would be punished for not clearing them up.

The recollection of his feet still appals me. They were in an awful state. His curled-up, twisted toes with their decaying yellow nails were the stuff of medical nightmares. It seemed they had got into such a state because he forced them into ill-fitting shoes and boots on a daily basis. John and I would often wonder how he could be a policeman with those feet. He couldn't walk any distance, let alone run after anyone. They were a cause of real discomfort, and the pain he suffered from them did arouse some sympathy in the house, although he did nothing to care for his feet; that was always someone else's job. The skin around his toes had a fungal infection and we were frequently called upon to clean off the hard skin and bathe his feet. It was a disgusting task. While we were busy doing such chores, he would sit in his chair in the living room, chain-smoking and watching television.

There was method in our madness; we did these tasks to keep him happy, and while he was sitting in that chair with his feet being fussed over, he wasn't beating or attacking any of us. It afforded us brief moments of respite, though neither John nor I could ever truly relax and I'm certain the same went for my mam. Life in our household was one continual state of crisis.

After my birthday in 1962, I became aware that John was increasingly distant and secretive, refusing to let Jack know anything about his life. It was as though someone had removed the power of laughter from him. I noticed that he was often sullen and quiet, and I worried further because I thought perhaps it was all my doing. John and I never did enter into any great discussion about what happened that day, although he did refer to it as 'the day when war broke out'. To me, it was the day a family died emotionally.

What John and I developed between us was an almost telepathic understanding. We were able to tune into each other's wavelengths; a solitary look or movement or a sign between us said more than a thousand spoken words. We could never share this understanding with anyone else; it was unique to us. This was our world and it meant much more than just keeping the odd family secret; to us, keeping what we knew secret felt like a matter of life and death, so keeping others (including Mam) out was a priority.

There were no more presents and no more nasty surprises on my birthday that year. I had acquired much more than I could ever have anticipated. What I got for my third birthday wasn't material goods. I was grateful for the ball and John's sweets. But the unwelcome gift of knowledge and awareness was to last much longer and affect me more than any ordinary gift ever could.

It was very uncomfortable living in that sort of environment. Strangely, I felt guilt and anguish knowing of the evil that existed within Jack. He was a cold, calculating and depraved man; he was the one with the problems, yet I felt tainted by his sick and repugnant behaviour. I know John felt the same. As innocent victims, we should never have had to endure any form of guilt or loss of self-respect, but Jack was expert at manipulating situations so that we believed everything was wholly our fault and that we therefore deserved any punishment that might be forthcoming.

I became consumed by the guilt and shame of what I had witnessed that day. I knew that I couldn't ever broach the subject with my mam or John, and definitely not with Jack. Seeing my brother so humiliated and degraded by someone who ought to love and protect him caused me a great deal of confusion and anxiety. I felt thoroughly demoralised, since it was clear that, as a result of Jack's actions, John was distancing himself from everyone within the home, including me. I couldn't cope with it and would shake and cry whenever I felt scared or under pressure. Worse still, I would wee myself.

The additional work that my incontinence caused, the constant changing of clothes, aroused concern within the house. It was extra work for my mam, and extra slaps and reprimands for me for not properly controlling my bladder. It got to the point where one day, about three weeks after my birthday, Jack heard Mam telling me off and volunteered to get involved. He called me to stand before him. I looked up at his angry face, his furrowed brow and his top lip curled up in a snarl. 'Why are you pissing your pants, boy? If I see or hear of you pissing your pants again, I will have to do something to stop it. I will sew up the end of it, do you understand what I mean? I will make sure it hurts you.'

My nerves were out of control. As I stood in front of him, I was trembling with fear; my head and legs were shaking uncontrollably. I was snivelling and continually repeating, 'Sorry, sorry, sorry.' Then I felt the warm sensation of wee running down the inside of my legs. I was doing the very thing I had dreaded and had been instructed not to do.

Jack saw it and yelled out, 'Stop it, you little bastard, you're pissing on the carpet. Stop it.' He lifted me off my feet and angrily stomped upstairs to the bathroom, carrying me under his right arm, all the time making more threats about how he was going to hurt me if I didn't stop it. I was paralysed by terror. I thought he was going to wee on me as he had on John. Instead, he took off my clothes, then rubbed my wee-soaked pants in my face before stuffing them into my mouth. The taste was disgusting, salty and sickly, but I didn't dare pull them from my mouth. I stood rigid, my whole body shaking, as he ran a bath.

The pants were pulled from my mouth as he lifted me in the air and literally dropped me into the bath. I landed with a splash and yelled out in shock as the ice-cold water hit my skin. I stood up as a reaction to the temperature, only for Jack to force me back down into the water, 'Lie down, you little fucker. Lie down. Damn it, you'll do as you're told or else.' I was now fighting against him and trying to force my way out of the water. My feet were slipping on the wet, sloping sides of the bath as I did all I could to rescue myself. Then, suddenly, everything went dark and quiet.

Chapter 3

My lifesaver makes an appearance

When I next opened my eyes, I was lying in bed. John was sitting on the bed next to me, looking at me with a worried expression. He stroked my face and asked if it was sore. At first, I couldn't understand why he was asking that. Then the pain arrived and it was all I could think about. It felt as though my head wasn't my own, as if something inside was banging and thumping to get out. I'd never felt any pain like this before.

Recollections flooded into my mind and I recalled where I was and what had been happening before I blacked out. In a panic, I asked where Jack was and John told me that he had gone out. I began to cry and told John I was scared. He leaned forward and hugged me and comforted me with kind words. He said that he was sorry that he hadn't been there to stop whatever it was from happening, that he would always be there for me in the future. It was good to know that the bond between us was as strong as ever, and for a brief time at least I felt safe. John said that Mam had asked him to get her when I woke up and we would all talk about what had happened. John told me that I had a large bump and long cut above my left eye. He told me not to touch it and that I wasn't to move while he was gone, since it would make me feel worse.

The Cupboard Under the Stairs

Mam came upstairs carrying a bowl of soup. She looked as if she was in a state of shock. Before I could say anything, she told me, 'You slipped as you were getting out of the bath.'

'No, I didn't. He did it to me. He pushed me down under the water. He was holding me under,' I responded.

'No, you've got it wrong. You slipped, Paul. Your father heard the splash when you fell. He came to help you. He saved you. He didn't harm you, and if he did, I'm certain he didn't mean to.'

I looked into my mam's eyes. They were sad, and she didn't want to hear what I was saying. I glanced over at John. He gently shook his head as a sign that I shouldn't pursue the argument. It was clear that the truth was so unpalatable that it was easier to ignore it or deny it. I closed my eyes and felt tears trickle slowly down my cheeks. This hell was never-ending. I believed I was destined for a lifetime of pain and torture, without ever being able to speak out about it to an adult.

Mam didn't stay long. She told John to look after me and to call her if she was needed. She told us that she had to go and make Jack's tea. He had gone for a ride on his scooter because he had a bad headache and needed to clear it, and he would expect his food to be ready when he returned.

I felt betrayed by Mam's response and was relieved when she went downstairs. I explained to John what had happened. He talked about how shocking the cold-water bath was, so I knew he too had suffered this punishment. John reiterated his desire to run away from the house as soon as he could. Again, those words frightened me. If he did that, I would truly be alone. I couldn't find the strength to express my feelings. My head was spinning and I felt confused. Too much had happened for me to be able to process it. I closed my eyes and fell asleep.

My lifesaver makes an appearance

The following few days remain a blank. I was bed-bound. I never once saw Jack during that spell, which was a great relief. A huge part of me hoped that he had left us. Sadly, that thought was dispelled when I heard the muffled tones of his voice downstairs, making his usual demands on the wife he seemed to believe was nothing more than his personal skivvy. I felt sick at the thought that I was part of this life. Jack was an adult, a parent, and he had hurt me, yet I would be the one who had to apologise to him. He knew what he had done to me, I knew what he had done to me, yet I had no voice.

John began to disappear out of the house for longer periods of time. He was out playing with friends (and imaginary friends) in a desperate attempt to keep to an absolute minimum the time he spent in the house. We never, after my third birthday, referred to it as 'home'. It was a house, an empty shell, a prison.

Spending some time in bed was great. It allowed me time to think and to try to make sense of what had happened. Like all good things, though, being given time alone, and more importantly without Jack, was a temporary respite. Whether I was regaining my senses more fully or whether the atmosphere in the house was deteriorating again, I cannot be certain. What I do know is that there seemed to be more 'vocal discussions' taking place downstairs; the insanity and chaos of everyday life remained.

The tranquillity of my bedroom was shattered when the door was flung open and there on the landing stood the scrawny form of my tormentor, Jack. 'Hands off cocks, on socks!' he shouted. This meant nothing to me and I wondered what he meant by it. I soon realised that it was an order when he returned and yelled at me, 'Get up, you lazy little fucker, or are you going to lie there till the sun burns a hole in your arse?'

The Cupboard Under the Stairs

I leapt from the bed not knowing what was happening or what I was to do. My head still hurt and I returned to a state of panic. I reiterated in my mind that I mustn't wee myself or shake, but my knees were already knocking and there was nothing I could do to prevent it.

No child should ever be placed in such fear, least of all by a parent. Even now, I get a sickly, nauseated feeling when I recall anything to do with my childhood and Jack. Now I tremble, as opposed to shake, when I consider what he did to me four decades ago. I am still frightened by him, although he is now dead and I am 53. The hold he had over me was so powerful that my entire life has been spent running away from him and my childhood. Imagine, then, how it was for me as a child physically living in that world, his evil world. I was without any choices and, all importantly, without any love. Every minute spent with him in that house was a trauma; I despised both it and him, and worst of all I despised myself.

I tried to get myself dressed, pulling random items of clothing from drawers and putting them on. There was no way I was going to go near the bathroom to wash or use the toilet when he was upstairs in the next room. The risk to my safety was too great, the memories too fresh. So, once dressed, I ran downstairs as quickly as I could, leaving him in his bedroom. My mam was sat in her chair. She took one look at me and told me to go back upstairs and get washed. Reluctantly, I did as I was told. As I reached the landing, I saw the naked form of Jack walk into the bathroom.

I pretended not to see him, ran into my bedroom and slammed the door in an attempt to delay the inevitable. I heard him call my name, instructing me to come and get in the bath with him. In a fleeting moment, a thousand thoughts flashed through my mind, none of them nice. I ran from the bedroom and down the stairs, through the living room and the kitchen, and outside. I turned right out of the front of the house and made a bid for freedom. I ran as fast as my legs would carry me and as far away as I could get from him and that house. It was about half a mile before I was running along country roads with cattle-filled fields and very little else on either side.

I knew that it wouldn't be long before someone came looking for me, so I opted to hide in some long grass in a hayfield. The blades stood tall and enveloped me. It was the perfect place to hide. I didn't stray too far into the field, just enough to hide from Jack and still be able to see the road.

I seemed to be there for an eternity, but there was no sign of anyone looking for me, not even John. I began to worry about what I was going to do when it got dark. Where could I go? Then I heard John calling out my name. I was relieved to see him looking for me; it gave me confidence that he truly cared. I stood up and waved to him. He came running, skipping almost, through the grass and over to me, and gave me a great big hug. 'They are going mad. The police are out looking for you and everything. Mam is crying and Jack is really angry. I'm sorry, but you're going to have to come back with me.'

I asked him if we could stay for a while longer since I was frightened to go home. John reassured me that the police were there, so Jack wouldn't be able to hurt me. He also said that Mam was really upset and that she would want to know I was safe. Begrudgingly, I walked home with John. The moment I saw the house, my heart began to race and I returned to my nervous state. An empty police car sat outside.

In the living room, a policeman in uniform was sitting drinking tea with my mam and Jack. There was no sense of panic or alarm. The policeman looked at me and commented, 'Well, well, well, the wanderer has returned. Where have you been?'

Jack jumped from his chair and slapped me hard across the face. 'You naughty little brat! Get out of my sight. See what you've done? The police are looking for you, your mother and your brother are very upset and you don't give a toss, do you? You selfish little sod! Now get up them stairs and don't come down until I tell you you can.'

The policeman was laughing. He had seen Jack whack me and wasn't particularly bothered about it. I trudged upstairs and waited for the worst to happen. Within seconds of the policeman leaving, I heard Jack stomping up the stairs. He walked past my bedroom and went into his own room without speaking a word to me. A few minutes later, he emerged wearing his blue police shirt and police trousers. It dawned on me that he was going to work. Within ten minutes, he was gone. He was on the back shift, 2 p.m. to 10 p.m. It was our favourite shift because we saw so little of him when he was working those hours.

Nothing was ever said about me running away. It was many years later that I realised why that was. Jack couldn't make a fuss about it, otherwise the truth about what he was might have been revealed by me. At the time, the episode simply reinforced to me the fact that no one (other than my brother), not even the police, cared. It was a frightening existence for one so young. I desperately needed someone to rescue me.

And in a way, a saviour had entered my world. On hearing the story of my childhood, one respected psychotherapist told me that this individual had saved my life. I first got to know of him while I was recuperating from Jack's bathroom assault. John brought me some comic books. He had been given them by one of his friends and thought I might enjoy looking at them while I was recovering in bed. I was totally captivated by the colourful image that appeared on the cover of one of them. It was an underwater scene featuring a great red sea serpent, dragon-like and looking menacing. In front of it were two people, one dressed in blue and grey with a mask and cape, the other in a garish red and yellow costume, both aiming spear guns at the sea serpent. There was something surreal about the image. It was a portrayal of good versus evil and it very much reminded me of my own battle against evil. To me, the two masked and caped people – the caped crusaders – represented John and myself.

Inside were pages of cartoon sketches telling how this pair battled against the bad and evil things of this world. It was a fantasy world, yet so much of it rang true. The frightening reality was that in the real world people lived and enjoyed everyday things and were totally oblivious to the dark side that existed just under the surface. Evil wasn't confined to comic books. So enthralled was I by the pictures that I asked John to read the comic to me. That was the first time I ever heard the *nom de guerre* used by the comic-book hero Bruce Wayne: Batman.

I wanted to know more of the exploits of Batman so asked John to try to get other comics for me to look at. The problem was they were made in America and had to be imported, so they were more expensive and much more exclusive than British comics such as *The Dandy* and *The Beano*. John did manage to get two or three others and soon I established my own ideas about what Batman represented.

I was captivated by the Batman logo, and I felt I could look beyond the sketch and the mask and into the soul of the character. Batman had no superpowers. He was a righter of wrongs, a role-model crime fighter if you like, doing the jobs the police and the authorities failed to do. As Bruce Wayne, he didn't swear and he didn't smoke; he simply made things better for everyone. As a little boy, I would gaze into the sky above our house, wishing that the Bat-Signal would flash across the night sky, allowing me to catch a glimpse of this superhero. I was certain that if I wished hard enough he might even come to rescue my mam, John and me from our living hell.

John recognised my passion for Batman and what he represented in my life. To satiate my desire to feel safe with Batman close at hand, he would draw the Batman logo on pieces of paper, and I would carefully colour these in. At last, I had something positive in my life, someone, even if he did not actually exist, who was truly inspirational. Batman provided hope that evil, no matter what form it came in, could be overpowered and beaten.

The three-year-old Paul Mason wanted to be Batman, and the fifty-two-year-old Paul Mason continues to admire what the superhero stands for to this day, although these days I view him in a more realistic and sensible manner. Batman has influenced my life in a greater and more positive way than I could ever have envisaged. It was only when I began to recount my childhood to the authorities that things began to fall into place and the role of Batman in my life became clear to me.

Back in 1962, John would make cardboard Batman masks that would be carefully tied to my head with wool, completely hiding my face from the outside world. To complete the image, a tea towel would be wrapped round my neck. This was, of course, much smaller than Batman's cape, but it did the trick, and in my own mind I looked just like the real Batman. None of this playful dreaming and fun was ever done in front of Jack. He was always absent when I went into crime-fighting mode –

naturally enough, since he was the evil one I was fighting. In the real world, I was a defenceless child and no match for his physical strength and manipulative ways; that, though, didn't prevent me from fighting battles with him in my mind.

Chapter 4

The learning begins

Jack would sometimes confine John or me to our bedroom for long periods, even days on end, as a punishment. We began to learn to use the time when he was absent from the house to our advantage, preparing in advance for these spells when we found ourselves eating, living and sleeping in one room until we were pardoned and granted freedom to use the rest of the house again. We would hoard sweets, biscuits, paper and pencils under the bed. The bedroom wasn't huge. It was big enough for two single beds separated by a bedside cabinet, with about a foot to spare between the edge of each bed and the walls.

John had the bed closer to the window, which looked out over the back garden. At the foot of his bed was a built-in double cupboard, where we stored virtually everything we owned: clothes, shoes, books, comics, old toys and lots of rubbish. My bed was directly opposite the door, which was often useful, since if anyone was loitering outside the bedroom door the shadow cast by their feet could be seen through the gap beneath from my bed – our very own early-warning system, if you like.

Next to my bed was a floor-to-ceiling built-in single cupboard. This was a definite no-go area for John and me. Jack stored his things in there. Secretly, when he was out and my mam was downstairs, John and I would open the cupboard and peer inside. It was full of camera equipment, lights and boxes of photographs and slides containing negatives of the images he captured. He was a keen amateur photographer and by all accounts a good one, too, making a few quid on the side taking portraits, wedding photographs and suchlike – at least that was what we believed he was doing.

The care and precision with which he looked after this equipment was obsessional. Everything in that cupboard was immaculately clean and had its own place. Tin boxes that had once contained tobacco were used to store various bits and pieces of equipment. There was always an acrid smell of chemicals, not surprising really, because he kept all of his developing fluids in there. They permeated the air in our bedroom. We often had headaches, not only because of the constant stress we endured but also as a result of inhaling these chemicals. When the air got particularly pungent, John would open the window to allow the smell to escape.

Jack developed and printed the photographs he took himself. Our tiny bathroom was often transformed into a darkroom. Carefully crafted blackout frames and curtains had been constructed for every possible entry point that light could creep through. With these in place, Jack would lock himself in the bathroom while developing his photographs. This meant that no one was allowed access to use the toilet for several hours at a time, which was extremely selfish given that this was the one and only toilet in the house. His obsession meant that he was consumed by getting images just right and finding new things to photograph.

Every so often, when he was on one of his days off, strange women would come to the house. They were generally by themselves. These visitors would be taken upstairs by Jack, to his bedroom, where John and I thought they were being photographed. Indeed, portraits from various shoots were often left lying around the house for us to see. As a result, we saw nothing sinister in this activity. What we didn't appreciate was that these images were deliberately left out as a smokescreen. Jack was taking other, more compromising photographs as well.

John, being older than me and much more streetwise, was forever going into Mam and Jack's room and searching drawers and cupboards. It was always when they were out, and rifling through their possessions had to be done with great care, since Jack left traps. He'd place items in certain positions and would know if they had been moved. While John went through their room, I would stand guard at the top of the stairs, peering out of the window and diligently watching for the unexpected return of our parents. It was dangerously exciting and made us feel as though we were clawing back some of the control from Jack.

During one foray into the bedroom, in the summer of 1963, John came rushing out and went to our room. He was shocked. He was clutching a pile of photographs. 'Look at these. They're rude. They were hidden under a pile of socks in Jack's bedroom drawer.' He tossed 30 or more black-and-white photographs onto his bed. I looked at the images but couldn't understand what I was seeing. I now know, however, that I was looking at various naked parts of bodies, fellatio and other sex acts; he had photographed lots of women's sexual parts being touched and interfered with. About half a dozen of the images showed different men and women intertwined, apparently wrestling.

The images aroused a feeling of revulsion in me. When I had secretly witnessed Jack weeing on John, I had been left with a feeling of sadness, which resurfaced now. That said, I didn't understand the pictures or find them remotely interesting. I don't suppose any three-year-old child would. John was clearly shaken by what we were looking at, though, so I recognised from that reaction that they must be bad things for Jack to have. I suddenly felt frightened and urged John to put the pictures back where he had found them and stop looking in their bedroom, which he did. Thankfully, Jack never realised we had been in there, let alone seen those disgusting photographs.

There was something about my mam and Jack's bedroom that I didn't like. Perhaps it was the fact that we were denied entry, unless ordered to go in for a specific purpose, such as getting Jack's slippers. More importantly, we were absolutely forbidden to look at or touch anything in that room unless we were told to. Such secrecy aroused curiosity, hence John going through their drawers and cupboards at every opportunity. I felt that John knew more about the secrets of that room than I did; he was invited in there far more often than I was, mainly by Jack. On occasion, he would be surreptitiously taken from our bedroom to theirs in the middle of the night, returning after a few hours. I was generally half-asleep when he came back, so never enquired about what he had been doing. I guessed that if it was interesting he would tell me. He never mentioned anything, though, which left me feeling slightly vulnerable, since I believed he was keeping something from me. These secret night-time visits and my exclusion from them added to my feelings of being alone and unwanted. I was soon to find out, however, that the intimacy of Jack's bedroom was something I was better not knowing anything about.

Late one evening, not long before my fourth birthday, I was forced to go into their bedroom because I had thrown up and still felt unwell. John was staying at a friend's house, so I was alone. I had been crying and calling out

The Cupboard Under the Stairs

for my mam for quite a while, but no one had come to my aid. With no option other than to go and find her, I jumped out of bed and ran from our room and out onto the tiny landing. I stood at their bedroom door. It was closed and for a moment I contemplated returning to my own bed and putting up with the sickness. However, I felt so poorly that I needed someone to help me. I gently tapped on the door and waited for a response. I knew that both my mam and Jack were there; it was just a matter of waking them. I knocked again. This time, I got a reply. It was Jack: 'What is it? What do you want?' Through the closed door, I said that I had been sick and wasn't feeling very well. He told me to come in.

As I walked in, I could smell an unclean, sweaty odour. Jack was alone in the bed and I immediately wondered where my mam was. It was dark and gloomy, and I moved to the side of the bed and innocently asked, 'Where's Mam?' Whereupon Jack threw back the bedcovers to reveal her crouched down between his legs with her head resting on his stomach. I was confused and couldn't understand why she was hiding from me. 'It's OK,' he said, 'your mam's just kissing me. Jump in here.' He patted the bed beside him. At this, my mam exclaimed, 'No, Jack, no. Not here, not now. Paul, go back to your room at once. I'll come through to you in a moment.'

I returned to my room and got into bed, pulling the sheets up as high around my neck as I could. What I had seen, and the way Mam had spoken to me, had made me feel very unsafe. She'd seemed scared; it made me feel scared too. I began to cry. My mam came through to check on me. She cleared away the sick and gave me some water to drink, telling me to go back to sleep and not to get out of bed again until the morning.

The door closed and again I was alone, frightened and in the dark. I was living in an ongoing nightmare, a life and a place where bad things that I didn't really understand continued to happen, things that made me feel very unhappy. Worst of all was the knowledge that no one seemed to want to stop what was happening. My mam and John both seemed to go through each day accepting that this was how it was and how it had to be. I didn't know any different. I hadn't had any kind of experience that had taught me that life could and should be different and more enjoyable. In my young life, there was no pleasure or joy, other than when Jack was at work. Even then, that was nothing more than temporary relief. The fear would return once a certain time came and we knew he was on his way home. My mam would go into a state of panic, cleaning and preparing food for his return. There was no obvious escape. I was still regarded as too young to play away from home on my own, because the roads nearby were busy. All I knew and had in my life revolved around that house and the tiny back garden.

Jack began to pay a little more attention to me and occasionally spoke to me. Not that he wanted to involve me in conversation; usually he just wanted to tell me off or frighten me. For example, he seemed to relish telling me ghost stories before I went to bed. One such tale of horror that I was forced to endure remains as clear to me today as it was when I was four. It went along the following lines.

At the back of our house stood a huge tree. I can't be certain, but I think it was a silver birch. This tree, Jack explained, was the last standing tree from a great forest that had existed in the area many years previously. The forest had been the scene of countless violent battles and over the years hundreds of people had been killed there, many slain by the notorious Border Reivers. However, this tree that stood behind our house was unique in that dozens of bodies of children had been found buried on the land surrounding it. This was the very same tree that I would hear creaking and groaning at night as it blew in the wind!

The police, Jack told me, were mystified by the discovery of the children's bodies, so they checked their records and, sure enough, in a file marked 'naughty children', they discovered that lots of children had gone missing from homes nearby, children who were never seen alive again. These were the bodies of those same children. The authorities sent people to try to find out who had killed the children, but no one was ever caught, and since the children were all naughty, nobody really cared about them or how they died.

At this point, Jack frightened me even more by holding a torch beneath his chin, lighting up his face from beneath. He then stared at me, expressionless, like a corpse. It gave him a hellish look that further instilled in me the belief that one side of him was bad, the other pure evil. There was no good in him at all. The story continued.

All was quiet until quite recently, when an old woman was found living in a cottage close to Crindledyke. She was Lizzie the Witch. Lizzie told the police that the tree was haunted, not by ghosts but by the Devil himself. It marked the place where evil lived and the entrance to hell could be found close by. The police report, which Jack claimed to have seen, explained that this was the place where the naughty children were taken and sacrificed to the Devil. The children, the police report recorded, deserved to die, since they were naughty and hadn't done as they were told. As for the old witch, she had died soon after, but her ghost still walked the area around the tree in search of naughty children to give to the Devil.

You can imagine how terrified I was on hearing this dreadful tale, but that was not enough for Jack. He grabbed me by the arm and pulled me towards the cupboard under the stairs. Outside, he stopped, bent down and whispered to me, 'If you listen carefully, you can hear the screaming cries of those children dying in pain. They are in here, in this cupboard.' He raised his finger to his lips and told me to shush as he listened intently to whatever it was that was in the cupboard behind that door. 'This is the entrance to hell. The Devil and his creatures are in there. Shall we look and see? Would you like to meet him, Paul? I'm certain he would like to meet you.'

At this point, I was screaming in terror. His amusement over, it was replaced with anger. He slapped me across the face in an effort to stop my desperate cries. It didn't work, so he opened the cupboard door, as though to release whatever it was that was in there. I instantly stopped crying and felt a warm, uncomfortable sensation in my pants, followed by the wet dribbling down my legs. I was weeing myself. I expected another slap and was shaking. Instead, Jack started to laugh at me. He called to my mother to come and see to me, saying, 'The little brat has pissed himself because he's so frightened. What a coward! If he does that again, he's definitely going in the cupboard under the stairs and staying there until the Devil takes him.'

My mam was angry, not at me but at him. She called him 'a cruel, nasty bastard' and hit him across the face; it wasn't a slap or a punch but more of a push. His head jerked back and I anticipated the row spilling over into a fight. My real concern, though, was my own vulnerability; I was standing directly next to the cupboard under the stairs. Jack could easily snatch me and put me in there with the Devil, so I moved myself away from the area, squirming away from my mam, who was trying to change my soiled clothing.

The Cupboard Under the Stairs

Jack saw the struggle she was having with me, so he picked me up and slapped my backside several times, telling me to keep still. It hurt a lot, but I had one eye firmly fixed on the cupboard under the stairs, making sure it hadn't sprung open and that I wasn't being moved towards it. I took the beating and was sent to bed. I was now terrified of several things: Brookie, the tree at the end of the garden, Lizzie the Witch, Jack and, most of all, the cupboard under the stairs. My world was a confusing mess, filled with nothing but fear, and it all stemmed from one source: Jack.

I asked John what he knew about the cupboard under the stairs, and quickly learned that it was a place he had tried to avoid for many years, ever since he had been told to get the Hoover from there by Jack. When he opened the door, he saw a huge spider sitting there. He described it as being 'as big as my fist'. He cried out in shock, and Jack, deciding that it would be funny, pushed him into the tiny space and closed the door behind him. John managed to force his way out and, in a state of panic, ran upstairs, vowing never to go near the cupboard again. Jack thought the episode was hilarious and, to exacerbate John's fear, later told him that the cupboard was haunted, claiming that there was a hole at the very back, immediately under the bottom stair. This, he stated, was the entrance to hell. To reinforce the terror, he told John that the spider he had seen was one of the Devil's guardians. Some time later, John saw Jack putting a sliding bolt on the outside of the door and, mistakenly, he believed it was to prevent the horrors contained within from getting out.

As children, neither of us had any reason to disbelieve what we were told. We were sufficiently naive to believe that adults, especially our parents, would speak only the truth. I cannot recall my mam ever trying to frighten us (as

The learning begins

I've said, I don't think that was her intention when she told us the story about Jack meeting the Devil). She may not have been the most strong-willed mother in the world, but she was our mam and we loved her very much. Looking back, I know she too suffered. At times, she did fail to protect us from him, but I am in no doubt that she too lived in fear of the man who was supposed to look after us.

There came a time, when I was about four, when Jack appeared to take a more relaxed attitude towards me. Never tactile or loving, he continued to deny me any support. Even when it came to playing with my ball in the back garden, he refused to join in, to kick or throw it for me. He refrained from any kind of activity that could remotely make me happy. However, he did seem less dismissive and less aggressive towards me. Then, one day, he told me that he was going to take some photographs of me, so I was going to have to be a good boy and pose for him. I was thrilled, because this surely meant that he did care.

Before the shoot, which took place in the front room, I was washed and dressed for the occasion by my mother. I was given a cowboy hat to wear. It wasn't my own; it was a prop that someone had given Jack for another shoot. The hat was stuck on my head and I was told to put on my best happy look.

Despite their best efforts, neither Jack nor my mam could get me to muster a smile or look anything like happy. I didn't want to be a cowboy, let alone be photographed as one. Jack got fed up with me looking 'so fucking miserable', as he put it, and threatened me with some time in the cupboard unless I at least tried to look interested. The end result showed the empty expression of a sad little boy. Despite this, Jack was sufficiently satisfied to develop the photographs. He took several in different poses, but each time a morose little boy peered back at the camera or off into the distance, blankly staring into space. My mind was engaged elsewhere and I was dreaming of escape. My sad demeanour was something Jack could never do anything about or disguise. Indeed, he once entered one of his pictures of me into a competition and one of the judging panel asked how he got the child model to look so unhappy.

Whenever I look through the old family photographs I own, it seems that in almost every picture I have a serious, vacant expression, my eyes empty, devoid of any happiness. To give you an idea of what it was like, imagine someone wanting to take your photograph when you are feeling and looking awful; your own thoughts and feelings don't matter at all. That's precisely how I used to feel all the time as a child: trapped and depressed. Not that it mattered one iota to my abuser; all that concerned him was how he felt.

A parent should never want to see their child unhappy or in distress, let alone make a permanent record of it through photography. Why would any father then think it right to show those images off to others? There exist countless photos of me with a forced smile on my face or an empty look in my eyes – eyes that are as hollow as Jack's morals. In some images from when I am about six or seven years old, my lips and the area around my nose and mouth are covered in large scabbed sores. These were in fact caused by herpes and I don't need to explain how that can be contracted. To have these wounds weeping all over my face caused me great shame and embarrassment. Other children and adults would comment on them, point at me and steer clear of any physical contact with me. The distress those scabs caused me was something I wanted to forget, but Jack recorded them for posterity.

To be entirely fair and to try to give as balanced an account as I can, there are some images where I don't look pained or racked with anguish or deep in serious thought. The closest I come to looking happy is in an image of me as a very young and innocent two year old holding a Yogi Bear pogo stick. Sadly, this was another prop. It belonged to someone else and was taken from me immediately after the picture was taken.

The truth is I have few happy memories of my childhood; the seeds of doubt were not so much sown by Jack as securely implanted from as far back as I can recall. Even birthdays and Christmas were not meant for the children; they were all about him, what we would all do for Jack, 'the Great Provider', as he would often refer to himself to justify the beatings he gave my mam.

The impact that seeing a uniformed policeman beating and abusing a woman and children had on me is hard to overstate. It created deep feelings of mistrust for anyone who was even remotely an authority figure. And while it's not healthy or normal for a child as young as three to harbour feelings of hatred towards an adult, I certainly did. I deplored everything about that excuse for a man: his attitude, his smell, the way he talked, the way he moved. He was vile.

I can still recall his smell, and the thought of it can still make me retch. It was a mixture of stale cigarettes, Brylcreem, cheap brandy and lubricating oil, all intertwined with a nasty whiff of Old Spice or Brut aftershave, which he used liberally in an attempt to disguise his natural body odours. It never fails to amaze me how such early memories can remain so vivid for an entire lifetime. To this day, I can't abide the smell of Old Spice or Brut, I am repulsed by even the sight of a bottle of Napoleon brandy (the only type he would drink, and which he consumed heavily), and Brylcreem is something I won't ever use. The last thing I would ever want is to be like him. As far as I am concerned, the only connection we have is our surname; we are totally different people and that's the way I want it to be.

Chapter 5

A whole new world

So we arrive at the point in time that I recalled in the introduction to this book, my first time in the cupboard under the stairs, which, for me, was to become the most fearful and intimidating place in the world. As Jack was so keen to remind me, it was the entrance to hell.

Jack continually told me that I was ugly, a nuisance, naughty, unloved, unwanted and a replacement. It was extremely hard to take and even more difficult to understand. I had no way of knowing what I was doing that was so wrong to make him think so badly of me. I desperately wanted validation from him, for him to pick me up and give me a simple cuddle. I wanted him to be a dad, but that was something he could never be. He failed on every count. It didn't matter what I did; it was never good enough for him. My development as a child was not so much stunted as non-existent, since I was never taught how to love, the meaning of love, the value of trust, friendships and relationships or family values. Instead, I was taught not to trust or confide in others, since they wouldn't believe anything I said, and that everything in life came at a cost, even love and compassion.

Now here I was, in the place I feared most, the cupboard under the stairs. A million thoughts went through my mind as the door slammed shut and I heard the awful noise of the bolt sliding along the metal into its housing. I hoped that my end would be swift and efficient. I didn't want to be devoured by the beast, the Devil, within that cupboard in a slow and painful manner; I wanted to die quickly. It's sad and sickening to realise that at just three years old I wanted my life to end. It may seem difficult to comprehend, but my life was so empty, so devoid of any love.

There was, I felt, no one there to protect me. It was impossible for John to be there all the time. Besides, he suffered too and it wasn't right that he should have to place himself in the firing line every time Jack felt like taking out his frustration on someone within those four walls. My mam, I still believe, was terrified of him. At important times in my young life, times when I suffered his abuse, she was absent. I think it was easier for her to hide than to confront it. She probably endured more beatings and cruelty from that creature than any of us ever knew.

I lay in complete darkness and cried. I believed I was literally waiting for death to take me. After a few minutes, I realised that my cries and screams were being ignored by the deviant brute who was sitting in the living room watching television. My tears stopped and I began to wipe the blood away from my face. The wound in my head was stinging. I could feel the gash beneath my fine blond hair. I felt sick and vomited.

I decided the route to my freedom might be to plead with Jack and beg for mercy. 'Dad, Dad! Please, Daddy, let me out. I don't feel well. I'm bleeding, Daddy, you've hurt me. Please let me out.' There was no response. Instead, the volume on the television was turned up. I spent a futile five minutes begging him. He ignored everything, even when I banged as hard as I could on the door. That feeling of being ignored hurt more than the slice of skin he had taken out of my scalp.

Eventually, I stopped and sat up in the tiny space. My legs and knees were bleeding. They had been split open by the impact when I'd hit the rough concrete floor and brick wall of the cupboard. The taste of him was still in my mouth; it was awful and again made me gag and retch. I knew what he had done to me was wrong and I had no idea why he'd done it. I could smell him everywhere on my body. I felt dirty, and silent tears began to stream down my cheeks.

Suddenly, from within the cupboard, there was a strange and frightening noise. It was a scratching followed by a guttural groaning sound. I imagined it was the Devil. I didn't dare move my body. My eyes were frantically darting about, desperately trying to catch a glimpse of the evil form that Jack had told us of, which presumably was the thing that was making the noise. It was as though my presence in the cupboard had disturbed something, causing it to give out warning sounds. Then there was silence. All that I could hear was my beating heart pumping like a ticking metronome.

Gradually, I began to consider how the situation had come about. What had I done that was so wrong and deserved such punishment? I began to think about what Jack had said. Who was Robert? Why could I never mention his name? What was so special about him? These were questions that I would ask John on my release. No matter how hard I tried to understand my situation, I couldn't. There didn't seem to be any answer other than, as Jack said, I got on his tits and he despised me.

I felt cold and frightened and began to shiver and shake; the shock and fear of my situation hit me hard. I felt dizzy and sick again. Everything was spinning. I managed to lie down and curled into a tight ball, hugging myself. I closed my eyes and whispered out to the Devil to come and take me to his hell.

A whole new world

I don't know how long I was in there. Several hours, perhaps. I was eventually freed by my mother. Jack had left the house and gone to work on the night shift (10 p.m. to 6 a.m.). The sudden burst of light that shattered the darkness as the cupboard door was opened woke me up. I couldn't see because the light was so bright. I could hear my mam saying, 'Come on, Paul, try and get up and climb out. He's gone now. You can come out.' I crawled out on my hands and knees. My head was throbbing and my legs hurt as though a thousand stinging nettles had attacked them.

When I stood up, my mam gasped in shock. John was there too. He shouted out, 'I hate him, I hate him! I want to kill him. Look what he's done to my brother. He's bleeding everywhere.'

My mam sat me on the edge of the kitchen sink and gently bathed the wounds on my head and legs with warm, salty water. I felt like I was in a bubble. Nothing anyone said seemed to matter any more. Although my mam asked what had happened, I felt so ashamed of what Jack had forced me to do that I couldn't tell her or anyone else. I was taken to bed. The strange thing was, although he wasn't in the house, I still felt unsafe. Everything had changed. I didn't want to talk about anything connected with the incident, but my mind wouldn't close down and banish it. The mental torment and anguish had begun to take root. My life would never be the same again; emotionally, it was over. There was no room for feeling sorry for myself. I was commencing a lifelong battle. It was about me and him now, and my aim was to avoid him at all costs. Of course, that wasn't possible, so I was continually waiting for the worst to happen.

The following day, John was like my conjoined twin. He never left my side. Although Jack was fast asleep in bed, having spent the night policing society, guarding the nation's security and acting like someone who cared, we still felt we had to talk furtively in whispers and creep around on eggshells. Although he was sleeping in a different room, he was still in the same house; his presence remained. The atmosphere was constantly depressing. Both John and I felt it would be better if he never woke up. In our bedroom, we discussed how we could rid ourselves of his presence in our lives. We could kill him: tie him up, perhaps, then shoot him or stab him with a dagger or a sword. John suggested poisoning his brandy; I wanted to lock him in the cupboard under the stairs so that the Devil could get him, but John reminded me that Mam had said he had made a pact with the Devil. It was all childish talk and dreams – and definitely not the sort of thing two young boys should be thinking about regarding one of their parents, but that's how abuse affects you. We needed to try to retain at least an illusion of having some control over our lives and our emotions, and fantasising about killing Jack was a way of doing this.

One good thing came about that day. It happened while Mam was busy preparing Jack's dinner in the kitchen. He was a creature of habit when it came to his domestic arrangements. Getting up off a night shift, he always rose at 12.45 p.m., expected Mam to take him a cup of tea in bed, then came downstairs at 1.20 p.m. He demanded his tea (dinner was at lunchtime, tea at what most people refer to as dinner-time) be served to him at 4.30 p.m. Monday was Sunday dinner leftovers fried, Tuesday was liver, Wednesday was kidney in a fry-up with chips, Thursday was home-made soup, Friday was mince and tatties, Saturday was pork chops and chips, Sunday was a chicken roast. None of which sounds anything like a healthy diet, but my mam was doing her best in difficult circumstances. In any case, as she was preparing his tea that afternoon, Mam, anticipating further problems for me, told me to go out and play with John, not in the back garden but out with the big boys! I had never been allowed to play outside before. Now, out of a crisis, came an element of freedom for me. Neither John nor I had to be asked twice; we were out of the house in a flash.

This was a whole new world to me. The only times I had previously been outside the boundaries of the garden were when I'd travelled with my mam to Carlisle and when I'd run away. John was like a tour guide. Grasping my hand firmly, he led me round Crindledyke Estate and the different places where everyone played. These were scattered around an area referred to as 'the back field'. I was amazed to find a fenced-off play area with a real metal swing within 20 yards of our house. This was set to the side of the block in which our house stood, so I'd never seen it before, and I couldn't believe it was there. I clambered onto the swing and was soon merrily swaying up and down as John gently pushed me. 'Come on,' he said, 'this is too close to our house and him. Let's go further away.'

We walked behind a block of concrete garages and out onto the back field. It was incredible. I can still remember the sense of awe I felt as I looked down from the top of the field towards the bottom. It seemed huge. At the bottom of this grassed area stood the blocks of houses that made up the front row of the estate. I took it all in, as John, still grasping my hand, explained the various areas. He showed me a set of home-made football goals, where the big boys pretended to be their sporting heroes. As we walked further down the field, we came to a horrible-looking pink-brick building, which he told me was very dangerous. 'This is what we call the powerhouse,' he told me. 'It's where the power for the estate is held and that's why it has caged-up windows and metal doors.' It looked like a dreadful place and I didn't like it at all.

John moved to take me behind the powerhouse. I

pulled back. 'What are you doing? Come on, it's safe, you're with me,' he reassured me. As we walked behind the powerhouse, he pointed to writing and drawings on its rear wall. 'This is where we [the big boys] hide when we don't want to be seen or found. No one comes behind here, only us. See these drawings and this writing? These are what we've done. There's stuff about him on here, how much I hate him.'

We continued on our journey, down into a narrow area of woodland and then beyond the houses that sat at the front of Crindledyke Estate. I was shocked. This all seemed a million miles from the dark and depressing hell that was our house. Everything felt bright and open. It was the summer holidays and there were children playing out at the front of the houses, laughing and enjoying themselves. John walked me along the pavement and we stopped where the children were playing. I had never seen any of these little people before; I didn't even know they existed.

One boy, a ginger-haired kid called 'Kirky', asked who I was and where I lived. 'He's my brother,' said John. 'He lives on the back row, in my house.' Kirky nodded his approval and asked if we wanted to play football. John explained that we couldn't but we would come back for a game later.

We must have met six or seven other children. They were almost all older than me, but it mattered little. This world offered a whole new opportunity for me to escape from our house as often as I could. This was the world where John existed; it was a world I wanted to be part of. A few minutes later, we were back looking towards our house. I told John that we needed to stay away and play out like Mam had said. He nodded and we turned round and went back to see the children playing on the front row.

John told Kirky to get everyone together for a game of

football on the back field. 'Can we take your ball with us?' John asked. Kirky kicked it to John and ran off to muster all the football-playing children he could find. 'Safety in numbers, Paul,' John told me. 'If we're surrounded by lots of children, they can't get to us.' I asked who 'they' were. 'It's his police friends and the people he knows from his club. They don't like children. They do bad things to them.' The other children we'd met didn't seem as quiet or withdrawn as we were. I was confused by their openness. The rolling orange ball that John kept kicking to me was the ideal distraction from my thoughts, though, and soon my attention was on the football.

After a while, we sat on the grass and waited for the other children to join us. I took the opportunity to ask John more questions about Robert. John answered everything. 'He was like you, really quiet and tiny. His hair was the same colour as yours, blond. You look like each other. Do you know about Elizabeth?' I had no idea who Elizabeth was, so I asked. John's response was mind-blowing. 'She was their baby that died in hospital when she was born. He always wanted little girls. He likes them better than boys.' I asked him if we were really still talking about Jack and our family. 'Yes, Elizabeth and Robert died when they were little. Elizabeth was born dead, I think.'

There is no right or wrong way to process such shocking information. As a child, it is difficult to comprehend death, unless you are pushed towards an understanding of it by your circumstances, as I was. My initial reaction was one of sadness for Mam. I also felt frightened knowing that two children in our family had died.

Eventually, we were joined by about a dozen or more children of various ages. Kirky, who seemed to be a little older than me, came over and sat down. We were joined by a couple of girls. The other, bigger boys played football, while we sat and watched and cheered our favourites.

John, it has to be said, wasn't a skilled footballer, though he was a decent runner and that made him hard to tackle when he set off on one of his loping sprints. I was very proud of him when he scored one of the goals, which he celebrated by wiping his nose with his sleeve and directing a jubilant smile towards me. He hardly took his eyes off me throughout the game, constantly checking I was all right and still there.

The match ended when some parents came out and watched for a bit before calling their children in for tea. Before too long, the others had all gone indoors. John and I were faced with going back to our house, where we knew Jack would be up and about making a misery of Mam's life. We trudged back, stopping to discuss what we would do when we got indoors. The plan was for me not to look at or speak to Jack and to go straight through the kitchen and up to our bedroom. John would follow a few seconds later, grab some food from the kitchen and sneak it upstairs for us to snack on.

I quietly pushed open the back door and walked quickly through the kitchen, trying to be as inconspicuous as possible. My head was down and I made no eye contact. The odour and haze of dozens of smoked cigarettes filled the air. I held my breath and quickly opened the door that led upstairs. As I pulled it open, I received a shock to see Jack standing on the other side.

'Who told you to get out of the cupboard?' he shouted at me. I began to stutter and tremble. 'Answer me, you little bastard. I never told you to get out, did I?' I wasn't able to say that Mam had let me out the night before, so I opted for silence and started to cry. Grabbing me by the hair, he dragged me upstairs and into our bedroom, where he pushed me onto the bed. 'Get your clothes off now, boy. Strip everything off and get downstairs immediately.'

A whole new world

He left the room and went downstairs. I was in a terrible state, shaking and very scared. I thought that if I left it for a few moments, Mam or John might be able to change his mood and save me from going back inside the cupboard. But he yelled up the stairs, 'Paul, get your fucking little arse down here now.'

I slowly descended the stairs, all 14 steps, and went tentatively into the living room. He was waiting by the door and grabbed hold of me, lifting me in the air. I glanced towards my mam. Both she and John were crying. I begged not to be put back in the cupboard. He rapped me on the back of the head with his knuckles. The blow made me dizzy. I heard the sound of water dripping onto the carpet. Once again, I was weeing myself in fear.

He dropped me from under his arm onto the floor outside the cupboard door, telling me, 'He's in here, I know he is, and he's waiting for you. Brookie wants to see you.' He bent down and pulled open the door. 'Get in. Go on, get in,' he demanded. There was no way I was voluntarily going into that place. I managed to get to my feet. Then came another smack to the head, this time from his left hand. My head flew forward and banged on the corner of the door. I could feel the warm sensation of blood running down my face. I hit the floor in an effort to protect myself and offered Jack as much resistance as I could. It didn't cause him any problems; using both arms, he picked me up by my waist and flung me into the cupboard. I landed in a crumpled heap, upside down and hurting badly. The door slammed shut behind me and I heard the bolt sliding into place.

I got into a seated position on the concrete floor. I heard my mam screaming and shouting, 'Jack, no! Stop it! No! Please stop it. You've hurt him.' Then I heard a slapping noise and her crying. Jack yelled, 'Both of you, out of my sight and upstairs now.' This was followed by the sound of footsteps climbing the stairs. Mam, John and Jack had all gone upstairs, leaving me alone downstairs in the cupboard. I tried to push open the door. It was solid and wouldn't budge.

The cupboard smelled of sick. My vomit from the previous night was still there. I felt ill. I had enjoyed a really good day with John, playing out for the first time and meeting new people – and now this! I wondered if the other children I had met would be locked in cupboards in their houses. Everything was quiet in the house. I decided I should curl up into a ball, since this had offered some comfort last time. I lay down and closed my eyes.

Suddenly, I felt a strange tickling sensation on my face. Thinking it was my hair, I raised my hand to move it. Then the feeling moved across my face and down onto my chest. It was a spider, and a big one by the feel of it. I screamed and screamed in the darkness. My mind was running riot as I imagined spiders crawling all over me. Despite my best efforts to attract help, no one came.

The next noise I heard was Jack getting ready to leave for work – another night shift. As soon as I heard the front door close, I expected to be released. Instead, I heard my mam fussing over John and getting him into the bath and bed. Only when this had been done was I let out. My mam leaving me in that place caused me much concern. My situation was important to me, yet she preferred to bath John. I didn't realise yet that his need was greater than mine.

When I was put to bed, John was crying and sobbing. He said he didn't want to talk to me about anything. I believed I had done something wrong, bad enough to get him battered. I wondered if it was something I'd done when we were out playing. I felt guilty that John and Mam were suffering because of me. Mam's face was bright red. She had clearly taken a slap or two to the face. She explained that I would have to go back into the cupboard before Jack got home from work. She gave us some toast and left. John was still crying and I was trembling at the thought of returning to that evil place. I told John how scared I was, but he was still sobbing and didn't hear or listen to what I said.

It was still dark when my mam came back into our bedroom and took me downstairs to the cupboard again. She told me not to make a noise and that Jack would be home soon and reassured me that once he was asleep she would come down and make us a nice breakfast, then we could go out to play. I was crying and begged her not to leave me, but she said she had to and pushed me towards the blackness beyond the cupboard door. She closed the door very gently and slid the bolt across. It was pitch black and very cold. I felt betrayed. The one person who could save me was equally frightened of the same evil that John and I feared.

I sat in the dark for a long time. Jack was late home from night shift, meaning I had to remain in the cupboard for longer than any of us had expected. I heard the sound of his boots stomping through the house. They passed the cupboard several times, once loitering outside before walking away. Finally, I heard him go upstairs and into his bedroom, the door banging shut. By the time I got out, it was daylight and again my eyes took a while to adjust to the light. John helped me wash and dress, while Mam made us a breakfast of boiled eggs and toast soldiers.

All night I had longed for the day and to get out of that house. Now we were outside and I could enjoy the freedom I had tasted the day before. I asked John if he had ever been locked in the cupboard under the stairs. He told me he hadn't been, except for that one time when he'd gone in to get the Hoover out, but that he had been locked in the coal bunker. Once he was inside it, Jack would jam the hatch shut so he couldn't escape. I asked if it was because he had been naughty. 'No, that's only what he says. He's the naughty one, Paul, not us. He's just a bad man. I think he's a kind of devil.'

We walked to the powerhouse and went behind it, sitting on the grass bank out of sight of the whole world. John told me that Mam had given him some money for us to get food from the mobile grocer's van that came round the estate several times a week. I felt comforted by the fact that we were not going to return to the house for the entire day.

It was great being out of the house, and for the first time in my life I was laughing and playing as a small child should. John and some of the bigger boys played football, while a small group of us played soldiers and a curious game called 'See Who Dies the Best'. This involved being goodies and baddies; as a baddie, you had to die in the most theatrical and spectacular manner possible. I was the youngest and smallest in the group and had no idea how to portray dying. I soon learned that it was quite a skill and, judging by the way some of the children enthusiastically threw themselves to the floor, there had been some practising done. When it was my turn to die, I fell to the floor in a collapsing movement. My effort didn't arouse a great deal of excitement among my peers, although I did get a round of applause, which gave me the motivation to improve my future performances.

There was a break in proceedings when it was announced that the grocer's van had arrived on the estate. Everyone rushed round to the front row of houses, where a small queue had formed behind a brown van that had its rear door open. The bigger boys lined up behind the van, while we smaller ones stood on the grass nearby. John asked me what I wanted from Mr Lowthian. I didn't know who Mr Lowthian was. 'It's the man who owns the van,' he said. 'Do you want a pastry or a cake and some sweets?' Jumping up and down, I excitedly screamed back at John, 'Yes, please! Yes, please!', which caused a burst of laughter from some of the adults in the queue. This was turning into the best day of my life and I didn't want it to end.

Once everyone had got their provisions, we retired to the field, where we sat in one big group and ate Mr Lowthian's wonderful food. It felt special to be almost anonymous, part of a group, with no one singling me out or shouting at me and telling me I was a horrible, ugly little boy, no one hitting or kicking me or treating me like a slave. These children said nothing nasty or hurtful to me. In fact, they seemed protective when I was with them. I felt safer than I ever had in my young life and I can't begin to tell you how good that felt.

The day got even better when, later that afternoon, my mam appeared on the back field and announced that our tea would be ready soon and we should both come in to have it as Jack had gone to work early since he was now on 12-hour nights (6 p.m. to 6 a.m.). John immediately put his arm around my shoulder and gave me a huge hug, and we laughed.

As we got up to leave, a few of the children asked if we were coming out to play the next day and said we should meet up at 9.30 a.m. on the back field. I didn't know whether we'd be allowed out, so looked up at John for a response. He looked perplexed and the sadness of our situation was reflected in his expression and his voice.

'I'm not sure. We'll try to,' he replied.

'Shall we come and call for you?' one of the bigger boys asked.

'No, don't do that. You might wake Jack up. He's on nights. We'll come out if we're allowed.'

This appeared to cause confusion among the group, so, before we had to answer any more awkward questions, we returned to our house, John firmly holding my hand.

In the house, my mam told me that she had cleared it with Jack for me to be freed from the cupboard. He had instructed her to tell me that if I dared upset him or cross him, I would be going back in there and this time he would make sure the Devil was awake and waiting for me. We had our tea and helped Mam wash the dishes. After that was done, she told John to go and run a hot bath for him and me and said we should then get ready for bed. It was wonderful. There was no tension or claustrophobia in the house. John and I had a bath together. It was fun and all very sensible; we chatted about whether we would be allowed out to play the following day. We desperately wanted to be, and he said that he would ask Mam before we went to bed.

Washed and bathed, we got dried and dressed for bed. John told me to get into bed while he went downstairs to ask Mam about the next day. I knew the answer before he got to the top of the stairs; there was a skip in his step and he was squealing with excitement. As he turned into our bedroom, he said, 'Mam says we can play out all day tomorrow if we like.' We slept very well that night, although we were both awake to hear Jack's heavy footsteps climbing the stairs at six. Thankfully, he went straight to bed.

The following day, true to our word, we were out on the back field by half past nine. We were greeted by smiling faces. The other kids seemed really pleased to see us. I felt a warmness inside. My only fear was of the unknown; I wasn't used to playing out and mixing with other children. I followed John's lead, as he seemed to be well liked by the older boys and girls. It was decided that we should play hide-and-seek, another game I didn't know. We split into pairs. I linked up with an older boy called Alan. He was John's friend, so he was my friend too. Alan told me that we were going to be the first pair to try and find the other children. I wasn't to leave his side unless he told me to. We went behind the powerhouse and looked out at the hayfield that backed onto the estate. Alan explained, 'We have to count to one hundred to let them find a good hiding-place, then, when we're finished counting, we go and look for them. OK?' I nodded. One hundred was reached very quickly and I suspected that Alan deliberately missed out a few numbers. We went in search of the others. It was excellent and we soon located all of them. Now it was our turn to hide.

Alan hid me beneath a tarpaulin and told me not to move. He said he would be close by; he was going to climb a tree. As I lay beneath the tarpaulin, it reminded me of the cupboard under the stairs. It was black and smelled of damp. Beyond the blackness, life was going on and no one knew I was in there. I could hear the other children screaming as one by one they were caught, including Alan. Yet no one had found me. I felt my heart beating faster and I became scared. The overwhelming sensation of being in that cupboard was too much. I screamed and tried to get out from under the tarpaulin. In my panic, I couldn't escape. I was turning round in circles and not getting any closer to the edge. My screams of terror grew more desperate.

The tarpaulin was lifted from me and thrown to one side. I felt terrified and was shaking. John picked me up and told me I was safe and not to cry. Everyone reassured me that everything was going to be OK and that I wouldn't have to go under the tarpaulin again. A few of the older boys asked John what had caused me to react like that. He explained that I was just a little boy and was probably scared by a spider or something. It dawned on me that both John and Mam continually lied to cover up Jack's disgusting actions. It didn't seem at all right that they should be doing that. It didn't help me and it didn't help them.

The Cupboard Under the Stairs

Later, I asked John why he lied to protect Jack when he hated him so much. John's reply was chilling. He told me that no one would ever believe us, no matter how much we cried and screamed and shouted. No one would ever believe that Jack was like that, evil. He was a policeman, someone everyone trusted to do the right thing and help those in need. Part of his job was to lock up bad people who hurt others or robbed banks or houses. No one would believe that he was the baddest man of all, that he hurt us. Even if they did listen, who would do anything about it? Everyone believes the police; they don't believe children at all. He could kill someone, kill his children even, kill us, and still everyone would believe that he didn't do it and he was a good man, all because he wore a uniform.

After the game of hide-and-seek, it was decided that we would go for a walk up to the farm, where I could see some cows and sheep and a horse. They made a bit of a fuss over me. I didn't want to be the centre of attention. I just wanted to forget my panic under the tarpaulin and go to the farm to see the animals. It was a real adventure, the like of which I had never been on before. To my surprise, the farm wasn't far away – a short walk along what was called 'the back road'.

I saw all the animals I'd been told about, plus ducks and goats, and there was a shiny red tractor. The farmer allowed us to feed the horse. This was what being a child was all about: discovering new things and creating positive memories. Not only that but also understanding the dangers that existed in everyday life, on the roads, on farms, through electricity (as in the powerhouse), in climbing trees. In the space of just three days, I had encountered every possible emotion and learned a lot about being a child and, importantly, about being Paul Mason.

Chapter 6

A malevolent spirit

Unfortunately, Jack couldn't be on permanent night shift and soon he was on rest days, his days off. Once again, the cloud of gloom, doom and despondency descended over our house. It was as though a heavy, coarse blanket were wrapped tightly around John and me, restricting us and preventing us from being children. My head always felt heavy when he was around, as though it were filled with lead. My mother's demeanour completely altered too; she became quiet and stopped showing us any attention. So much sadness in one house would be a cause for concern for a caring man; not for him, though. He revelled in that environment.

Throughout John's summer holidays, he and I remained in our bedroom, the door closed to exclude him from our space. On one occasion, my mam came in to tell us that she and Jack were going out for the day on the scooter and we were to take care of ourselves. We were to be in bed when they got back, which would be evening. We were elated, not at all fazed about being left alone. John was able to make us beans on toast or a sandwich, and, of course, it meant we had the run of the house.

They had hardly been gone ten minutes before John started to poke around in the drawers and cupboards in their bedroom. He told me he was looking for the odd penny or threepenny bit to get some sweets when Mr Lowthian next came to the estate. I preferred to keep out of their bedroom, since it had Jack's smell. I was downstairs when I heard John excitedly cry out, 'Paul, Paul! Come quickly, come and see this.' I wondered what he had found and hoped deep inside my heart that it wasn't more of Jack's pictures.

When I walked into the bedroom, John was looking inside the built-in cupboard and pointing to something. I peered round the door, but all I saw was a folding table.

'Do you know what that is?' John asked.

'It's a table,' I replied.

'No, it isn't. It's much more than that.'

He bent forward and slid the table out. It was square, the size of a card table. He carefully opened it out and stood it up. 'It's a table, John. Put it back,' I said. John, in his eagerness, was panting with excitement. He pointed to the writings, etchings and drawings on the tabletop. They meant nothing to me; they were just symbols and letters from the alphabet. In the centre of the ring of letters and etchings, though, I saw something that took my breath away: it was the face of a monster. John said it was the face of the Devil.

It was a grotesque, red face, sharp-featured, with two small horns, a pointed chin and eyes that bored deep inside your head. I was scared by the image and told John to put the table away. He didn't listen; he was too intrigued by the object. 'I know what this is. It's in some of my comics and books, and I've seen books that Jack has in his drawers that have stuff like this in them. This is a Ouija board. You call dead people from it and speak with them. I can't believe he's got one of these.'

Talking to dead people was not something I wanted to know about and, again, I asked John to put the table back. Hearing the panic in my voice, he folded it away, returned it to the cupboard and continued on his quest for pennies. He pulled out a box that sat next to the table. In it were several decks of cards with terrifying images on them – spirits, buildings on fire and what seemed to be people suffering. The contents of the box caused John to blurt out, 'This is Jack's box of black-magic stuff. It must be how he calls up the Devil and puts him in the cupboard under the stairs.' On hearing this, I was petrified. Initially, I'd thought he meant that Jack could do magic tricks; it was only when John mentioned the Devil that I understood he was talking about a different kind of magic.

I didn't want to know any more, so I left John and went downstairs. To make myself feel safer, I looked through the pictures of Batman in my comics. I was desperate to understand the words, so when John came down I asked him to help me learn to read. It also distracted him from talking about Jack calling up the Devil or whatever it was that lurked in that cupboard under the stairs. We sat together and he began to educate me in the ways of words and language. Over the months that followed, John taught me more and more and I was soon able to read a sentence and write a few basic words.

With John back at school, I missed going out to play and asked my mam to let me go out in search of other children my age to play with. She would always ask where I was going and each time I would repeat the same answer: 'On the back field.' It was good, because all the children who were out there now were pre-school age too, so we liked the same kinds of games.

Matters within the house didn't improve. In fact, as far as I was concerned, they got much worse. Since the day when he had forced his penis into my mouth, Jack had clearly lost any respect for me and didn't see me as his child or even a human being. He paid me no attention whatsoever, acted as if I didn't exist and spoke to me only through my mam. It was a situation that I couldn't understand. I don't know what was worse, being completely ignored or being shouted at and hit. The reality was that it was another form of abuse, another way to break down my resistance and cause me to do as he wanted.

One evening, John and I were put to bed early. Jack was showing signs of excitement about something that was occurring that evening. I heard him tell John that it was Friday and that Friday night was regarded as the most common time for ghosts and spirits to walk the earth. I remember he said something along the following lines: 'It does you good to understand that there is a balance between good and bad. You gain far more rewards from evil. You can be rich beyond your wildest dreams and have everything you want any time you want through dealing and dabbling with the Devil. With God, you are punished for wanting or needing rewards and riches, so it's best to pretend you are on the side of God but really work with the Devil. I do, and it's done me no harm at all. Look at me, I've got a house, a good job with a good wage, and I have everything I want for my hobbies and to keep me happy. I have people, others who are like me, who are in high places, and they look after not only me but lots of others. I have some of these people coming to see us tonight. They're important people and they don't like children, so you and your brother had better keep quiet and not bother us at all.' It was a threat. John told me that what Jack meant was that he was part of a gang and they were cruel to children because the Devil told them to be. He said that this must mean that there were other children suffering like us.

That night, as John and I sat in our bedroom, we heard various people arrive at the house. John had seen Jack take the Ouija board and the box of black-magic stuff downstairs earlier. Eventually, the noise and chattering downstairs went quiet. John crept out onto the landing to try to hear what was happening. He looked out of the window and saw several cars parked in the road outside the house, so we knew the visitors were still downstairs. I came out of the bedroom too and together we sat halfway down the stairs, trying to hear what was going on. Then a voice neither of us recognised repeated several times, 'Is there anyone there?' I thought we had been rumbled and that the person was referring to us. I wanted to go back to the bedroom, but John held on to me and assured me the voice wasn't speaking to us. I asked him who it was speaking to. The answer was not something I wanted to hear: 'They're calling out to the dead, Paul.'

John told me to sit tight while he went further down the stairs to the door leading into the front room, where the visitors were gathered. I didn't dare move and sat silently waiting for John to return. There was much commotion downstairs – people making wailing noises, and men and women speaking in different voices. I couldn't hear Mam, but Jack's voice was prominent. John came back to me. He was shaking. He said we had to go back to the bedroom straight away. He looked frightened, so I knew that something had happened that wasn't very good.

Once we were safely in our beds, John told me that the door to the front room had been ajar and he had peered round to look into the room. 'They were sat round the Ouija board in the dark, with candles around them. Mam and Jack are there, and Jack has got a weird sort of dark blanket draped around his head and shoulders. They were chanting quietly and there was a man who was speaking to them all. He seemed to be in charge. He was asking questions of the Devil and the ghosts. I think that's what they must have been, because I couldn't see anyone and they were pushing something across the table that spelled out different words. It was freezing cold in there and I think I saw something dancing in the shadows behind them. I think it was the Devil.'

John jumped into bed beside me and we pulled the sheets over our heads and held on to each other tightly. We never discussed the matter again, though such gatherings and events were reasonably frequent in the house. We never ventured close to them again either, fearing we would come to harm if the Devil discovered us listening to or spying on him.

Jack gradually began to acknowledge my existence again, giving me the occasional dirty look or making the odd nasty comment, such as asking if I had pissed my pants again. Eventually, because of the way his and Mam's shift patterns worked out, it was just him and me again, with John at school and Mam at work. He would lock doors and hide keys to prevent me leaving the house. At least once a day, I would be locked away in the cupboard under the stairs, sometimes for a few seconds, other times for much longer periods. Every time he threatened me, I would cry and wee my pants. This, he seemed to think, gave him the right to strip me naked and put me in there.

I told John what was happening and his advice was to stop weeing my pants, as he felt this was what was causing Jack to flip and lock me away. It wasn't something I could control. Fear is fear, whether you are young or old. If you are so frightened that you cannot control your bodily functions, there is nothing that can be done to prevent it.

As a child, it's not easy to confront and overcome your fears, especially when the person terrifying you is someone as close as a parent. I was a form of amusement to Jack. He would tell me horrific ghost stories about creatures that lurked in dark corners of our house and how they were watching and waiting for naughty little boys who didn't do what they were told. All the time, I could see in my mind the image of the Devil on the Ouija table in his bedroom. As far as I was concerned, that table was real and so the things that were etched onto it existed. Not only that, they were in our house.

One afternoon, things completely changed. At first, it was no different from many other days. John was at school and Mam was at work. Jack had told me he didn't want me around him and had stripped me naked and locked me in the cupboard under the stairs. I was reminded that the Devil was getting ever closer and that he had spoken with Jack and told him that very soon he would drag me to hell.

Jack, as far as I knew, was upstairs. I had heard his footsteps climbing the stairs shortly after he put me into the cupboard. Then, after a while, I heard a noise coming from beneath the bottom stair. It sounded like something groaning in pain. I sat very still, listening intently, believing that the Devil was there and my time had come. I started to cry because I thought I would never get to see John or my mam again. Then I heard a cough that I knew all too well, coming from the same place, underneath the bottom stair. It was Jack! I knew he wasn't in the cupboard with me, so where was he? I worked out that he must be on the floor of the hall, at the foot of the stairs. I couldn't understand what he would be doing there, until I heard a ghostly voice crying, 'Paaaaul, Paaaaul.' It was him, I knew it was. He was trying to frighten me even more. I realised it must have been him who'd been making the horrible noises at the bottom of the stairs the first time I'd been locked in the cupboard. I said nothing and for the first time in my life I found I was able to switch off my mind from everything going on around me. I stared into the dark and thought about anything but being where I was.

The Cupboard Under the Stairs

When I was eventually released, my father was wearing nothing but his string underpants. He reached into the cupboard and dragged me out and onto my feet. 'Get up them fucking stairs now and go into my bedroom.' My heart sank. His bedroom was an awful place where bad things were kept and seemed to happen. I slowly climbed the stairs, wishing that John or my mam would come home and rescue me and stop whatever he was going to do from happening.

As I got to the bedroom, I saw a blue sheet laid out across the bed. Jack followed me into the room, walked to the curtains and pulled them closed. It was winter, in the early afternoon. Daylight permeated through the curtains and kept at bay the darkness I so detested. Jack placed a tea towel on the bed and removed his underpants. I kept my head bowed and stared at the floor. I knew how repulsive the sight of him naked was. He climbed onto the bed. I stood in the nude before him, scared to look up and deeply worried about whether he was going to wee into my mouth. I felt sick and began to gag.

'Stop that, you little twat, and don't piss yourself either, otherwise you'll lick it all up, do you understand? Come and lie on this sheet on the bed, lie on your front, face down.' He patted the bed and smoothed out the sheet with the palm of his left hand. I clambered onto the bed. The feeling of fear was now overwhelming. I coughed in an attempt to hold back the sick I could feel rising. 'Lie down,' he said sternly. I flopped onto the sheet, as instructed, face down. Every muscle in my body tensed up as I lay completely rigid like a plank of wood. I was silently crying into the sheet.

To my surprise, Jack's voice seemed calm and not at all irritated. His tone was almost reassuring. 'You're going to feel a cold sensation in the middle of your back, OK? It's lotion that I'm going to rub into your body. It won't hurt. I do this to your brother too. He likes it, so I'm sure you will too.' The cold sensation caused me to gasp in shock, but it didn't last long as he gently and gradually began to rub the stuff all over my back. Slowly, I started to unwind and relax my muscles. I tensed up very quickly when I felt him change his position on the bed. He moved from lying beside me to kneeling over me, his legs astride my torso. He worked his hands all over my back, his fingers probing into muscles. Within moments, he was fondling the cheeks of my buttocks. He climbed off me and lay beside me again. His right hand was kneading each of my bum cheeks and the actions were becoming much more vigorous.

Instinctively, I tensed up, as something didn't feel right. There was a sudden pain that seemed to be coming from my stomach. I moved to roll over to try to stop the pain. 'Lay still. Don't you dare move now,' he said angrily. He was still lying down beside me. 'My tummy hurts a lot,' I told him. He told me, 'OK, it'll stop in a minute. Just lie still for now.' All of a sudden, my bottom felt very sore. I moved my hand to see what was causing it and was obstructed by his right hand. His finger was inside and moving in circular motions. The pain increased. It was like a red-hot poker being forced inside. Then it stopped and I felt his finger withdraw from me.

The tone of his voice was altogether different now, malicious and more intense. 'Paul! Paul, sit up and come here.' I turned my head to look towards him. He was lying on his back, his penis stiff, stroking it with his hand. I really didn't want to go anywhere near it. 'Here,' he said, 'take it in your hands and rub them up and down like this.' He took my hands and showed me what to do. 'That's it. Move them up and down, up and down.' It felt disgusting. I averted my gaze and tried to focus on being in another place. I was obviously doing something wrong, because he lost patience with me and harshly pushed me away before moving to a kneeling position. He then told me to lie back down on the sheet. He was kneeling over me. I became frightened when he began to talk to himself. The words were vile and therefore never forgotten: 'Come on, you fucker, come on. I'm going to cover you with my juice, you little bastard.' I didn't understand. All I knew was I didn't want him to wee on me again. His body jerked and I managed to move my head, preventing anything from landing on my face. 'You bastard!' he yelled. 'Lie still.'

I jumped off the bed and saw blood on the blue sheet where I had been lying. I felt something running down the back of my legs and looked down. It was blood. I was bleeding from my bottom. I ran to the bathroom and sat on the toilet, wiping away the blood with toilet roll. Jack followed and grabbed me by the hair, dragging me back into his bedroom. 'I didn't tell you you could leave. Get back on that sheet. I don't care if you are bleeding, I'm not done with you yet.' He threw me onto the bed; my face landed in a wet patch. Roughly, he forced his finger back inside me. He was standing by the bed masturbating with his other hand. I felt dizzy and was crying for him to stop. He didn't.

He attended to my bleeding, taking a small box from my mother's bedside table. He produced a small white tube. 'This is a magic bandage for your bottom. It's to stop you bleeding. I'm going to push it inside your bottom. Keep perfectly still until I come back and take it out.' He wiped himself down, dressed and left me in the bedroom.

The emotion and the horror of it all were too much for me. I burst into tears and sobbed. I didn't dare move from the bed. My bottom was stinging. I hated it. I hated him. I hated my life.

When he came back into the bedroom, he wasn't gentle. He removed the magic bandage and told me to go into the bathroom and wait for him. 'I'm running you a bath so you can clean yourself up. It'll help stop the bleeding as well.' I was then promptly dumped into a bath of freezing-cold water and ordered to sit upright until I was told I could get out.

The hellish nightmare that was my life wasn't improving. There was no John or Mam to help me. It was just me and him. John was right, Jack was every bit as evil as the Devil. My spirit and will were broken. There was nothing I could do to prevent him from defiling me. I had no say. There was so much bad stuff happening that I couldn't think, I couldn't see a way of escape. He was barely giving me time to breathe. The cold water turned crimson as the blood from my bottom seeped out in strange swirling patterns. The coldness of the water itself was painful and I was shivering, probably through fear and shock.

I tried to forget my situation and focus on the thought of Mam and John getting home. I imagined myself tucked up in a warm bed, safe and protected. Jack was at work. John was in his own bed reading his comics. Mam was downstairs watching television. We were all at peace and it was an OK world. I was thrust back into reality when Jack pulled me from the water, threw a towel at me and told me to dry myself and get into bed, adding, 'I don't want to hear another noise out of you today, do you understand?' I dried myself as best I could before running from the bathroom to the relative sanctuary of my bedroom and closing the door behind me. There was still blood coming out of me, it was all over the towel, so I wiped myself again, put my pyjamas on and climbed into bed. I felt so disgusting and ashamed that I couldn't bear the thought of other people knowing how bad it was. Part of me understood why John and Mam didn't speak out about Jack. The shame and embarrassment I felt were incredible.

The sexual assaults by Jack in his bedroom continued

every week. Mentally and physically, I was sickened by him touching me in any way. I somehow resisted his efforts to force me to kiss his lower regions. He seemed more focused on hurting my bottom. Initially, it was his fingers, but this changed. Various awful-smelling creams and rubs were massaged in before things such as a stainless-steel ring similar to a napkin holder were inserted. This would be left inside for long periods. Each time he finished abusing me, he would insert one of the magic bottom bandages to help stop the bleeding and strengthen the muscle grip there. I didn't feel like a little boy. I was nothing but a plaything for him to experiment on, a toy. The way he looked at me changed too; he seemed altogether more sinister and dangerous now he had done this to me.

My only respite was when he was on night shift. Then I could go and play with the other children and put Jack and his disgusting ways out of my mind. Then I could try to be the child I was.

Chapter 7

Starting school

There were no playschools or nursery schools in the Crindledyke area, meaning that my first encounter with education was my first day at school. I wasn't alone; some of the other children I played with in the back field were starting too. The school I was to attend was tiny, and was situated close to a church.

For me, religion was a non-starter. I didn't believe in God. Why should I? If he existed, why would he put so much pain into my young life and give me so much suffering? Why would he let Jack get away with hurting his family so much? I wasn't particularly bothered about which school I went to. For me, it solved one problem: I would get to spend less time alone with Jack.

I often heard John speak of school, and by all accounts it was a good place to be, better than being in that house at Crindledyke, for sure. John had become one of the big boys and moved to another school by the time I started. He was at Carlisle Grammar School 'because he's clever, like his father', I would often hear Jack say.

To get to school, I had to travel from Crindledyke by bus. On my first day at school, I was five years old. I was the only child who wasn't accompanied by a parent to the gates. Instead, I walked behind some of the other children. I was nervous yet excited, and when I walked into the school yard I immediately felt intimidated by the walls and fencing that surrounded the playground. Other than through the main gate, there was no escape from this place.

As I walked through the main door, I was greeted by countless adults. The ladies smiled and took our bags and coats, then showed us to our individual pegs, where we were to hang our coats and bags each day. I was then escorted into a huge room, our classroom. It smelled damp, which reminded me of the cupboard under the stairs. It was quite dark. The tall ceiling and narrow windows meant that a limited amount of light reached the room, which made it even more intimidating. We were sat at desks, introduced to various people who would be in charge of us and informed of the rights and wrongs of school behaviour.

I felt uncomfortable but tried to embrace it and make new friends. The girl sitting next to me was friendly, so I talked to her. Whack! I felt a smack across the side of my head. I had broken the first rule of school: you don't talk during a lesson or when the teacher is speaking. I looked up at the woman who had hit me and flinched in shock; she looked like a wicked witch. I decided I would not cross her again, as she had a menacing appearance that sent a shiver down my spine.

At breaktime, we were given milk. In fact, it had to be paid for, at least that was the general idea. But I was rarely given any milk money and, thankfully, the school was prepared for such situations and gave milk free to the children who came from poor families. Naturally, with this handout came a stigma, and an opportunity for better-off kids to bully and mock those less fortunate. I never thought of our family as poor, with Jack being a policeman and Mam working part time; I believed we had money. The truth was, we did. It was another case of

Jack being too selfish to put his children first.

That first week at school was a real struggle. The other children in my class seemed so free, reckless almost, whereas I constantly carried worries around with me like excess baggage. No matter how hard I tried, my life at Crindledyke with Jack was always on my mind. I was preoccupied and would drift into deep thought, not paying attention to my surroundings. This was viewed as rudeness and insolence by the teachers, and that meant trouble and a poor reputation for me.

Each night, a group of us would be walked to the bus stop by a lovely woman whom I can only describe as my guardian angel, Mrs Hogg. She was a helper at the school; I suppose today she'd be called a classroom assistant. She was everything I wanted a parent to be: happy, caring, attentive, interested, supportive, understanding, knowledgeable and, importantly, she listened. There was something that made her different from other adults. I felt she understood me, knew that things weren't right at home, yet never once did she speak out of turn or do anything to jeopardise my trust in her. She was one of the loveliest, nicest people I have ever met in my life.

Mrs Hogg would put us on the bus, instructing the driver to drop me outside 14MU. The driver would tell me when to get off. On arrival at Crindledyke, other children would get off the bus and run home. As soon as the bus pulled up, I felt my stomach tighten and knot; my head would ache and I became nervous and timid. Walking as slowly as possible, once at the house I would creep in and go straight to my room. Other than after my first day at school, Jack never asked how I had got on.

I gradually settled into school life as well as could be expected. I wasn't the most academic of children and struggled most with arithmetic. Figures and sums are something that I have never understood. I found them boring then and still find them mind-numbing now, so much so that I get confused and switch off when confronted with a report or communication that consists of numbers.

One teacher in particular was very strict, and she regularly gave me a good slap across my head to remind me that she was in charge. She had previously taught John and would remind me how quick John was at learning and what a clever boy he was. Despite the obvious failure on her behalf to take into consideration my feelings, she actually meant no harm by this comparison; I believe she was trying to motivate me to do better. What she didn't account for was that I didn't care. Where John was concerned, he was my hero and first role model; he was my older brother and I could see no wrong in him, so when others rhapsodised over how clever he was, it just made me feel proud.

The headmaster was an altogether different character, a horrid man. I never felt comfortable around him, and especially not after he punched me on the thigh for going out of school (to retrieve a football that had gone over the fence) without asking a teacher.

The amount of bullying that took place in the school playground surprised me. At playtime, it was a free-for-all. Pupils from all classes were put out together. Generally, the smaller, newer children were forced to the edges of the playground, while the bigger children played football, or sometimes netball. At the rear of the playground stood the bike sheds and the toilets. This was where the bullies led their prey and intimidated and beat them. I quickly learned to avoid this area like the plague, as I witnessed countless children punched, pinched and kicked for any money they had on them. Once targeted, those children were consistently picked on. No one ever reported such matters, as the prevailing wisdom was that it would only make the bullying worse.

Starting school

Not long after I started school, an older boy targeted me. His name was Gordon. At breaktime one day, he dragged me to the bike-shed area. He grabbed my jumper and threatened to hit me unless I gave him whatever money I had in my pockets. I told him I didn't have any and he threw me to the ground. 'Get up and empty your pockets,' he said. In my most angelic and non-threatening way, I stood up and walked towards him. 'Empty your pockets, I said,' he told me. I stared at him without uttering a word. 'Come on, what's up with you, you freak? Empty your pockets or I'll hit you.' I couldn't speak because I was so scared and concentrating on not peeing my pants. Then he spat in my face. It was like showing a red rag to a bull; I exploded into a rage. I pulled back my left hand, formed a fist and smashed it into his face. He fell to the floor as though he had been hit by a steam train. I returned to the playground and joined a game of football.

Within minutes, it was like a siege. Teachers and other staff came running out of the school and surrounded me. I was taken to the headmaster, who, understandably, demanded an explanation. I told him the truth. I explained that the boy had tried to bully me and had spat in my face, so I'd hit him as hard as I could.

'Gordon's father is one of the school governors. He has never bullied anyone before; no one has reported him bullying anyone before. That's because he didn't do it – you are the bully, not Gordon. I can tell that I am going to see a lot of you. Now hold out your hand.'

I raised my left hand in the air and held it out. The headmaster produced a long, thin stick, which he whipped in the air, making a whooshing noise that in itself was frightening. He manipulated my hand into the best position for him to whack it, then unleashed the cane onto the insides of my fingers. It stung horribly. Three times he caned my left hand, followed by a further three to my right hand. I did my best not to cry, but the pain was so great that I couldn't contain myself and the tears began to flow. It wasn't only my hands that hurt. Inside, I realised that I was being punished for telling the truth. I was confused by the injustice of it all. Without listening to my version of events, or taking the time to assess the facts, the headmaster had judged me guilty.

Gordon the bully never came near me again, nor did any of the other well-known school-yard thugs. Smacking him wasn't something I was proud of, nor did I think it was right and proper for me to do it. It was the first time in my life I had stood up for myself and lashed out, and it didn't feel that great.

Chapter 8

I love you, Leeds, Leeds, Leeds!

School wasn't something I enjoyed. It was, however, a means of escape from the torment I endured at Crindledyke. My performance in the classroom was poor. When it came to reciting the various times tables to the rest of the class while standing on a chair, I wasn't the best. My talent was to be found elsewhere: on the football field.

Twice a week, we had outdoor games. We would have to form a crocodile as we were marched to the sports field, generally by the headmaster. For me, it felt wonderful to escape from the confines of the classroom, and once at the sports field I became a different person. I was a small and scrawny-looking child, with skinny legs and knobbly knees; Charles Atlas I was not. Being slight in build had its advantages when it came to sport, though. For a start, I could run like the wind, and with a ball at my feet I soon learned the art of playing football and the joy of scoring goals.

Every boy at our school seemed to enjoy football, and each had his own favourite team and player. The vast majority followed whoever was in vogue at the time; Manchester United was a favourite team, and so was Tottenham Hotspur. I had no real understanding of which team was the best or worst or why to follow them, but at a tender age my lifelong love affair with Leeds United began. Nobody else in the school supported Leeds, and this made me feel unique and different. Outside of Leeds, they were unpopular for their ruthless professionalism. The team captain was Billy Bremner. He was a fighter, with determination, passion and commitment; to me, he epitomised all that Leeds United were about. Being a Leeds fan is something I still take great pride in, more so as Leeds and their support are generally reviled by fans of other clubs. Playing football was much more than simple escapism for me. The football field was the only place I could really express myself, a place where I could be judged as an equal and excel.

Sport provided a great distraction from the daily torment I felt inside. More and more of my time in class was spent thinking about what perils awaited when I got back to Crindledyke that evening. The situation had not improved. The outbursts of violence continued. If Jack was good at one thing, it was making his family feel constantly ill at ease. Every evening, I would enter the house and walk into the living room, where he would be sitting in his chair. More often than not, he would simply cast me a glance, a dirty look that told me to keep quiet, go upstairs and keep out of his way.

On one occasion, I came home from school and as usual went straight to my bedroom. On my bed I saw a pile of magazines and immediately thought that John had got me some more Batman comics. I couldn't wait to look inside the colourful front covers, so, as quickly as I could, I took off my school uniform and got changed into my house clothes. Sitting on the edge of my bed, I pulled back the cover of the first magazine and was mortified to see a nude woman looking back at me. The pages were filled with women in various states of undress, some completely naked.

I love you, Leeds, Leeds, Leeds!

I felt the familiar tingle of fear running down my spine as I heard someone come into the bedroom behind me. I quickly closed the magazine and looked at the floor. 'What are you doing with my magazines? Did I say you could look at them?' It was Jack. I kept my back turned towards him and said nothing in reply to his question. I could tell by the tone of his voice that he was angry.

'Stand up, you little bastard. Stand up and look at me when I'm speaking to you.' I stood up and turned to face him. He was standing naked in the doorway. I hadn't expected to see his revolting nude form and my nerves got the better of me; I did the worst thing possible: I giggled. He lifted his shoulders and expanded his chest as if to show me he had a body that ought not to be laughed at. I could see the furrows in his forehead as he angrily considered his next move. I was motionless, looking past him, desperately hoping that Batman would appear behind him, pick him up and snap him in half.

'Are you fucking laughing at me? Right, get your clothes off now.' I undressed under his watchful gaze. He walked over to the bed and threw open one of the magazines. He made a curious purring sound as he looked at the image of a nude black woman. 'Come here and touch this.' He had his penis in his hand and pushed it towards me. 'Stroke it,' he demanded. I was temporarily paralysed and didn't move. Then he hit me, a full-blown smack across the face. I tasted blood in my mouth and fell to the floor, more in self-protection than through the force of the smack. I hated the bastard so much, yet all I wanted was for him to stop treating me like he did and to give me a hug.

I was lying in a crumpled heap on the floor at his feet. It was, I felt, the safest place to be. I felt liquid raining down on my head. It smelled horrid. It was pee. I looked up and got a face full. It seemed to last for ever and I could sense another part of me destroyed. I felt dirty and helpless. He was laughing. 'You, my lad, are my toilet, my very own piss-pot. Get in the bathroom right now.'

The bathroom! How I despised that place. It was at the very heart of his nefarious activities. Not daring to cross him any further, and believing that I warranted punishment for looking through his magazines, I walked through to the bathroom and stood in the middle of the floor. He came in behind me and pushed my head forward. 'Bend over the toilet now.' I had no idea what was going to happen. At least I was on my feet so I could offer some resistance if it was something awful. He placed my hands on either side of the toilet bowl and kicked my legs apart at the ankles. I felt very exposed and vulnerable and was trying to imagine what he was doing behind me. Incredibly, he left me standing there and started to run a bath.

It was nothing more than a brief respite from the torture he enjoyed inflicting on me. I yelped with pain as he again defiled me with his hands. Afterwards, I was dumped into the freezing bathwater and told to remain there while he got dressed. I was shivering with the cold when he returned. 'Get out and stand on the rug,' he instructed. I climbed out of the bath and waited for the towel that would provide some temporary warmth as I dried myself.

No towel was forthcoming. Instead, I was taken downstairs and forced into the cupboard. 'Get in and keep quiet. Do you understand? Quiet!' The door slammed shut and was locked. I couldn't move. My bottom was stinging. His assault had left me cut and bleeding. I could still smell him on my body. I cried out for help. None came. Mam and John hadn't come home from work and school.

It was bitterly cold in the cupboard. My toes felt like

blocks of ice. With nothing in there to keep me warm, I tried to rub them, but I couldn't position myself so I could reach them. I was shaking with cold and still bleeding. At the back of the cupboard, I could hear something moving. I felt sure that it wasn't my imagination or Jack trying to frighten me, that this time there actually was something there. I yelled for Jack to let me out, and for a moment thought my wish had been granted as he approached the outside of the door. However, he just told me to shut up. Through great sobs, I told him that there was something in the cupboard with me, that something was moving about at the back of the cupboard, a monster or something. He laughed and dismissed it, informing me that it was a big black rat he had caught in the garden. 'It's not been fed for a week, so it'll be nice and hungry now. It'll start with your toes, then it'll eat your eyes for its pudding.' He sniggered and walked away.

There was nothing I could do to defend myself. The feeling of vulnerability overwhelmed me. I was naked, freezing cold and blind in the pitch dark. I tried to kick the door open, but I couldn't get any power in my kick. I heard the scurrying of tiny claws moving through the darkness, and every sound was amplified as I tried to recognise where it was coming from. My breathing became shallow and my heart was thumping. I had cried so much that I didn't have another tear to shed. I was in a state of sheer panic and sat rigid and silent.

I recalled listening to one of the teachers at school discussing religion, good and evil. We were forced to say prayers and to revere the Lord. I was told by the teachers that praying to God in times of need would help us, give us strength, and that he would listen and support and guide us. In a state of desperation, I prayed to him and begged him to help me, and to get Jack to stop doing bad things to me. I said, 'Amen,' and waited and waited and waited . . . The salvation I sought through prayer didn't materialise. I remained locked in that place without light or sustenance of any kind. The teachers hadn't told the truth and I wondered why adults could be so horrible to children and lie to them so readily.

Eventually, I heard the back door open and close. I recognised my mam's footsteps. 'I'm home. What would you like me to do for your tea tonight? Chops?' she asked Jack. I didn't hear a response, and it struck me listening to her that she probably worried about returning to the house too. I heard her ask, 'Is Paul home yet?' There was still no reply.

I forced a cough, hoping she would hear and know I was in the cupboard. There was a quick tapping on the outside of the cupboard door – Mam letting me know she knew I was there. A few moments later, John was in the house. He went directly upstairs to our bedroom. He was back downstairs within seconds. 'Where's Paul, Mam?' he asked. 'He isn't in the bedroom and his clothes are on the floor.'

I coughed again and was surprised when the cupboard door suddenly burst open. It was John. 'Oh my God, look at him. He looks terrible. He's turning blue and shivering.' I tried to get myself out of the cupboard, but before I could stand up the door slammed shut and again I was locked inside. I heard a slap and Jack's voice boomed out, 'You little fucker, how dare you open that cupboard? Now get upstairs to bed and don't come down until I tell you.' I heard John's desperate cries as he scampered upstairs. Then there was nothing but an eerie silence.

My visit to hell lasted longer than ever. I remained in the cupboard for what seemed an eternity. John didn't resurface after being sent upstairs. Mam had made the tea and gone for a bath. Downstairs, there was just him and me. I imagined having the strength and resolve of

Batman, donning my superhero outfit and being able to quietly get out of the cupboard, creep up behind my captor and kill him, releasing us all from the nightmare he created every day of our lives. Sadly, I wasn't Batman; I was the snivelling little boy that Jack had created. I existed, yet had no real reason to be alive on this earth. I hated myself for being so horrid and awful, for being the child that no one wanted. I had no idea what it was that I was doing that was so wrong and made me so abhorrent to Jack and my schoolteachers. With no help at hand and no sign that I was going to be released any time soon, I stared into the cold darkness and closed down my thoughts, imagining myself outside, playing football with other children in the sunshine . . .

I emerged from my dreams when the cupboard door opened. There was no light outside, but I could see the shadowy form of my brother crouching in the doorway. 'Paul, come out. It's OK. Everyone's asleep. You need to go to bed.' I asked where Mam was. I'd expected it to be her who released me. 'There's been another argument, a huge row about you. They're both in bed now. Mam was begging Jack to let you out of the cupboard, but he wouldn't. He said you were a horrible child and had been naughty, you needed to be taught a lesson.' My sadness hit an all-time low when I heard that. It wasn't John's fault; he was just telling the truth. I was sad because it seemed to reinforce the fact that we were all trapped, suffocated by this one man who controlled every aspect of our lives and had no scruples about the level of cruelty he displayed or how it affected us. I blamed myself for being the cause of all the hatred in the family; if I wasn't alive, then no one would suffer. I wanted to die.

I didn't sleep for the remaining hours of darkness, worried by the thought that Jack might surface and drag me back to the cupboard. Dawn was breaking when I heard him clumping about the house, getting ready for work, I suspected. I hid beneath the covers of my bed, trembling as I waited for the bedroom door to open and him to grab me. It didn't happen. I breathed a huge sigh of relief when I heard the front door slam as he left the house. I must have drifted off to sleep because the next thing I was aware of was John shaking me and telling me to get up and dressed for school, that Mam was downstairs putting out our bowls of cereal. He reminded me to wash myself and told me to come down quick as we were running late.

When I came down, Mam was putting on her coat; she was off to work too. She told me to eat up my breakfast and make sure we washed up our dirty dishes afterwards, as Jack would be the first one back and he wouldn't like it at all if he came home to dirty dishes. It's a terrible thing, but the mention of his name caused me to shake.

As we left the house, I felt wretched, tired, cold and anxious about every part of my life. I asked John if he thought other children were treated like we were. He told me that I should never mention it to anyone else, as Jack had told him that if he did they would take him away to a terrible place called Dothy Boys Hole, where children were stripped naked, placed in chains and hung from stone walls. They would be whipped until sores opened on their bodies and slugs put into the wounds to eat them alive. The look on John's face as he told me this detail was one of terror. I agreed with him: I shouldn't ever tell anyone if that was what would happen to me if I did. (John and I always thought of this terrifying place as 'Dothy Boys Hole', but I've since found out that in fact Jack was referring to Dotheboys Hall, a brutal school for unwanted children that appears in Dickens' *Nicholas Nickleby*.)

More terrible still for me was what he said next: he thought that while we were children it would never end. I told him I didn't want to be a little boy any more. He smiled and gave me a reassuring hug, adding, 'We've got each other, Paul. That's all that counts. I'll look after you as best I can.'

When I arrived at school that day, I climbed down the steps of the bus and onto the pavement, where Mrs Hogg was waiting. She greeted me with a beaming smile. I felt myself welling up inside and burst into tears.

Mrs Hogg bent down in front of me and sympathetically looked me squarely in the face, asking, 'Are you all right? You've got awful dark circles round your eyes. Did you get any sleep last night?' I desperately wanted to tell her about my situation, but then I thought of Dothy Boys Hole, so, instead of pouring out my sadness, I merely nodded my head and said I was OK. I could see in her eyes that she didn't believe me, but for whatever reason she didn't push me. Instead, she took me by the hand and said she would tell the teacher that I wasn't well and ask if she could stay with me during the day.

I didn't really want any attention. I just wanted to be left alone, with time to think about what was happening and somehow try to understand why things were like they were. Learning sums and spelling was the least of my worries and therefore relegated to being an unimportant aspect of my life. For me, it was all about survival and trying to get Jack to like me, so that he wouldn't send me to the cupboard under the stairs, hell or Dothy Boys Hole.

School was terrible that day. With Mrs Hogg acting as my nursemaid, I received much unwanted attention from my classmates and the various teachers who came into the classroom. Being under such scrutiny meant that I felt suffocated. I wanted to scream and scream, but I was sure that even if I did no one would hear or listen.

It was something of a relief when the school bell sounded and that was it for another day. Mrs Hogg had protected me and looked after me as best she could, and when I'd cried she'd told me I would be all right and things would get better. She said that she would send a letter home with me to give to my mam about me being ill and that if I wasn't feeling well enough to come in the next day then I should go to the doctor. Inside, though, I knew that I would be at school the following day, no matter how ill or exhausted I was. There was no one at home to look after me, so I'd have to go to school anyway. In any case, if Jack was off work and at home, I would rather be at school; I would rather be anywhere than with him.

When I got home, I had to wait on the back doorstep for John; he knew where the key was kept, whereas I was considered too young for such responsibility. To be fair to my mam, she did arrange for me to go round to Mollie's to wait. However, despite Mollie being really nice, I now avoided going to her house. Jack had told me that Mollie was a witch and her budgerigar was her familiar. He said that if I upset her, she would get the bird to peck out my eyes. So I felt it was in my best interests to wait outside for John to come home.

John was his usual attentive self when he arrived. He asked if I was OK, how my day had been and whether anyone had said anything about how I looked. I explained that Mrs Hogg had and a letter had been sent home from school for Mam. John told me to make sure I handed it to Mam and not to Jack. Mam was soon home and I handed the letter to her, expecting a fuss; instead, there was silence. I heard nothing more about it, other than being put to bed even earlier than usual, which I didn't complain about since it kept me out of Jack's way.

My first few months adapting to life in school hadn't been what could be classed as typical. I was really struggling, as some of the teachers, especially the headmaster, seemed to have a particular dislike of me since I'd laid Gordon out with a solitary punch in the playground. For one reason or another, I found myself getting the cane at least twice a month, and of course with that came a reputation as a troublemaker, which I always felt was unfounded.

One day, we had the headmaster in class all day as our teacher. He had assembled a slide projector and screen to give us some kind of presentation and we were told not to touch the screen. It had moved round and wasn't straight, so a few of us were looking at it from an awkward angle. When the teacher momentarily left the classroom, I jumped up and tried to move the screen back to its correct position. I had barely touched it when I felt a piercing smack to the back of my neck. It was the headmaster. His face was red and he was very angry with me. 'I told you not to touch anything. What are you doing? Why are you touching the screen? Get out of here and wait for me in there.'

He ordered me into an adjoining classroom and shortly afterwards followed me in. I saw the familiar wooden cane in his hand. I stood in front of him and begged him not to hit me with it, saying I was sorry. I tried to explain why I had moved the screen. He wasn't interested. He wasn't even listening to me.

He told me to bend over and I heard the whooshing sound as the cane was brought down on my bottom with force – six times in quick succession. I screamed out at the first couple of whacks; after that, I was able to shut down and put myself somewhere else. It hurt much more than it did when I was caned on my hands.

After lunchtime, I was allowed back into class, but my buttocks stung so badly that I could hardly sit down. We had games in the afternoon and I was entirely focused on running about the field with a football at my feet. As we got changed and went up to the football field, my classmates showed me some support. They respected the way I'd handled it all. The headmaster realised what had occurred as a result of his disproportionate disciplinary action against me, and he clearly didn't like it. I'll never forget the look of disdain on his face as suddenly I was given some regard.

I scored six goals during that games session and each one was disallowed by the headmaster. I was a child, but he was doing a damn good impression of acting like a baby. From that day forth, it was always going to be difficult for me to have any respect for him. He helped fertilise the seed of suspicion for people in authority that had been sown by Jack. I still feel wary of those who exercise power over others today; most cannot be trusted.

Chapter 9

Defiled and reviled

By now, I had managed to get some sort of protective routine in my life, although it was, of course, impossible to avoid a parent altogether while at home. John and I would spend evenings in our bedroom pretending to do homework and discussing the various methods we used to avoid drawing attention to our existence. John was much more academically inclined than I was. He threw himself into his schoolwork and gained some excellent qualifications. The sums I found impossible to understand he could answer without any real thought. Because he was so clever, I believed he could find an answer for everything, even Jack and his cruelty.

One technique I used in order to distract Jack and make him forget about my existence was to deliberately break things in the house. This meant that he would have to take time to repair them, thus he would forget I was there. It wasn't anything major, and it was always things that belonged to him, so that he would make mending them a priority. The simplest thing to do was break connections on the wires that made his transistor radio work. When the television wasn't switched on, he almost always had this thing blaring out, so I expect when it failed him it hurt, like he had lost something important in his life. He would spend hours repairing it, all the time ignoring the rest of the family. There were only so many times I could break or damage things and make it look like an accident or a failure, though, and I think he may have become suspicious about the regularity with which objects belonging to him stopped working and needed attention. After a time, things like the transistor radio were locked away in drawers, presumably so that prying little fingers couldn't break them.

Every so often, John would withdraw from me, usually when Jack had been alone with him. John would spend time with him in the darkroom and in his bedroom. After such periods, John went quiet, whereas Jack was overly attentive to him and seemed to reward him. I hated those times. Mam went missing and I spent hours alone, often locked in the cupboard under the stairs, and I could hear banging and knocking coming from upstairs, where John and Jack were. I imagined them having fun, perhaps repairing something or making some kind of magical toy that we could play with. Deep down inside, though, I knew there was no toy, nor were they likely to be repairing anything or doing anything that could be remotely regarded as fun for John.

John was a great brother, and during those formative years he was my superhero. I so wanted to be as resilient as he was. When he was on form, without pressure and focused, he was more than a match for Jack, not physically but through what I would describe as his clever strategic tricks and superior intelligence. Jack wasn't bright by any standard, although he was devious, cunning and selfish. Everything in Jack's world was about him, so his weakness was his tunnel vision, his inability to think about anybody else.

To give an example of his self-centredness, I remember one occasion when he hit me across the face with the handle of a knife. I had failed to eat a meal of fried liver and had dared to comment that it tasted horrible and made me feel sick. I was only speaking the truth; it remains one of the foulest-tasting pieces of food that I can think of. Jack thought this was disrespectful of me, so he did what he was best at: he used violence. Without a care as to the consequences, he lashed out with the knife and caught me above the eye, opening a cut. Then, as if nothing had happened and I didn't exist, he continued to eat his meal.

Meanwhile, I was sitting at the table crying and reeling from the blow. Mam spoke out and said, 'Jack, we need to treat that. Look at his eye.' She began to cry and he told her to 'shut the fuck up'. My mother looked as frightened as I felt. She stood up from the table and left the kitchen. His face changed into a scowl of contempt as he looked at me. 'See what you've done now? You've caused another argument and more trouble. You are a bad boy and I wish I'd never had you. John does as he is told. You piss me and your mother off. Go and get your clothes off and wait outside the cupboard. You're meeting the Devil this evening.'

Mam heard what was going on and returned to the kitchen. She told me to go upstairs and get ready for bed while she talked to Jack. I ran up the stairs, clearing two at a time, and closed the bedroom door behind me. Downstairs, I could hear Mam telling Jack that he was too quick to use his hands and he had to stop hitting me with things. He told her I deserved all I got and the only way I would learn and do as I was told was if it was knocked into me. 'He will do what I want, whenever I want, and not when he wants.'

Mam came upstairs, put a cold wet flannel over my eye and told me to try to go to sleep. My head was thumping and, because it was swollen so much, I couldn't actually see out of my right eye. She was clearly distressed by my appearance and I recall her saying to me, 'Oh, Paul, what are we going to do with him?' I gave her an answer; it was an ideal solution: 'Kill him, Mam. I want to kill him.'

The following morning, I got up for school as usual. My injured eye was now completely closed by the swelling and my head was still pounding. John let out a scream when he saw me that morning; he had been out when Jack had struck and didn't know anything about it. He called Mam and told her to come and look at my face, as something was wrong with it. When she appeared, she told me, 'You can't go to school with an eye like that. You'll have to stay at home until the swelling disappears. John, I want you to stay at home with him. Don't let him go out and don't let anyone see him looking like that.' While I'm sure her only intention was to protect the family (and Jack in particular) from awkward questions, these words hurt me, making me feel like some grossly disfigured creature that no one could bear to look at.

In the build-up to Christmas that year, I asked John if there really was a Santa Claus and how he managed to get round all the children in the world in one night; I wondered if his journey was made easier because he didn't have to visit the naughty children like me. This irritated John, who assured me that I was not a naughty boy as Jack said. He explained that at Christmas there were no naughty children, but there were evil people who wanted to stop children having fun and enjoying themselves. 'People like Jack want to spoil Christmas for us. Mam does her best, but Jack takes all her money off her and doesn't allow her to get presents to send to Santa. It's the only way Jack can make sure he gets presents, to force her to get them for him. Santa wouldn't give him any because he is so horrid.'

I asked why, in previous years, John always seemed to get presents and I got none or his old toys to play with.

'Jack takes them from you. You're better off not having any presents from him. He doesn't give them because he cares about us or anyone else. He does it to buy us and get our trust. He's a liar and I despise him.'

At school, Christmas was celebrated in many ways. The build-up to the event was something I had never encountered before. There was a nativity play that we acted out before teachers and pupils in assembly. There was another event, which parents were invited to attend; it seemed that everyone's parents came except my own and those of a girl whose family were Jehovah's Witnesses. There was even Christmas milk: the tinfoil bottle tops had images of holly printed on them. Finally, there was a carol service at a nearby church. I had never been inside a church before, and as we were walked to it I worried about what it was all about and how it would affect me, especially as I had the Devil living in a cupboard under the stairs at home!

As the class walked into the church, the air was cold but stuffy and there was an overwhelming atmosphere of serenity. The vicar was there to greet us, dressed in his robes and looking like one of the saints I had seen in the school's religious storybooks. He shook our hands as we entered through the old wooden doors. I was worried that he might sense that I was the naughty boy Jack assured me I was and therefore cast me out. Thankfully, he didn't; instead, he smiled and told me to take a seat on a pew with my friends. Everywhere I looked, I saw magnificent colours, windows that told stories and odd images of faces carved in stone. It was an incredible place and I wondered if God and Jesus lived in this very building.

The vicar explained to us that we would be singing carols in front of family and invited guests from the congregation and asked if we had any questions. Seizing the opportunity to find out where God and Jesus were, I asked him if they lived in his church. I was shocked when he confirmed that they did live there; in fact, he added, 'They are all around us now, protecting us all and keeping us safe from evil. They are with good people and children all the time, looking after us in our homes, as we eat, play and sleep.'

I found that hard to believe and told him so. 'I don't think they live at my house because the Devil lives in a cupboard under the stairs where I live.' The vicar ignored this comment, although it clearly stunned him, since he looked at the teachers as if to say that he felt I needed to be told not to speak of such things in his church. One of the teachers immediately took me by the arm and ushered me to one side, where I was told not to talk such nonsense and to keep quiet.

I was surprised that a vicar should say something that clearly wasn't true. My reasoning was that if God and Jesus had been with me or John or Mam, then none of what was happening at that house would have taken place.

The practice began and we all learned the words to various hymns and carols. The excitement and anticipation of Christmas began to build in everyone. The vicar was very pleased with our singing and actually singled me out as having a beautiful voice. This was all a bit embarrassing, since being a good singer in a choir wasn't appealing to me or any of my classmates!

The carol service went well on the day, and I actually enjoyed the singing, since the congregation listened and smiled at us all the way through and genuinely seemed to enjoy hearing our voices, something I had never before experienced. Slowly, I began to understand that a church was most definitely not a place where 'little boys should be seen and not heard'. On the contrary, our voices were welcomed there. After the service, the vicar gave each of us a gift, a small book – the New Testament and Psalms

– and wished us all a very happy Christmas.

We returned to school and, to my utmost surprise, a party was thrown in the classroom – sandwiches and cakes and orange juice for all of us. Some of the teachers asked what we wanted Santa Claus to bring us for Christmas. I told Mrs Hogg that I wanted a daddy like the other children had. She cried and gave me a big hug. Soon, the school bell rang signalling the end of term. We wouldn't return until after Christmas. My classmates screamed with excitement, but I didn't make a murmur. I was dreading it. The thought of spending more time in the house with Jack made me very sad.

As Mrs Hogg walked us to the bus stop, I told her that I wanted her to have a happy Christmas and that I would pray that Santa brought her all the presents she wanted. I asked what she wanted most of all. 'I want to see you smile and for you to have a happy time.' There was a silence between us and I began to shake. No one other than John had ever said that they wanted to see me smile. I said nothing but lunged forward and gave her a massive hug, throwing my arms around her waist. The bus arrived and I climbed up the steps and took my seat by the window, frantically waving goodbye to the lovely lady who was making me realise that not all adults were bad.

At Crindledyke, the gloomy atmosphere in our house continued. John broke up from school at the same time as I did, so that at least offered some consolation, in that I wouldn't be alone in the house with Jack too often. We resorted to our usual routine, doing everything we could to avoid being anywhere near Jack, who, in fact, turned out to be at work for much of the time anyway. John and I tried to help Mam as much as we could with the household chores.

When Mam asked John to help her get some boxes out of the loft, John seemed to get a little excited. I was told to wait downstairs while this was done. My eyes lit up when a few moments later I saw them both emerge with a Christmas tree and boxes of decorations. We spent a whole afternoon blowing up balloons, hanging decorations and making the house look more festive. It was the first time I can remember us laughing and having fun as a family; it was no coincidence that Jack was absent. Despite everything that had happened in my brief life, I was getting excited about Christmas and Santa Claus coming and the thought of presents.

In the run-up to the big day, each night before going to sleep, I asked Santa Claus to bring me a new daddy, one who cared about his family. That was all I wanted; that was all any of us wanted: to feel safe and comfortable in our house, to feel wanted and properly loved by a real father. What we had instead was a man who demanded respect but deserved none and ultimately got none.

On Christmas Eve, the festive activity within the house increased. Jack returned in a police car and brought with him a turkey, a horrendous-looking creature that was to be served up for our dinner the following day. I was stunned to see him carrying a dead bird through the house and upstairs to the bathroom, where he ceremoniously laid it out in the bath. I had never seen a dead thing before, and I had certainly never connected the food we ate with the idea of animals being killed. Jack told John that he would be helping him to pluck the turkey and prepare it for Mam to cook. He ordered him to go upstairs and take his clothes off, as there was sure to be a lot of blood when they butchered the bird. Poor John, he looked horrified. I was glad I didn't have to do it. Mam told me that I could watch her bake in the kitchen while they were preparing the bird.

It seemed an eternity before John came back downstairs. He was naked except for his underpants, his face and chest were covered with blood and he was crying. 'He's put blood on me, Mam. He's put turkey blood all over my face.' Mam ushered him to the sink and told him to wash his face in warm soapy water. It was a shocking scene. Seeing John's face plastered in blood frightened and confused me. Surely this wasn't what Christmas was about? Everything I had been taught at school was contradicted by what was happening in our house. Jack came downstairs, laughing and calling John 'a poof' for throwing up and being frightened of a dead turkey. 'Wait until I tell your friends you cried and were sick when you had to touch a dead bird, you bloody poof. What did you think it was going to do, eat you? It's fucking dead, boy. You'll be eating it tomorrow.'

We could tell by the tone of Jack's voice that he was keyed up and liable to erupt at any time. Mam gave me one of those looks that told me I should keep out of the way. I became very anxious. Jack was standing in the doorway of the kitchen; the only way out was to go past him and there was no chance of me doing that. I felt my best course of action was to sit tight and hope he wouldn't notice me – quite a ridiculous notion in a kitchen that was barely ten feet long and six feet wide.

My strategy worked, however. He didn't pay any attention to me. Instead, he told Mam he would bring the turkey down from the bathroom so that she could stuff it and get it in the oven. He turned and went back upstairs. I jumped down from the stool and ran into the living room, hiding behind a chair at the far end. I knew he was going back into the kitchen. When he did, I would take the opportunity to creep upstairs to our bedroom. I was relieved when I got up to the room and closed the door, shutting out the horrific memory of the dead turkey as I did so.

I was expecting John to follow me up, but he was stuck

downstairs. I felt sorry for him. Mam came and told me to get dressed for bed and go to sleep as soon as I could, since Santa Claus was on his way and wouldn't want to catch me awake. I asked her when John was coming up and she told me that John was clearing up the bathroom with Jack, then he would be coming to bed. I got into bed, pulled the covers over my head and lay there in the dark. I must have fallen asleep, because I was awoken by whispering in the room. I was still under the covers. It was John. He sounded scared and I heard him say, 'Dad, no, please don't. I don't want you to do this to me, Dad. Please, no. It really hurts.' I heard a slap and John cried out in pain. Jack told him to shut up or he'd wake me up with his crying.

Unbeknown to either of them, I was wide awake. I slowly lifted the covers from the side of the bed. I didn't want them to see me peeking, so I was careful not to make a noise or to move the covers too much. I was shocked to see John on all fours on the end of his bed, facing the headboard. He was naked. His face was racked with pain and terror. He was silently sobbing and I could see tears pouring down his cheeks. Behind him stood my father, with no clothes on. At first, I'd thought maybe they were playing cowboys and Indians and John was pretending to be a horse and Jack was riding him. The look on Jack's face was the most sickening sight I have ever seen. It was filled with pleasure, yet he was clearly hurting John, whose face was contorted in agony. I felt hopeless, helpless and weak, and I dropped the covers. I felt sick and began to shake with fear. I wasn't at all sure what I was witnessing, but I knew it was grotesque. I knew that Jack must be the Devil to hurt one of his own children this way.

It went quiet and he told John to stay still while he got a towel. I gently lifted the covers again. I wish I hadn't.

John was still on his hands and knees on the end of his bed. The look on his face was hard to determine. I saw vulnerability, shame, disgust, hurt, pain. But it was his eyes that frightened me the most. They were black, cold and lifeless. He looked as if the life had been removed from him. I heard Jack coming and dropped the covers. There was some whispering and then I heard a loud slap and John crying out. Jack blurted out, 'Get in the bathroom now and get into that bath.' The bedroom door closed and I was alone with my thoughts. Quietly, I cried and cried.

John came back into the room. I could hear him shivering with the cold. I sat up in bed and asked if he was all right. He asked how long I had been awake. I couldn't tell him the truth – I thought it would hurt him – so I said I had just woken up. I climbed out of bed and wrapped one of my sheets around his shivering body as he sat in his bed. I managed to get him to lie down and told him to close his eyes and get some sleep. I stroked his face in an attempt to soothe away his sadness. We were both crying, so I climbed in beside him and held him as tight as I could to try to make him feel safe. In the back of my mind, I was hoping that Santa Claus wouldn't arrive at our house until we were both asleep, since he wouldn't be very happy to see two frightened little boys crying on Christmas Eve and he might tell us off.

I still hadn't gone back to sleep when I heard the sound of footsteps climbing the stairs. It was Mam and Jack coming to bed. Before Mam came to check on us, I leapt out of John's bed and back into my own, somehow managing to pull the covers up over my head, and pretended to be asleep. She whispered in my ear, 'Sleep tight and remember I love you,' before gently kissing me on the cheek and moving over to check on John, where she repeated the words and the gesture. I knew John was awake, but he didn't let Mam see; he lay perfectly still until the door closed and we were back in the dark.

We sat up and whispered to each other. 'I think you should stay in your bed,' John advised me. 'It'll be safer for you. If Jack comes in and finds you in with me, he'll hurt you.' I wanted to kill Jack. I sat in the dark, clenched my fists as tight as I could, scrunched my face as tight as I could, and prayed to God that he would make him die that night. I have never wanted anything so desperately. Finally, I lay down and fell into a fitful sleep.

It was daylight when Jack woke us up, throwing open the bedroom door and shouting at us, 'Come on, you pair. Hands off cocks, on socks. I think Father Christmas may have been to our house.' Neither John nor I wanted to get up. There seemed no point. I lay on my back, staring at the ceiling. I considered Jack's statement and thought to myself, 'No, Santa hasn't been. If he has, why are you still alive?' I turned to look over at John. He was lying on his side looking over at me. We smiled and wished each other a happy Christmas.

Almost grudgingly, we rose from our beds and slowly made our way downstairs. John led the way and I was happy for him to do so, since I didn't know how to react or what I was to do. The house was completely silent. I thought it was like being inside an empty church. It felt a cold and thoroughly miserable place at the best of times, but today it seemed more desolate and chilling than normal.

As we entered the living room via the door at the foot of the stairs, the first thing I saw was the back of Jack's head. He was reclining in his usual chair and he made no effort to turn to greet us. The room was filled with cigarette smoke; both he and Mam smoked heavily. The smell given off by Senior Service cigarettes was horrible: strong, sweet and sickly. Every item we owned was infused with the acrid smell of stale cigarettes.

John walked through into the lounge and stopped behind Jack's chair. I was right behind him, peeking round. Mam sat facing us, staring intently at Jack. There we stood, silent and motionless. For all of a minute, no one spoke. At the far end of the room I could see a huge pile of presents. To my right was the cupboard under the stairs, where a smaller pile lay. Jack moved, pointing over to the huge pile behind Mam: 'John, your presents are there. Paul, you haven't got many because you are a brat. Yours are by the cupboard over there.' My heart sank. He knew I feared that place so much – he had caused that – yet my presents were laid out there. 'Open them one at a time and play with each toy for ten minutes before opening your next one.'

Neither John nor I felt any kind of excitement or joy. Calmly, we both quietly walked over to the areas where our respective presents were. I ripped open the first one and found a jumper that I had seen Mam busily knitting over several weeks. I held it up in the air and thanked her. I then sat for ten minutes until Jack told me I could open another present. I was surprised to find three Tarzan jigsaw puzzles. They were used and had clearly seen better days, and they were meant for older children, but the sentiment was fine and I appreciated them. Next was a knitted teddy bear dressed as a policeman, which caused Mam to comment, 'Look, it's dressed like a policeman, like your dad.' I wondered to myself why she thought I would want anything that was in the image of him or any policeman.

To be honest, I wasn't particularly bothered about what presents I received. The one I wanted and had asked Father Christmas for had failed to materialise. Jack was still alive, sitting with a big smug grin on his face. I'd hated him before I saw him hurting John the night before; now I despised everything about him.

I remember there being a strange atmosphere. We were forced to sit and watch Jack open his presents. His demeanour changed to one of excited joy as he looked at the quantity Mam had bought him. She had made the effort to buy individual presents from John and me for him. I had no idea what I was supposed to have got him and I doubt whether John knew what his gift was either. When Mam handed Jack the present that was supposed to be from me, he tossed it onto the chair behind him, with the comment, 'I'm not bothered about that one. It's for the rubbish bin.' I didn't know whether to laugh or cry. I felt an immense feeling of sadness watching him enjoy himself and damn the rest of us.

Once his presents were opened, we were told to take our gifts upstairs and play until we were called down. This was the instruction we wanted to hear, and John and I gathered up our presents and trotted upstairs to our bedroom, where we closed the door. John looked terrible. His face was an odd shade of green and his eyes looked black and empty. I doubt I looked any better, but my concern was for John. I couldn't get the images and sounds of the night before out of my mind. We both sat in absolute silence. There was no sensation of happiness, just a flat, tense feeling of being frightened, trapped by a real-life monster.

After several hours, John was called down by Mam and asked to help prepare the table for Christmas dinner. I felt drained, so I lay down on my bed with a colouring book and some crayons. I couldn't focus on neatly colouring in the shapes and outlines in the book, and soon I was staring at one page in particular and rapidly scribbling out the facial features of a drawing of a laughing policeman. I saw Jack in the figure. It reminded me of pain and the awful things he did. I wanted to hurt him the way he hurt John, so I defaced the image's head and drew a knife through its chest. It gave me satisfaction to vandalise that cartoon figure of authority.

I got a fright when the bedroom door burst open. There stood Jack. 'What are you still doing up here, you lazy little fucker? Get down those stairs and help your mam and brother now.' I jumped from the bed and went to the kitchen and asked Mam what I could do to help. 'Nothing, darling, just you go and play.' I told her Jack had said I had to help, to which she said, 'The best way you can help is to keep out of the way, darling.' I didn't know what to do. I was scared to go anywhere near Jack, scared to be seen not doing what he'd asked. I panicked when I heard his heavy footsteps coming down the stairs. My situation wasn't helped by the sound of him shouting, 'Paul! Paul, come here right now. What have you done to this book?'

Moments later, he was standing above me, angrily waving the colouring book at me. 'Why have you done this, you little shit? You don't deserve any presents or kindness. Go to your bedroom and wait for me.' I ran past him and straight to my bedroom. I could hear his footsteps behind me. 'Off with your clothes. You're going to hell, you little bastard.' I screamed and yelled and pleaded, but, as was the way in our house, it went unheeded. I was forcibly dragged down to the cupboard under the stairs and thrown inside. As usual, the door slammed behind me and the bolt slid across.

I heard him say to Mam, 'He stays in there until I release him, understand? No dinner, no nothing. This time, I'll teach him a lesson. He'll do as I say and that's the end of the matter. Leave him to me now. Just look what the ungrateful little bastard's done to this picture of a policeman. It's treason, bloody treachery. He should have his throat slit or be locked up in prison for doing something as bad as that.' Mam tried to defend me by telling Jack that I was a child, not an artist, and that it was Christmas and I should be allowed to play and have fun. She said it was nothing but a piece of paper, nothing to get so worked up and angry about. Jack would have none of it and said he wanted to kill me. I sat in the cupboard wishing he would; death seemed a better option than the life I was having forced upon me.

I made my sadness known to all; I sat wailing and sobbing for some time. I continued until my throat was dry and sore, and my eyes began to sting from my hands rubbing the tears away. I felt as though I was living in a different world from everyone else, cut off from my family and excluded from everything they did. Sitting in the cupboard on Christmas day was different; I expected to be released any minute because I'd been told at school that this was a time for families, for little children to play and enjoy themselves and for everyone to laugh together. I decided that these were more adult lies, because Jack's intimidation and abuse of me reached a new level that day.

Every so often, Jack would come to the cupboard door, crouch down and remind me that the Devil was with me and his creatures were watching me. He told me to look out for their bright-red fiery eyes in the darkness. Terrifyingly, he told me that the day before he had released several huge black 'man-eating' tarantulas into the cupboard as food for the Devil's creatures. He was sure they would still be about, since they were so big that even the Devil's beasts couldn't eat more than one a day. The spiders, he said, would be looking for their Christmas dinner. They enjoyed eating naughty little boys. On another visit to the door, he told me to be careful of the 'biting worms' that were in the cupboard. Apparently, these horrid-sounding creatures would try to get inside my body, through my bottom and my ears, and eat my insides. On hearing this, I immediately placed one hand under my exposed bottom to prevent the 'biting worms' from getting inside. 'Don't make a sound or they'll hear you and come for you. Be quiet and don't talk or they'll have you. Once they start eating you, others will hear and they'll come from miles around to finish you off.'

I was rigid with fear and didn't so much as blink for long periods of time. I was worried that if I did, I would be pounced on by one of the awful beasts that he had introduced to the cramped space. I couldn't understand why the world I lived in was so full of horrible nasty things. There didn't seem to be anything that was associated with that house that was nice. Even the garden seemed a bleak, cold place to play. Flowers rarely bloomed; more often they died. The apples on the tree were rotten and filled with worms. Then there was that huge tree that towered above the house at the end of the garden, the haunted tree.

The discomfort of sitting in a distorted position caused cramp throughout my body. After a couple of hours, it became difficult to sit tight and not move. I desperately wanted to stretch my legs and back and be able to stand up and reach out my arms, upwards and sideways. Sadly, the most movement I was afforded in that space was bending my upper body forward and shuffling my legs about to stop the cramp. I was made all the more uncomfortable because I had to keep one hand firmly clamped to my bottom as a barrier against the biting worms.

Outside the cupboard, life went on. I could smell the Christmas dinner being prepared. Mam was busy creating her culinary delights and I was filled with anticipation at the thought of getting out of that prison and eating the food, which smelled so good. Every so often, John would secretly tap on the cupboard door as he walked by. The noise reassured me that I hadn't been totally forgotten and I thought that, with Christmas dinner being served up, my release must be imminent. I sat and waited for the door to open, but nothing happened. I heard Jack yell out to someone, 'Leave him, I said. He stays in there until I'm ready.'

The clatter of knives and forks filled the air. They were eating and I was still locked away in the cupboard! In a desperate attempt to escape, I lunged at the cupboard door, shoulder first, hoping to smash it open. Then surely they would let me join them for dinner. My tiny frame had little or no impact on the tightly secured wooden door, leaving me totally dejected, frustrated by my weakness and vulnerability. I stared towards the back of the cupboard, into the darkness where I believed the entrance to hell to be. I whispered to the Devil and asked him to come and take me, to end my miserable existence.

He seemed a far more real entity than Santa Claus or God, since he had made his presence felt each day of my life. Maybe, instead of resisting him, I should embrace him, try to understand him and accept that I was the world's naughtiest little boy and deserved everything that was happening to me. I pondered whether I should tell Jack that I understood why he had to treat me so badly, that I had come to realise that I was unwanted and naughty and that from now on I would be the good, subservient child he wanted. Perhaps he would then begin to like me.

My emotions flitted from sadness and feeling sorry for myself to anger at being ignored and left to fester in this filthy pit while the rest of the family ate Christmas dinner and pulled Christmas crackers. I tried and tried to forget the outside world, but it wouldn't go away. I heard John ask if he could let me out, as he was worried that I might be hungry. There followed a resounding 'no' from Jack. Christmas dinner over, I could hear the sound of dishes being washed in the kitchen by Mam and John. I stopped responding to John's knocking each time he walked past. Christmas was over for me and it would be a pointless exercise pretending otherwise. I was devastated and felt let down by the entire family, John included. My exclusion from the family cut deep and scarred my emotional connection with everyone. I understood now that there was no one I could rely on to free me from hell. I was on my own.

Having got myself into that frame of mind, free of emotion and caring, I was able to shut down my mind and mentally remove myself from the cupboard, to a place where I felt safe. That in itself was no easy choice, since I couldn't think of anywhere I felt safe; in the end, I opted for the church where we'd had the carol service. As cold and gloomy as it was, I hadn't any recollection of experiencing suffering or pain in that place, so I imagined myself in there, the wooden door firmly locked behind me and the key safely held in my pocket. I fell into a deep sleep.

I don't know how long I was help captive in the cupboard. It was a long time, that's for sure. I was awoken by the sounds of shouting and crying from the living room. It was Mam and John. Jack was evidently on the warpath and looking for a sacrificial lamb. For once, I was relieved to be in the cupboard. He would forget me and focus his anger elsewhere. Not that I wanted Mam or John to suffer, but I couldn't take any more. I was struggling to understand why my life was so awful. I recognised the sound of a beating. I heard slaps, and cries from both Mam and John. The physical abuse ceased and was quickly followed by more shouting and name-calling, foul and offensive threats.

I heard my name mentioned by Mam, and she said,

The Cupboard Under the Stairs

'Let him out of the cupboard now and let him go to bed. Jesus Christ, Jack, he's just a bairn. You can't starve him, he's a child.' The sound of a heavy smack – fist to face, I believed – ended all such debate.

'He can come out, but he's coming upstairs with me. You two can get out of the house. Go and say happy Christmas to Mollie next door. Leave me alone with him.'

I began to shake as I wondered why we were going upstairs and why Mam and John had to get out of the house. I decided the best thing to do on my release would be to tell Jack I was a naughty little boy and thank him for my wonderful Christmas presents.

Mam and John left the house, and I heard her tell Jack that they would be back from Mollie's within the hour. Now it was just me and him. I mentally readied myself for our next encounter and planned my apology. When the door opened, he was standing in his string underpants. The smell of cheap brandy, stale cigarettes and sweat hit me full on and I gagged. 'Out now,' Jack said. I tried to blurt out my apology, but before I could say a word I was slapped across the face, a blow that knocked me from my feet. 'Stand up. You're not a baby any more. You're a child, a naughty little boy. Get up them stairs and wait by your bed.' I was scared and he knew it.

In the bedroom, I noticed that two pillows had been placed at the foot of my bed on top of the covers and I wondered what they were there for. Jack walked into the room. He was playing with himself. I was told to bend over the two pillows and lie face down on the bed. A lump appeared in my throat; I knew this was going to be a painful experience. I lay down and felt liquid being rubbed on my bottom; it was cold at first but soon warmed up. I began to cry. This was Christmas day and here I was being hurt by Jack.

Suddenly, I felt Jack collapse onto me, his body

wrapping around my tiny frame. 'Don't cry, Paul. Don't cry.' I was confused because he was showing me some care. Then he said, 'Keep still. Keep still, Robert, you little fucker,' as he pulled me about like a rag doll. The pain he was inflicting was so bad that I felt as though I was going to burst wide open. He had called me Robert. He didn't even know that it was me, Paul, he was defiling. I wanted to shout out, 'I am Paul,' but the pain was so searing that I couldn't speak. Without any voice, I was helpless. No matter how I tried, I couldn't get my breath to scream. I would have done anything to get him to stop and release me from his vice-like grip. I was overcome with a dizzy sensation and began to feel the room spinning around me. It was like being on a merry-go-round spinning at a frightening rate and not being able to stop it or get off.

Involuntarily, I vomited all over my bed. Despite the mess and smell, still he didn't stop and the pain got much worse. I wriggled and squirmed and somehow managed to find the strength to cry out, 'Mam! Mam! I want my mam. Get off me, please. Please. You're hurting me. I want Mam.' He then let out a yelp, a squeal, and dropped me from his grip. I collapsed onto the bed, my face sliding into a pool of sick and saliva. I couldn't move and could hardly breathe. There was a strange sensation of shame. I felt dirty and used, and, despite the fact that my face was surrounded by vomit, I just lay there confused and completely devastated.

I didn't know it then, but my life would never be the same again. The small and innocent child that was Paul Mason was destroyed that day, raped and humiliated and without any real identity. I was mentally and emotionally traumatised, and, as a child, I had no options or alternatives available to me. The heart and soul had been ripped out of me. I had been betrayed by someone who should have protected and cared for me. I was punished simply for being alive and being a child. Love became just a word; hate became a much more real and tangible emotion. Never again would I be able to trust a living soul, particularly one who was any kind of authority figure. I truly was alone.

Chapter 10

Water, water, everywhere

Jack stood up. I hadn't the strength or will to move my head or even my eyes to look up at him. I stared blankly into space, wondering when Mam and John were coming back and what was going to happen to me now. I realised that what I had witnessed happening to John the night before in this same room had just happened to me. I was crying and felt sick. I wished I was dead.

Behind me, Jack was getting dressed. He continued to ignore my presence; as usual, he was too busy thinking about himself. I had served my purpose and now he could go and have a cigarette or a glass of brandy to celebrate. I glanced towards the bedroom window. The curtains were drawn and it was clearly dark outside. Christmas had been and gone and I had spent most of it in the dark, literally. I had no idea what was meant to be so special about it. From what I'd seen of it today, it was a time for pain and despair, a day when children were hurt and the Devil came out to play. After what I had just gone through, I would always regard it as one of the worst days of my life.

I heard Jack go out into the bathroom and start running water. I couldn't move. I felt drained; there was a dull but severe pain in my stomach and I felt that any movement might make it worse. The worst thing about lying there in that pit of filth and degradation was his smell. It lingered. His body odour was like old sweet potatoes that had gone bad; his stale-smoke-and-brandy breath seemed to fill my nostrils. It felt disgusting. Being covered with and surrounded by those smells was like being part of Jack himself, and the idea of that revolted me.

There was no central heating in the house. Downstairs was heated by a coal fire and upstairs there was nothing but a tiny electric wall heater, which didn't work. In winter, the windows beyond the front room would all be frozen, inside and out. I remember John scraping a hole on the ice on the inside of our bedroom window so he could see if it was snowing. We often went to bed with our clothes on – anything to keep warm. The bathroom was by far the coldest room in that cold house. It had a tiled floor and lots of ceramic fittings. It was like a block of ice during winter, and we took relatively few baths because it was so cold and unwelcoming. Having been forced into a cold bath by Jack more than once before, I dreaded what was coming.

My entire body was trembling. I was shaking uncontrollably. Jack returned. 'Get up, you dirty little sod. You stink to high heaven and I'm putting you in the bath.' I didn't move. My legs and arms felt numb and lifeless, and my brain was confused, battling with a million thoughts. I felt him pull at one of my legs, and he told me to get up or suffer the consequences. Still I couldn't move.

He became angry and grabbed hold of me by the waist, lifting me from the bed and carrying me the short distance to the bathroom, where he stood me up on the floor. I had switched off, and I suspect I looked as lifeless and emotionless as one of those cheap dolls that do nothing except move their eyes to a closed position when you lay them on their backs.

I recall Jack turning off the water, lifting me up and

dropping me into the bath. I screamed out as the freezing water hit my skin and frantically I began to fight to get out, pushing him away and screaming, 'No, no, no! Let me go, let me go!' This achieved nothing, except to further rile Jack and cause him to force me down into the water. It felt as though I was fighting for my life, but I realised that I was in no position to overcome his strength, so I accepted my fate. I managed to get into a seated position so as to keep my head and upper body above the water.

The stinging sensation that the ice-cold water caused to my damaged bottom was unbearable and I was in a state of panic, experiencing an overwhelming feeling of suffocation and anxiety. I wasn't certain what Jack was trying to do or wanted me to do, which made me even more frightened. I sat in the freezing-cold water, both hands firmly grasping the rim of the cast-iron bathtub. By this stage, I was sobbing uncontrollably and my shivering was exaggerated by the freezing temperature. Jack scowled at me and told me to sit there until he told me I could move. He switched off the light and left, locking the bathroom door. Once again, I was trapped alone behind a locked door.

It sounds strange, but I could smell blood and knew by the sensation in my bottom that I had been ruptured in some way. During the frenzy to get me in the bath, I had seen drops of blood on the tiled floor, so I realised I had been wounded. But all the sobbing and crying in the world wasn't going to help me or resolve matters. Jack didn't care and Mam and John were still round at the neighbours' house. The only thing I could do was sit tight and accept my situation. Jack had all the control; everything depended on him. Sitting there in a bath of cold water in the dark somehow focused my mind. I kept telling myself that this wasn't a permanent situation, I would be released and over time the torture would cease.

I imagined being a giant and in the position where I could retaliate and inflict pain on him. Once again, I moved my mind into my own world, forgetting Christmas, forgetting the hurt and pain, imagining having the power to lock and unlock doors myself, thus being able to create barriers to defend myself.

I jumped with shock when the bathroom door flew open and the light was switched on. Jack marched purposefully over to the tub and I anticipated him lifting me out. Instead, he grabbed me by the shoulders, threw me backwards and downwards, and for a few seconds immersed my head under the water. I was too tired to fight back or struggle, and in my panic I swallowed a mouthful of water and immediately began to cough and splutter under the water. This made it worse, since I was taking in more water. I felt a numbness in my head and a pain behind my eyes. He pulled me up and I had just enough time to spit out the water and gasp for air before he thrust me back under the water, holding me there for several seconds. I was frightened and tried to get his hands off me. My arms and legs were thrashing about and I was wriggling like an eel. I couldn't see anything, since water was bubbling and splashing in front of my eyes. Then he pulled me up and lifted me from the bath. I was coughing and vomited on the bathroom floor. Jack wasn't at all disturbed by this and, roughly throwing me onto the floor, he tossed a towel on top of me. 'Clean the fucking mess up, dry yourself and get to your bed,' he said, before walking out of the bathroom and leaving me to my own devices.

Scrambling to my feet, I rubbed the towel over my body in an attempt to rid myself of the cold and shivering. My hands were shaking so violently that they could hardly hold the towel and seemed to have a life of their own. I couldn't understand the horrors I had just endured.

The bathwater was stained crimson. It was blood, not just a few drops but a lot of it. The white towel I was using to dry myself was covered in blood too, and when I looked down between my legs, I could see streams of blood running down the inside of my thighs. The strange thing was it didn't hurt. The cold water had numbed the pain but not stemmed the flow. I got a wad of toilet paper and inserted it between the cheeks of my bottom to soak up the blood.

I was really worried about the towel. It was a real mess, so I decided to hide it since it would probably make Jack even more angry when he saw how I had ruined it with my blood. I felt so ashamed and wanted to pretend it had never happened. To do that, I needed to hide all traces of it from Mam and John. I also knew that I didn't want to leave any reminders for Jack to see, in case it prompted him to do it to me again. To prevent him thinking about it, I had to erase every piece of evidence. He had told me to clear up, so I reached into the bathtub and pulled out the plug. I watched the bloody water swirl around the plughole as it drained away. I wished I could escape from my hell so easily.

With the bath cleaned, I made my way into the bedroom and saw the aftermath of what had happened. The pillows were still strewn at the foot of my mattress, the bedcover was saturated with sick, and everywhere there was that disgusting smell of Jack. I cleaned up the bed as best I could, removing the soiled cover and hiding it in our built-in cupboard. Out of sight, out of mind. Then I climbed into bed.

My mind was spinning with terrible thoughts. I wanted to die, and again I wondered why, if there was a God, he would allow such atrocities to happen, on Christmas Day of all days. The only logical conclusion I could reach was that Jack was right: I was a horrible little boy who deserved to suffer. It seemed clear to me that the Devil was stronger than God, that, as Jack said, he was everywhere and watching me very closely. I wondered what it was that made me so different; I seemed like the other little boys at school, apart from the fact that I wasn't liked by the headmaster. And he wasn't someone who should have been protecting and caring for me; he wasn't family and didn't really know me at all. Jack, meanwhile, lived in the same house as me and should have had some paternal inclination towards teaching me the right things and providing an element of security. Instead, he hated me, he wanted to hurt me, he was ashamed of me. There had to be something wrong with me for him to want to inflict pain on me and lock me away in the cupboard under the stairs.

I didn't feel safe. I needed to sit upright and see everything that was happening around me, so as to defend myself against any further attack from Jack. I don't know how long I sat staring into space before I heard Mam and John come back into the house. There was very little conversation downstairs. I knew that Jack would be in his customary place, lounging on his chair, accompanied by his best friends, brandy and cigarettes. John came straight upstairs to the bedroom. He didn't ask what had happened; it was as if he knew. He sat on the bed beside me and hugged me tightly. I cried into his warm, reassuring chest, aware that, for now at least, it was over and he would keep me safe.

John reached into his trouser pocket and pulled out some sweets and chocolate. 'These are from Mollie and Eddie next door. Eat them. Have you had anything to eat while we've been out?' he asked. I shook my head and returned it to the safety of his chest. I could sense that John was thinking up some plan. 'Wait here. I'll go and sneak some turkey up for you to eat. There's plenty of it and you must be hungry.' Food was the last thing on my mind; I would have given anything to be invisible and be the last thing on Jack's mind.

John came back with a small side plate of turkey meat, a few slices. He whispered that Mam had cut it for me and not to make a noise in case Jack heard anything. I wolfed the lot down in a few seconds. The back of my throat still hurt from the coughing and vomiting. John was amazing. He had a glass of orange juice waiting by his bedside and passed it to me to drink. Neither of us spoke, and John held my tiny hand and stroked my hair as I sat and silently cried. Through my own tears, I could see that he was crying too. That was the first time in my life that I understood what love, unconditional love, was. My brother John always seemed to be there for me. He instinctively knew how I was feeling and what had happened. He wanted nothing in return for his kindness – just to see me happy and to keep me safe.

'I wish he was dead, Paul, but the Devil never dies, does he? We can't kill him. We will just have to keep running from him.' Prophetic words, as five decades later, I feel that, emotionally at least, I have never stopped running from Jack.

Chapter 11

Happy New Year

Boxing Day was, understandably, subdued. I spent most of it in my bedroom trying to hide my shame and escape any unwanted attention that Jack might want to force on me. I longed for the holidays to end and to get back to school, to a place where I could try to be normal. While I was in the house, there was to be no escape. Over the days that followed, Jack was attentive, not in a good way but touching me sexually. He had this terrifying, sadistic way of looking at me and licking his lips; it made me feel dirty and scared.

On New Year's Eve, it was revealed that Jack and Mam were going to a party and wouldn't be back until the following morning. The party wasn't local and John, who was to be my babysitter, told me they would be gone a long time, so it would be just him and me at home. It was the first time over the festive period that I'd felt any sense of happiness. It was only lunchtime, yet John was busy planning the evening's activities for us: games to play, food to eat and things to do. Mam had given him some money and he went out to get crisps and snacks for us both, with a stern warning from Mam: 'Don't let Jack know I've given you any money or what you're doing.'

It was almost as if Jack had a psychic side to him. That afternoon, while I was sitting in my bedroom, he came in and sat on my bed. He was fully dressed and didn't have the seedy look in his eye, so I felt reassured that at least I wasn't about to be raped. He said he wanted to tell me a special New Year's Eve story. It was of course no ordinary story but a frightening ghost story in which a small boy is in his bed on New Year's Eve and is visited by different ghosts who punish him for all the naughty things he has done that year. If he has told lies or betrayed trust, one ghost will come and stitch up his lips; if he has eaten food that he wasn't allowed, another ghost will come and chop off his fingers; if he hasn't done as his daddy wanted, a ghost will come and cut off his willy; if he has seen something he shouldn't have, a ghost will come and poke out his eyes with a sharp stick. The story was horrific and it ended with Jack standing up and sniffing at the air around the room, as though he was trying to track down a certain smell. He stopped and, staring at me in a cold and calculating way, he told me that the bedroom was full of ghosts who would visit me that night; he could smell them and hear them whispering my name. His parting shot was: 'I wouldn't want to be in this room tonight.'

I began to scream in terror. I imagined the ghosts coming out of the walls, from beneath the beds, dropping through the ceiling. I was inconsolable and it took a hard slap around the face from Jack to stop me crying. Mam came running up the stairs and demanded to know what was happening. She asked Jack what he had done. He leapt towards her and punched her on the side of the head, knocking her down and sending her sprawling across the floor. Blood was coming out of her ear. 'How dare you accuse me of making the little brat scream? He does it because he's a little bastard. He doesn't want us to go out tonight. He says he's frightened. He's trying to manipulate what we do now. Well, fuck him. He won't do that to me!'

The Cupboard Under the Stairs

Jack was irate. He stepped over Mam and went downstairs, where I could hear him chuntering and swearing about me. I had no idea what he was going to do. I was petrified. Mam sat up and asked if I was OK. She told me I had upset Jack so it was best to stay in the bedroom until she sorted it out. I tried to tell her that he had frightened me with scary stories, but she was preoccupied with trying to calm him down and didn't hear what I was saying.

I waited for what seemed an eternity. There wasn't a lot of shouting, so I imagined things must have calmed down. John came up and said I should stay where I was. I told him about the story and he reassured me that ghosts, if they existed, couldn't hurt anyone, they just floated about and made wailing noises to frighten people. I wondered why so many horrid things existed. The world seemed such an awful place, filled with nothing but misery, especially for little children.

Jack came back. He had a grotesque spring in his step, his deformed feet bounding up the stairs. He was clearly very excited about something. He literally skipped into the bedroom, grabbed hold of me and swept me off the bed. He had me gripped tightly beneath his arm. He carried me downstairs, taking two steps at a time, and dropped me outside the cupboard under the stairs. He seemed pleased with himself and was grinning from ear to ear. I tried to look beyond him towards my mam, who was sitting with her head in her hands. I could see she had been crying. John was there too, sitting on the couch and looking down at the ground. Neither of them made eye contact with me. I knew that whatever was coming, there would be no escape. The only one looking at me was Jack. I didn't like to look into his eyes, as I found it intimidating and scary. It is perhaps the worst feeling in the world a young child can suffer: to look into the eyes of a parent and see nothing but hatred. It's like having vertigo, standing at the very top of a tall building; you feel frightened and very vulnerable.

Jack crouched down so that he was at my eye level. He moved towards the cupboard door to show me a shiny new lock. He handled it. 'Do you know what this is?' he asked. I nodded, as I was too scared to speak. He closed the cupboard door, slid the shiny new bolt across, then reached into his pocket and took out a padlock. It was a fearsome-looking thing, huge, tarnished and ugly. I could see the easily recognisable crow's-foot stamp that marked it as MoD property.

Jack insisted on showing me how the lock worked, snapping it closed then pulling at the cupboard door to show how secure it was. For a time, the purpose of this exercise was lost on me. It was only when he removed the padlock, opened the cupboard door, told me to get undressed and threw me inside that I realised what his performance had been about. He commented for everyone in the room to hear, 'You can stay in there until tomorrow when I get home and get up. You've upset both your mam and me, and your brother doesn't want you about tonight. He's coming with us now, so you're here alone with the ghosts and the monsters and the Devil. If I hear so much as a peep out of you, there'll be trouble.'

I was gasping for breath and then I wet myself. The warm sensation quickly turned cold in the freezing cupboard. After all John's efforts and preparations, I'd fully expected that he would be there to let me out if Jack locked me in the cupboard before he and Mam went out. Now John was going with them, and even if he'd remained behind he wouldn't have been able to get round the padlock. Despite my constant sobbing, I was ignored and I could hear that they were all getting ready to go out. I heard my mam pleading with Jack to release me, but he was having none of it. I could hear John being sick and asking Jack if he could stay at home. The answer wasn't what either of us wanted to hear.

I didn't believe at first that they would really all go out and leave me alone in the house, but they did. I suppose my mam and John had no choice in the matter. I heard Jack shout out that the taxi had arrived and then the front door slammed shut. Instinctively, I tried, as I'd tried in the past, to kick open the cupboard door, but I had no more success than before. I got the shock of my life when I heard someone fiddling with the padlock and the door suddenly opened. Jack was standing there, his face contorted. He leaned towards me and pinched my leg with his fingers, making me squeal with pain. 'Shut that bloody noise up! If you dare make a sound, the ghosts will come for you. The Devil is going to stand guard outside of this door. If he hears you, you will suffer. Now be quiet.' The door slammed closed and the padlock snapped shut. Again, I heard the front door bang and the house fell silent.

In a strange way, I felt safer locked in the cupboard than I would have done if I'd been left alone with the run of the house. I had become used to the contours of the inside of the cupboard; I knew where every sharp area of each brick was and how to avoid them. My senses improved after a while, although the pitch black still frightened me. In the dark, I felt tiny creatures run across my hands, spiders and other such insects. It was me and them; this was our place. I didn't mean them any harm and I'd begun to realise that they didn't mean me any, although I still disliked them.

The one thing I wouldn't do was go near the very back of the cupboard, at the base of the stairs, the place where Jack insisted the entrance to hell lay. It always seemed frightening and mysterious. I'd heard Mam say to Jack that she'd seen a mouse there. Mice were an altogether different matter: they had sharp teeth. I wasn't certain how you could tell the difference between a mouse and a rat, but they were all potential biters. I curled up into a ball and imagined myself as Batman. In my mind I played out scenes where I was the Caped Crusader, fighting enemies and locking them up. It's sad to think that I would never kill Batman's foes in my imaginings, yet Jack I killed in my fantasies a thousand times a day.

I must have fallen asleep, because the next thing I recall is the cupboard door opening and breakfast being cooked. No words were spoken. I could barely move my legs, neck or back. They were stiff and painful. My body had been contorted for at least half a day in the tiny cupboard. I could barely open my eyes as I crawled out into the daylight. I felt like some kind of troglodyte emerging from its cave. No one paid me the slightest bit of notice; it was as though what had happened was normal.

My throat was parched and I was desperate for a drink. I was struggling to function. Because of the pain, I was unable to stand up, so I remained seated on the floor. The silence was deafening and, from the look on Mam's face and John's, it was clear that all was not well. They looked really worried. I was afraid that this was because I had done something else wrong and was going to suffer further. Mam and Jack left the kitchen, Jack giving me a hefty kick as he passed by me on his way to the living room. John bent down and lifted me onto a stool. Nervously, he whispered to me, checking I was OK, and he apologised for not having been able to prevent what had happened. To be honest, I had been asleep and oblivious for most of the night. I was exhausted and aching, though. With everything that had happened in the previous few days, my body and brain had shut down. I was still very tired, confused and distressed.

John told me that Jack had said to Mam that he wasn't yet finished with me and he was going to make sure that I understood my place in the house. Mam had apparently pleaded with him to stop hurting me and leave me alone. Jack had laughed at this and reminded her that it was 'his house' and he would do what he wanted to whoever he wanted whenever he wanted. John told me to expect Jack to return me to the cupboard as soon as breakfast was over. My heart sank.

Sure enough, Jack returned to the kitchen. I was still sitting naked on the stool. He gave me a knowing wink as he approached. 'What's up with you?' he asked. 'You look like you don't know whether your arsehole's been bored or punched.' I hadn't a clue what he meant by this. It was a term he would often use, and as I grew older I began to understand it as his sick way of referring to my obvious confusion.

'Get out of my sight, you little sod,' he told me. I jumped off the stool, ran from the kitchen and began to make my way upstairs. I had hardly climbed two steps when I heard his booming voice: 'Paul, who gave you permission to go upstairs? Get your arse down here now and get back in that cupboard.' As I returned, he was standing by the cupboard door, a nasty grin on his face. He pointed to the inside of the cupboard and I reluctantly climbed inside and curled up into a ball.

My eyes were closed by the time the door slammed shut, followed by the sliding of the bolt and the snapping of the padlock. My stomach began to ache and my head felt as though it was about to explode. No matter how hard I tried, I couldn't understand what it was I had done that was so bad. I opened my eyes and stared into the black gloom. I was certain I could see a pair of beady red eyes staring back at me. I hoped it was the Devil seeking me out and coming to take me, to release me from the awful life I had. I held my breath and waited in anticipation, but nothing happened.

Chapter 12

Help me, please!

When Jack and I were in the house at the same time, I knew that I might be locked in the cupboard at any moment. I soon learned that it mattered little what I had done or how I had behaved: if Jack wanted to put me in there, he would. The one saving grace I had was that he worked shifts, and so was often in bed or at work when I was at home.

I made every effort to be like the other children at school, yet somehow I always seemed to be separated from them by an invisible barrier. I don't think anyone likes to think of themselves as different. However, in hindsight, I didn't form the close friendships other children seemed to have, and my relationship with the staff (with the exception of Mrs Hogg) was far from good. There always seemed to be problems and my relationship with my first teacher wasn't helped by her constant humiliation of me in front of the entire class.

The first occasion I was made to feel and look completely stupid was when we were asked to do some simple sums. It was addition. John had taught me how to add up numbers using my fingers – it was simple – but the numbers our teacher wanted us to add up totalled more than my ten fingers. So I did what I thought was right: I removed my shoes and socks and used my toes. I was concentrating so hard that I didn't notice the teacher standing next to my desk. The class was silent. 'What do you think you're doing? Why have you taken your shoes and socks off?' she asked. I explained that I was using my toes to find the answer she wanted. 'Are you thick? It's rude to expose your bare feet in class. Put your socks and shoes back on and come to the front of the class. How stupid you are.'

The others were laughing at me as I fumbled about trying to replace my shoes on my feet. I walked to the front of the class and looked at her. 'I'm here, miss,' I said.

'I told you not to be rude. Don't interrupt me when I'm writing on the blackboard,' she snapped, and slapped me across the head. A ring on her finger caught the top of my ear and cut it open. The shock of being hit and the stinging sensation it left made me burst into tears. I was told to return to my seat and shut up.

At playtime, news of my counting technique spread around the school yard like wildfire. It seemed that everyone was laughing at me and making fun of me. I did my best to ignore it and pretend it didn't hurt, but each jibe ripped into my self-confidence and destroyed yet another part of me. Mrs Hogg did her best to support me and explained that little boys and girls mustn't remove their shoes and socks in public unless they had to, for example if they were getting changed to play sport, and certainly not in class. She told me to ignore the other boys and girls laughing at me and that the matter would soon be forgotten.

It was, but only because I once again erred. I got so fed up with the teachers bringing up the shoes and socks incident that I got up and ran out of class and school. I headed off along a busy main road but was chased after and returned by a staff member. I was taken before the headmaster and whipped six times on each hand with the cane. I was given no chance to explain or apologise; the punishment was delivered without any discussion.

It seemed that no matter how much effort I put into being good and trying to fit in with everyone else, I failed every time. At home, John was gradually growing up and finding new friends and gaining more freedom to get out of the house. This meant that I became a sitting duck for Jack's unwanted attention. Unbeknown to me, the school had been sending a letter home to Jack each time I did something wrong or stepped out of line. I wasn't aware of this until I told my first-ever lie. It wasn't a lie that was meant to cause harm or hurt; in fact, the only person it hurt was myself.

It was revealed that our class would be visiting a pool to learn to swim. The news was received by the class with great excitement and soon everyone was asking one another how far they could swim. For me, it was another nightmare. Jack had submerged me in freezing-cold bathwater many times, and the thought of being in what I thought of as a vast expanse of water with other people genuinely struck fear into me. I was determined that I would not be going to the swimming baths or anywhere near them. On the day of the visit, I bunked off school. I left home as normal but didn't get the bus. The following day, I told them I had been ill and was asked for a letter to confirm this. Naturally, no letter was ever provided, but the school wouldn't let it drop and wrote to Jack. The end result was that I received the cane. This time, it was delivered in front of the class. Jack didn't think this was sufficient punishment, though. He spelled it out on my bare bottom with his hands, slapping out each syllable: 'Paul is naughty. No one likes Paul. No one believes Paul.'

The swimming was a fortnightly event and my terror was evident for all to see. The instructors could see that my fear was very real and gave me all the encouragement they could. Nonetheless, I would go into a complete panic when in the water and wouldn't let go of the side of the pool. So much concern was raised about this that a letter was sent home asking if I had suffered any water-related trauma. Naturally, Jack lied and said that there was no reason for me to have such a fear. He dismissed it as another example of my bad behaviour. It took a great deal of courage, but I kept going to the swimming classes and did my best to overcome my phobia, although I rarely ventured beyond the shallow end and never went far from the side of the pool.

My life was torture. It was filled with so many dreadful experiences: Jack's abuse, the cupboard under the stairs, school, the cane, water and the fear of drowning. There seemed to be so little room for me to be a child; everything seemed to involve confrontation, to require inner strength and determination – and for what purpose?

One Saturday afternoon, something unexpected happened to change my life. Jack was on the back shift, and Mam, John and I were in the living room with the television on. The TV was black-and-white and the picture was nowhere near as clear as today's images. I can't remember precisely what I was doing, but whatever it was I stopped and focused wholly on the television when I heard the name Batman mentioned. This was a character I had only seen in comic books, as a cartoon, so to see a live-action version was incredible. It made him more real than ever. My eyes never moved from the screen as I caught my first glimpse of the Caped Crusader, dashing about in a wonderful car and fighting evil as only he could. Everything about him – his secret identity, the Batcave, the Batmobile, good overcoming evil – captivated me. His companion crime fighter, Robin, didn't have anything like the same charisma and didn't particularly interest me. Batman seemed an altogether more believable character to a young boy.

One of the attractions for me was the mask. It disguised his true identity and when he put it on it changed his personality, giving him strength and determination. He had suffered as a child, but he used that to his benefit later in life; it inspired him to fight crime and such devilishly charming yet evil characters as the Joker, the Riddler and the Penguin. When the credits rolled, I learned the names of the actors involved, including Adam West (Batman), Burt Ward (Robin), Alan Napier (Alfred), Madge Blake (Aunt Harriet), Frank Gorshin (the Riddler), Cesar Romero (the Joker) and Burgess Meredith (the Penguin) to name but a few. They gave something to my life, something I had never before encountered: hope!

My mam thought my love of the comics and the TV series was just a typical childhood passion. I could never turn to her and say that my identification with Batman was much deeper than ordinary, childish hero worship, that I had an affinity with him because I too had been forced to face real evil. The Batman logo and other images from the cartoons and the programme were permanently etched in my mind and I unsuccessfully tried to replicate them in drawings. These sketches were a helpful distraction for me. I could never watch the programme when Jack was about, but the episodes I did see gave me focus, inspiration and determination. As silly as it sounds, I realised that if Batman could survive the traumas that life had thrown at him, then so could I.

The re-emergence of Batman in my life, while it meant a lot to me, did nothing to stop Jack's abuse. In his life, there was no place for anything other than Jack and his own fulfilment. But his image and how others saw him was important to him, and that made him vulnerable and weak. Even as a child, I recognised this and tried to use it to stop the abuse, trying to please him by keeping out of his way and always doing as I was instructed by him, even when I hated what he wanted me to do. It was a constant battle, not that he saw it that way; he was too self-obsessed to consider my perspective. What he had in his favour was total control. As a child, I had no voice and I offered no challenge to his adult size and strength. The fact was that, no matter how much mental resolve I had, no matter what strategies I tried to use to keep the abuse to a minimum, Jack raped and abused me whenever he felt like it and realistically there was nothing I could do about it.

One afternoon, Jack told me to come into the covered passage that ran along the side of the house, to help him repair a small wooden stool he had acquired. It was a grotesque-looking thing, angular and square. It had felt glued to its unpadded seat. To me, it appeared home-made; it looked distinctly useless as a seat. I could never have described it so at the time, but in hindsight it had the appearance of an instrument of torture.

As Jack stood there looking at it, I saw that sadistic look in his eye and recognised that this stool was not simply a seat. It had some other purpose. I was made to watch as, with great care, he attached four leather straps, complete with buckles, to the base of each stool leg. With these secured, he told me to face the stool and place my feet by two of the legs. I did this and he moved swiftly to secure the buckles round my ankles, firmly strapping me to the legs of the stool. He then told me to bend over the stool and take hold of the bottom of the other two legs. I had no idea what was happening. Jack wrapped the straps round my wrists and secured them tightly. I couldn't move and struggled to keep my feet on the ground. I was in the most vulnerable position I could imagine, and being bound made me feel even greater panic. I had no idea what it was all about. At no point did I consider that this thing would be used in defiling me. Jack was making sure it was the right size for me and would meet his requirements. Over the space of three years, at the end of which I had outgrown it, I got to know that stool all too well.

Jack wasted no time in trying out his new toy. He had gone to work on the back shift, so we all felt relatively safe, knowing he wouldn't be back until after we'd gone to bed. When he returned that night, it was gone 10 p.m. and I was asleep. He removed me from my bed and took me downstairs. I saw John murmur and look up at me, his face grief-stricken. We both knew he could do nothing to prevent Jack from having his evil way.

The house was silent and there was no sign of Mam. I asked where she was and what was happening. I feared I was going into the cupboard. 'Shut up. Your mam's in bed asleep. I don't want her woken up, so no screaming or crying, do you hear?' he told me. There, in the middle of the front room, was the stool. He took off my pyjamas and strapped me over the stool. Then he raped me. The pain and fear were even worse than before. The smell of stale cigarettes and alcohol from his breath filled my nostrils. He made no effort to ease my pain and forced himself onto me, telling me I was a 'good boy' and a 'nice boy' for not crying out. He had his hand clamped over my mouth and was talking to the back of my head. If he had seen my face, he would have seen a little boy destroyed. Tears were running down my cheeks and my face must have been distorted with pain. If he had looked into my eyes, he would have seen a cold black stare, lifeless and without emotion.

I stared at the carpet and imagined myself as an adult, able to defend myself. I imagined myself with a gun held to his forehead and him pleading for mercy. I felt guilty for thinking such nasty thoughts, yet, all the time, he was raping me and enjoying every moment of it.

Help me, please!

Afterwards, he left me strapped to the stool. I was quietly sobbing and hating my life and myself while he cleared up the mess he had made on the carpet. The feeling of sickness overwhelmed me and I vomited all over the place. He made no comment and cleared it up. I was released several minutes later and taken upstairs to the bathroom, where the cold bath was run and I was again submerged. This time, I offered no resistance. I simply let him push me under the water and hold me there, partly because I hadn't the strength to fight and partly because I wanted him to end my life. Because I didn't struggle, he seemed less interested in or pleased with what he was doing and instead of keeping me there until I was desperately gasping for air, he pulled me out. I believed I had learned something: resistance gave him more pleasure and satisfaction; submission didn't excite him and therefore he lost interest.

No matter how much I washed after an attack, I still felt dirty and ashamed. One day when I was out in town with Mam, my auntie commented that I rarely looked into adults' faces and stared down at the ground too much for someone my age. She said it was as though my self-confidence had disappeared. She was right. I hated looking into the face of an adult in case I saw the sadistic and grotesque lustful look that sent me into a panic. I despised being looked up and down by adults in a way that made me feel frightened and cheap, as though I was some kind of doll for them to play with. By now, I hated being anywhere near Jack. His smell, appearance and general demeanour sickened me. It was wrong for a child to think so badly of his parent, but I really hated him for what he was doing to me.

My attitude at school had begun to change. Instead of feeling happy or excited or enjoying different subjects and games, I lost interest in getting involved in anything.

My schoolwork deteriorated, as I would spend entire lessons daydreaming, thinking about different things that could make my life better – running away, Mam and Jack splitting up, Jack dying – none of which, as far as I could see, was realistic or likely to happen.

The worst was when the headmaster would take the class. He was a peculiar man, unforgiving and rigid in his attitude towards me. He had said from the outset that he thought I was a bad boy and that bad boys needed to be punished to make them stop being bad and to do as they were told. He seemed totally humourless and he didn't like the fact that I occasionally whispered to others during lessons. I wasn't having full-blown conversations; I was just looking for the answers to questions I didn't know.

One day, when our usual teacher was absent and a substitute teacher was taking our class, it was wintertime and the radiators weren't working. The classroom was freezing cold and a paraffin heater had been brought in and placed near the teacher at the front of the class. We had been given tests to complete and told to take them to the front for him to mark. I joined the queue at the teacher's desk and saw him putting ticks on the papers of the kids in front of me. I was pleased because I knew I had got many of the questions right and he would be giving me ticks too.

When it was my turn, I handed the teacher my book to mark. He took one look at the front cover, which had a pencil sketch of the Batman logo on it, and flew into a rage. He took hold of my wrist and slapped me a couple of times around the head with his free hand, reprimanding me for defacing the workbook. It was an overreaction, as other children had drawings on their book covers and had not endured any kind of punishment or telling-off. I told him I would rub it out straight away, as it was only drawn in pencil, and said I was very sorry. He slapped me in the face again and I began to cry. It was humiliating. There is only so much animosity and cruelty you can take from adults as a child before it begins to destroy you.

My sad state did nothing to lessen this teacher's anger, and he put both hands on my chest and pushed me backwards. I was skinny and weighed next to nothing, so I was unable to prevent him from sending me flying backwards. I fell onto the red-hot paraffin heater, it fell over and I landed on top of it. At first I felt nothing, but other people in the class were screaming and the look on the teacher's face told me he was worried. He leapt to his feet and ran towards me. In my panic, I thought he was coming to hit me again, so I moved to stand up. It was then that I felt a searing pain in my right leg. It was stuck to the paraffin heater; my skin had literally melted onto it. The smell was disgusting. The teacher dived on top of me and demanded that I lie still. He shouted to one of the other children to go and fetch Mrs Hogg and to tell her that Paul Mason had burned himself. My leg felt as though it was on fire and I instinctively reached down to touch where it hurt. It felt wet and had the texture of a gooey mess.

Help was there quickly and soon I had calmed down. The teacher repeated like a mantra that it wasn't his fault, I had stepped back onto the heater, he hadn't pushed me at all. I looked into his eyes. He was lying and yet there was no remorse or guilt there. Mrs Hogg carried me through to another room and laid me down. I saw the extent of my injury. The burn was circular and about four inches across, covering the width of my leg. It was seeping blood and other fluids. I looked at my guardian angel and she assured me that I would be all right, she would make it better. Those were the last words I heard before I passed out.

When I came round, my leg was smothered in cream

and bandaged. It was still painful, but the cream was cooling and made it less uncomfortable than it could have been. Mrs Hogg said she would come home with me on the bus after school to explain what had happened. I told her that the teacher had pushed me into the heater and that it wasn't my fault. She reassured me that she understood that and told me not to worry because I wasn't in trouble and no one was going to tell me off. She didn't know Jack, and I didn't want her to meet him. I was scared he would harm her or call her names like he did Mam. I begged Mrs Hogg not to take me home and told her I would be OK. She said she would write a letter to my parents explaining what had happened.

I managed to get home without incident. Mam was panicked by the state of my leg. She bathed and treated it and put me to bed. When Jack learned of my injury, he wasn't bothered. He laughed and dismissed it as nothing serious, and told me that would teach me not to play around hot paraffin heaters, or fire, ever again. I'd believed in this case he would surely show some care and sympathy towards me, but he failed to step up to the mark and once again let me down.

Looking back, it was a serious incident and could have been a whole lot worse. If my uniform had caught fire, I might have been permanently maimed or even killed. It shows how times have changed. If something like that were to happen today, I would have been rushed to hospital. All manner of paperwork would have had to be completed and criminal charges might have been brought against the teacher. Yet, as the situation was, I was the one who was made to feel guilty, even though I was only a little boy eager to please his teachers.

I was granted a couple of days off school so that the wound could begin to heal. It was something I needed, a bit of space and time to think. Jack was out at work for most of the time, so it was good, and I got to spend two whole days with Mam. Unfortunately, instead of being able to relax and bond with her, I recognised in her a fear similar to that which I lived with. She was constantly on the go, never sitting still, always fretting over whether Jack would like this or expect that, or want something altogether different when he came home from work. She was living (maybe 'surviving' would be more accurate) on the edge, chain-smoking and genuinely frightened of her own husband. I desperately wanted to be able to tell her to stop worrying, that John and I would make it all right for her, that we would sort Jack out. It was the first time in my life that I felt I had failed my mam. There was nothing I could do, and I realised that there was nothing she could do either. Like John and me, she was trapped in her own nightmare.

Once again, John showed his strength of character through his attentive care and understanding of my needs. He was angry about what the teacher had done to me, and said he was going to come in before school to remonstrate with him and make his feelings known. When I returned to school, everyone was talking about my brother turning up and heatedly speaking to this teacher. That's the sort of thing you would expect a father to do. John was in every way a more responsible and caring brother than Jack could ever hope to be a father.

This wasn't all John did for me. One evening, he sat down with me and told me of a grand plan he had that would make my life so much better. Secretly, he was going to transform the cupboard under the stairs into the Batcave. He would draw Batman logos and leave messages on the wooden undersides of the steps, out of sight of Jack, should he ever poke his head inside the cupboard. He would even create a Bat-Torch, a Batman sweetie bag and a Batman book box with comics in it. Each of these items he would hide at the very back of the cupboard, so that when I was locked inside I would have light, comics and sweets, and I could pretend I was Batman inside the Batcave. Jack would never know; it would be our secret. It was a fantastic idea and one that thrilled me. It felt like we were getting one over on Jack. We were transforming a place where evil lurked into a place where hope existed.

Chapter 13

Monsters all around

To say that I avoided the cupboard under the stairs at all costs would be an understatement. It terrified me. Yet knowing that John had been inside and had created something unique and special for me in there, I began to feel an element of curiosity and wanted to take a look. My imagination was running wild. I wasn't willing to risk taking a peek, though. It was our secret alone, and I could never betray the trust John had placed in me. If Jack found out what we had done, he would hit the roof and punish us both very badly. So my curiosity had to be harnessed until Jack felt the urge to imprison me in there again.

In the meantime, I was shocked and more than a little scared when one weekend I was told that a friend of Jack, a teacher, was coming to pick me up and take me to his house. He wanted to help me in my schooling. Jack seemed thrilled about it and thought it would be good for me. I was told that other children would also be attending, so it wouldn't be just me and this teacher. 'You'll learn a lot from this,' Jack said gleefully.

It concerned me that he was suddenly interested in my life. Something didn't seem right about the whole affair.

A car pulled up outside and driving it was a stern-looking man. Jack took me out to the car and was assured

I would be home in good time. The drive to the teacher's house was a long one.

He walked me round his garden. Afterwards, we went inside and he gave me some orange squash and assured me that the other children would be there shortly. It was then that I had the courage to look up into his face. I began to think of him differently; he seemed like a nice man. However, my blood ran cold when I saw in his eyes the look that terrified me. I could sense his eagerness and tried to keep distance between us.

I was given sweets and generally made a fuss of until I found myself trapped in a room with him. He caned my bottom six or seven times, making sure I was under his complete control, before raping me. It was over quickly. I never spoke. He told me that it was all OK because Jack had said it was all right for him to do it to me. I cried. I was sore and I knew I was bleeding. The sick feeling in the pit of my stomach propelled itself upwards, hurling itself through my body and onto the floor. The man furiously cleaned up the mess and told me to go and stand outside his house. I wanted to run away, but I had no idea where I was or where I could go.

Soon after, he appeared and told me to jump into his car and he would take me home. Not a word was spoken between us throughout the journey. He was sweating and I could smell his fear. He knew what he had done was wrong and perhaps he felt guilty and wished he hadn't done it. At least that was what I hoped. When we arrived back at Crindledyke Estate, he told me to remember that it was our secret and that Jack had said it was OK for him to do it, so no one would believe me if I said it wasn't what everyone wanted. I got out of the car and walked back into the house. Jack rushed past me and went out to speak to the man. I stopped on the stairs and watched them both from a window. He handed Jack some money, pound notes. I wondered what it was for. Maybe it was a present for me, I thought; perhaps it was another way of saying sorry for what he had done to me. They laughed as they talked, and as Jack stood up, he slipped the money into his pocket. I never saw it again.

I went into my bedroom and was soon joined there by Jack, who told me to strip off my clothes and get into the cold bath he was going to run. As usual, I was lifted into the bath and made to sit there for what felt like for ever before Jack reappeared and submerged me, all the time reminding me that it was my fault these things happened to me, it was because I was a bad boy, a naughty boy who no one liked, and bad boys have bad things done to them. I wasn't prepared to be submerged, so when he took hold of my shoulders and forced me under, I let out an almighty scream, so loud that it was heard outside the house. A neighbour, alerted to the sound of a child's terror, knocked on the front door and enquired if everything was OK. Jack assured him it was and said it was 'Paul being a naughty boy and demanding attention'. He apologised to the man for my bad behaviour and disturbing him.

I had got out of the bath and was drying myself when Jack stood in front of me and said, 'Don't bother getting dressed. You're going in the cupboard for the rest of the day.' I shivered with fear and felt myself begin to shake. Jack was furious with me, and when we got to the cupboard door he grabbed hold of my hair, yanked my head forward and pushed me into the dark space before me. I fell onto boxes and the floor, the door slamming shut behind me and the bolt sliding into place.

It took me a while to calm down. What had happened had been too frantic and chaotic for me to take in. Now here I was, locked away like a prisoner in a tiny cell. I was in solitary confinement. Outside the cupboard door, I could hear life going on without me. It felt like no one cared, or if they did they were powerless to help me. Then I heard John walk by the door. He was humming the *Batman* theme tune, reminding me of what he'd done inside the cupboard. Suddenly, I felt my heart begin to race with excitement.

As quietly as I could, I felt about in the dark, seeking out the Bat-Torch John had said would be in a gym bag close to the back of the cupboard. I found it, gently slid the on switch forward and the cupboard lit up. On the lens of the torch, John had drawn a red Batman logo, which created a shadow like the Bat-Signal. As I shone the torch on the wooden underside of the steps, I caught my first sight of John's artwork. It was fantastic: a red Batman logo and lots of other images too, the Batmobile and writing. As I moved the torchlight further round, my delight was abruptly ended as my eyes focused on a huge black spider in its web. There were often spiders of all sizes and types in the cupboard, and the joy of having a secret Batcave that only John and I knew about diminished as I realised that I was still a prisoner in a place filled with real-life horrors.

For a moment, I wondered whether I would have been better off not knowing that the huge spider was in there with me. The torch, while being a great asset, had in fact created new nightmares. I backed away as far as possible from the spider and sat watching it, waiting for it to move. One of the big problems I had was returning the torch to where I'd found it. This would have to be done in the dark and meant my head coming within inches of the spider. I had no option, I had to do it, but it was hardly the most calm and coordinated move I have ever made. I closed my eyes and held my breath as I leaned forward and put the torch back. Now, of course, I was in the dark alone with a huge spider that I couldn't see. That fear was nothing more than a distraction, though. Soon I remembered what had happened to me. My bottom was still sore and my stomach ached as though it had been punched or kicked.

Jack didn't let me out of the cupboard until he was going to bed. I was hungry and tired and my body ached from the contortions forced upon me by the cramped space. I could never admit that to Jack, though; that would be seen as a weakness and further expose my vulnerability. He told me to go to my bed. In my bedroom, I went to put on my pyjamas only to be stopped by John. He grabbed hold of my arm and told me that there was blood coming out of my bottom and that the backs of my legs were covered in it. John cleaned me up as best he could and put me to bed.

The following morning, the blood was still dripping from my bottom. We had no alternative but to tell Mam, as it was clearly not going to stop. Jack was alerted and at once said he knew what to do. He laid me on my front and inserted a 'magic bandage' into my bottom. He told me to lie there on my front until he was certain the blood had stopped. I lay still for several hours. Every so often, he would return to the bedroom and replace the dirty, bloodstained bandage with a clean one. I cannot recall Jack ever being as gentle with me.

It was several years later that I realised that the so-called 'magic bandage' was nothing more than a tampon, and the reason he was being so gentle and caring was not through genuine love but because he realised that if any internal damage had been caused to me it would require hospital treatment. That, in turn, would reveal what was happening to me and, of course, he would have to face a lot of questions and be in big trouble.

The blood did stop, though my stomach pains persisted. Jack dismissed the pains as my muscles stretching through overuse. He told me that it would be good for me to use my muscles and that one day I would grow into a big strong man like him. That thought repulsed me. The last thing I ever wanted to be was anything like him. It was around this time that I suspected that every adult male in the world wanted to hurt little children and see them cry. I couldn't understand that Jack and his teacher friend were both sexual deviants who had recognised each other's desires through some social chemistry or law of attraction.

Jack began to push the boundaries further and further. Understandably, I was a depressed child who struggled to trust anyone, especially adults and authority figures. For some reason, he felt it proper to record my sadness; he took photographs of me during some of the most distressing times in my life. Once, when I was pushing a swing, the seat flew back and hit me in the mouth, knocking out my front four teeth and cutting my lips and gums wide open. Before I was taken to the dentist and doctor by a neighbour, Jack had me pose for a picture.

He had no idea of morality where his family was concerned; both Mam and John were forced to act on his every whim or suffer the consequences. John, however, was beginning to turn rebellious and outspoken. As he grew older, he was less and less the target of Jack's unwanted attention. I remember one evening John being sent to the airing cupboard to fetch a tea towel. He returned not only with a tea towel but carrying a briefcase. 'Look what I found at the back of the airing cupboard,' he said excitedly, thinking he had happened upon some missing treasure or something. He opened it up and inside were a pair of brilliant white gloves, a sash and an apron. 'What's this stuff?' he asked out loud. Jack turned to see what the fuss was about and at once leapt from his chair and grabbed the briefcase from John. 'Don't touch that. That's stuff for my club. It's not for your filthy little fingers to touch.'

John was curious and asked what sort of club it was where men wore aprons and gloves. 'A band, perhaps? What musical instrument do you play?' he gleefully commented. I was horrified by the response. Jack punched him full-on in the face. John shot back across the floor and fell to the ground. He didn't move. He was knocked out. I immediately began to cry because I thought John had been killed. Jack walked calmly into the kitchen and returned with a tumbler full of water, which he threw over John's face, causing him to stir and wake up. His lips were swollen and blood covered his face.

What happened next will live with me for ever. John stood up with not a tear in his eye nor a quiver in his voice and stared deep into Jack's eyes, saying, 'You'll never get the chance to do that to me again. I hate you, you evil bastard. One day your time will come and I will enjoy every moment of it, watching you squirm and shrivel up like the old toad you are.'

Jack was clearly as shocked as I was, yet his response was swift and succinct: 'Get out of my fucking house and don't ever come back, you horrible little bastard.'

John replied, 'I will and then it'll all come out. Mark my words, it will all come out.'

Jack suddenly changed his attitude. He chased after John and asked him to stay and sort things out. John agreed to stay, but only until he left school and was old enough to get away from him. Jack accepted that and thanked him, telling him that he had turned into a fine man and how he would make a great father one day. John retaliated with a very cutting and direct, 'Yes, like you would know what makes a good father.' He walked out of the room and upstairs.

That confrontation released John from Jack's clutches

and left the focus of attention very much on me. I was frightened about what the backlash was going to be. If someone angered or annoyed Jack, someone else would suffer. John went out with his friends, leaving just Mam, Jack and me in the house. The tension in the air was obvious, and I was shaking, waiting for the situation to explode. On this occasion, it was Mam who took the punishment. I only witnessed a small part of what happened, but he battered her – and I don't use that description lightly – he literally battered her into submission. There wasn't any reason for the assault; it was his way of dealing with things. I saw him punch her in the head and about the body and kick her as she fell to the floor pleading with him. I began to cry and took hold of his trouser leg and begged him to stop. With one slap, he knocked me to the floor.

Mam was on the floor too, her face bloodied and her eyes swollen. She yelled at me to get out of his way and go to my bed. I didn't want to leave her alone with him. He was standing over her with the look of a deranged monster on his face. He bent down, took hold of her blood-covered white blouse and ripped it open. He then pulled at her bra until he managed to yank it off. I was confused and struggling to understand what was happening. I thought he was going to kill her and I involuntarily emptied my bladder. Mam was begging him to stop and by the tone of her cries I knew she was hurt. I stood there helpless and really scared for her. She turned and looked over at me. 'Please, Paul, please, go to your bed now,' she wailed. Jack turned to me and snarled, 'Get out of my fucking sight. Go to your room and wait for me. You're next.'

I ran as fast as I could to my bedroom and slammed the door closed behind me. I slid down the door to the floor and held my hands over my ears to drown out the sounds of the pain being inflicted on Mam downstairs. I didn't understand it then, but she was being raped by her husband. There was no escape and I knew from what Jack had said to me earlier that it was only a matter of time before he came in search of me. My eyes were tightly shut and I was sobbing hysterically. Then I remembered Batman and asked myself how he would have handled it. The young Bruce Wayne could have done nothing more than I had. As difficult as it may be for some to understand how a child could consider such things, I seriously wondered how I could kill Jack. I wanted him to stop hurting us, leave Mam alone and let us be a proper family.

It was much later when I felt someone pushing at the other side of the bedroom door. I was lying behind it, forming a barrier. I was rigid with fear, as I thought it was Jack. Then I heard John whisper, 'Paul, what's going on? Open the door. Are you OK?' I moved and John burst in and lifted me onto the bed. I could hardly speak as I told him what had happened after he'd gone out. 'Where's Mam?' he asked. I told him she was downstairs with Jack. John looked worried as he told me that there was no one downstairs. He rushed out of the room and to their bedroom door. It was locked from the inside. 'Mam, Mam, are you in there? Are you OK?' he yelled through the keyhole. I heard my mam reply to his question, saying everything was all right and telling him to go to bed. It was obvious from her voice that everything was not all right, so John threatened to go and fetch a policeman, one of our neighbours. Jack must have leapt out of bed and opened the door in one move, since he was suddenly face to face with John.

'Paul said you've hurt Mam. I want to see her,' he told Jack.

'Paul's nothing but a liar. He's making things up because he's a bad boy and he wants all of my attention. He doesn't like me loving you and your mam,' Jack told him.

The Cupboard Under the Stairs

I felt a lump in my throat. My own father was telling lies about me to my brother. Then I heard Mam speak out: 'It's all right, John, I'm not hurt. I think Paul might have been frightened because Jack and I were having an argument. It's all OK.' The shock of hearing Mam telling lies and dismissing what I had witnessed as a mere argument really hurt. What I didn't understand was that she was trying to protect us all from Jack by minimising the severity of the situation.

John returned to our bedroom. He didn't believe any of it and told me to go to sleep as we had school the following day. At breakfast the next morning, we were both shocked by the state of Mam's face. Her eyes were black and blue. They were nothing but two slits in her head. Her nose was swollen and there was a huge yellow bruise on her cheek. I rushed up to her and held her tightly and began to cry. She told John she had fallen down the stairs in the middle of the night and not to say anything about it to anyone; she was going to take a few days off work and Jack was going to contact them to let them know about her fall. As she told us this lie, her eyes were filled with tears. There was no sign of Jack. He was still in bed. As we were about to leave for school, John yelled out from the foot of the stairs for everyone in the house to hear, 'We love you, Mam,' then, 'I fucking hate you, Jack.'

At school, I was thoroughly miserable and inadvertently made matters worse for myself. The teacher asked us to write a story about something memorable that we had done ourselves or as a family at the weekend. I saw this as my opportunity to speak out against what Jack was doing, so I retold the details of what had occurred: Jack battering Mam, tearing her clothes off and telling me he was going to hurt me next. When I handed it in, I saw the look of disbelief emerge on the teacher's face. Her eyes opened wide and her jaw dropped as she gasped for air. She rushed from the classroom and apparently went straight to the headmaster. There were a few minutes of silence before the headmaster appeared at the classroom door. He looked directly at me and waved his finger, telling me to go with him immediately.

I was taken to his office, where he asked me why I had chosen to write the things I had. I told him it had happened. He told me that he didn't believe me. I felt sure that anyone I tried to seek help from would take Jack's side and dismiss what I was saying as not being true. After school, Jack was contacted and made aware of what I had done. On returning home, I was stripped naked and thrown into the cupboard under the stairs, where at least, despite the brute of a spider watching me from its web, I could become Batman.

Chapter 14

The flying Scotsman

As I grew older, I was allowed to exercise my freedom a little more than I had been before. Other children would come to the house and call for me, asking whoever answered the door if I was 'allowed to come out and play'. I often arranged for them to do this, so I could get out of Jack's way. Living in the countryside, there was very little in the way of amenities for us children, so we would invariably end up playing hide-and-seek and football. I loved it. Being part of a team and treated as normal was wonderful. Once I was out of the house, I would stay out for as long as possible. The other children would be called in for meals or to watch a favourite television programme, whereas I stayed out on my own, often in the rain, kicking a football or amusing myself by playing on the communal swing and seeing how far I could jump from it when the swing was at its full height.

However, as I got older, I was also introduced to a whole raft of new experiences against my will. One evening, when I was six or seven, Jack told me he was going to take me to a club on RAF 14MU that I would enjoy. It was a model-railway club and other children apparently went there. I was somewhat confused by this, since I wasn't especially keen on trains, whether model ones or full-blown steam engines. The extent of my interest was a children's television series about a railwayman, *Casey Jones*. Not that I was a fan, particularly, it was just one of those programmes that was on and I liked the theme tune. Jack had his own model-railway set that I was not allowed near, its track neatly nailed to a hardboard base. The engines and trucks were kept in the loft. John had often shown an interest in it when he was secretly rooting about up there, but to me it was Jack's toy, and I wanted no part of anything that was connected with him. For a start, it was boring and far too intricate, and all model trains did was go round and round the same piece of track.

In any case, I was forced along to the RAF 14MU model-railway club. It was held in an old cream-coloured Nissen hut. Jack was keen to introduce me to the people who owned their own model-railway exhibits. As soon as I walked into the place, I knew it was going to be full of people with whom I had nothing in common. On tables along two sides of the main hall were various model-railway layouts, each with its own adult operator excitedly flicking switches and turning knobs so as to make the tiny trains go faster, reverse or puff out smoke. The place had a foul smell of lubricating oil and the people who operated the train sets were in a world of their own. Some had created entire model towns around their railways. I found it all quite scary and couldn't understand what pleasure an adult could get from such activity.

My lack of interest must have been clear, since I was virtually ignored the entire time we were there. Jack had to go to a special adult meeting in a room at the back of the club, so he left me to my own devices. I went up to some other children who were there, none of whom I recognised or knew. None of them was playing or seemed remotely interested in the train sets. I asked if they liked trains or had their own model railways. None of them had. It was a decidedly strange place and I was spooked by the dull atmosphere and the unhappy look of the other children present.

After about an hour, Jack reappeared and told me I was now a member of the model-railway club and that I would attend every week. I was underwhelmed by the news, though it hardly surprised me that I was again being forced to get involved in something I had no interest in. At home, I told John about the model-railway club and how Jack had enrolled me as a member. He thought it was hilarious and laughed at me. Each week, I was taken to the club and made to look at the sets and layouts around the room, watching the trains go round and round while Jack attended his meeting in the back room. Over time, I began to notice children emerging from the room crying and appearing to be very upset. When one of these children came out, an adult would take them outside and I wouldn't see them again until the following week. I was curious as to what happened in the room, especially as Jack had told me that it was where the adults met.

I asked one of the other children what happened in there. She was pretty girl called Lindsay and I felt strangely attracted to her in a childish sort of way. She ignored my question and instead asked me which school I attended and how old I was. Her father was a police officer too and she said she had met Jack. This took me by surprise, since I couldn't see how she would ever have met him. He was hardly an approachable sort of adult. I asked how she had met him and she pointed towards the door of the room. 'In there. I've met him in there.' I recognised the look that flashed across her face. I knew it myself. It was a look of absolute hatred, not of anyone else but of oneself. I asked what happened in the room, upon which an adult appeared and intervened in our conversation, telling me not to be so nosy and to leave

Lindsay alone as she was wanted in the back room. I watched her being led down the main hall and through the door, looking down at the ground the whole time.

Lindsay had hardly been in there a few minutes when Jack came out. He told me that it was none of my business what happened in the room and if I was so interested he would take me in on our next visit. I immediately suspected that something very wrong happened in there and saw it as a threatening place, a larger version of the cupboard under the stairs, if you like, a place where evil lurked.

My next visit to the club was a fortnight later, since Jack had been at work and we had missed a meeting. This time, when we arrived, I was told to go and sit on a chair at the back of the hall and wait to be called into the room. Jack told me I must call all the men in there 'sir' and that the women were to be referred to as 'ma'am'. I was told that I should not ask any questions and speak only when I was spoken to. When someone told me I could 'move on' I was to say, 'Thank you for your time.' I wondered what it could all be about and what was going to happen. I was a bit excited – perhaps, despite my gut instinct, it might be something fun – but also apprehensive and nervous.

The door opened and a woman appeared. She was very pretty and smiled and called out my name. I went to her and she led me into a small area behind some screens. The woman told me to take off my shoes and socks and place them on the floor behind me. For a moment, I wondered what all this had to do with a model-railway club. The lady told me to undress but to leave my underpants on. She told me to stop shaking and assured me that everything would be fine; I wasn't to be scared. 'The people in here are from the RAF and they're policemen and women and all kinds of people who don't want to hurt you. They want to play with you.' I felt sick as it dawned on me what she meant when she said they wanted to play with me. She meant it in the same way Jack did. I was told that every ten minutes I would change station; effectively what this meant was that I would move to someone different, the next adult waiting around the room. I was petrified by the thought of what was going to happen to me. The pain of being raped by Jack and his teacher friend was unbearable. What if these people were all going to do that to me, one after the other? I wanted to run away, but they had removed any chance of that by stripping me to my underpants. I was trapped.

A man called out, 'Next!', and the woman told me to quickly go to the next person. As I stepped out from behind the screens, I saw half a dozen other children silently moving round the room. Each one looked dreadful, as though they were in a nightmare. As I entered the next area, I was confronted by a fat man sitting on a chair. He was completely naked and his feet were in a bowl of hot water. He asked my name and began to touch me. I pulled away from him and his grip tightened around my arm. 'Come over here, Paul. I'm not going to hurt you, I promise. I want you to wash me. Take that cloth and wash my legs and feet for me. Be my slave.' It was a strange request and I asked him what he meant, at which point he slapped me hard around the head. 'Don't ask questions, boy. Just do it.' I knelt before him and did as he asked. He gestured to me and told me to gently wash the tops of his legs, specifically around his private parts. He was right: I didn't at all feel like a little boy, I felt like a slave. I was pleased when the authoritative voice bellowed out, 'Next!', and I could get away from this horrible fat person. I said, 'Thank you for your time,' and left.

In the next area, I was thankful to see a woman waiting. She looked anything but threatening or intimidating; in fact, she looked the sort of trustworthy person I could tell about everything that was happening in my life and she would sort it out for me. Again, I was wrong. She was very pleasant and nice, but I was forced to touch her in places I had never before encountered. She was wearing a dressing gown, beneath which she had no clothes on.

There were six or seven stations we each had to visit. In each one, further degrading and disgusting sexual acts took place. There were men and women of all ages. Finally, I reached an area where a number of children were sitting on chairs. Here, no one looked at anyone else; eyes were fixed firmly on the floor and no words were spoken. This was the final station, and the sounds of pain emerging from behind the screen frightened me.

One by one, the children were taken away. Each time one disappeared behind the screen, we had to move up a place, until finally I was next in line. I glanced up and saw Lindsay enter the area. Our eyes met and, for a fleeting moment, the sadness we both felt gave us a connection. Then I was pulled from my chair and taken behind the screens, where another friendly-looking woman waited. She looked much younger than the other woman. She removed my underpants and washed me all over. She defiled me with her fingers. I was told not to shout or scream, as it wouldn't help, and if I did as I was told it would be over very quickly and there would be a nice surprise for me at the end that would make me feel better. I nodded and was pushed through a curtain.

Behind it, a man who I can only describe as looking like the cartoon character Willo the Wisp was standing with his private parts in his hand. He moved towards me and told me to touch and kiss them. I moved away from him, but a wall prevented me from escaping his clutches. He grabbed hold of my head and forced me onto him. I gagged, as he was almost choking me. I was scared and felt myself weeing on the floor. I was pushed onto a bed face down and raped. I bit into the blanket and stopped myself from screaming out as he repeatedly abused me. It was over very quickly and afterwards I felt disgusting and dirty.

The rapist grabbed hold of me and told me to say thank you. I looked at him, and no matter how much he tried to make me say it, I couldn't bring myself to thank him. He pushed his face close to mine and angrily said, 'I said, say thank you, you disgusting little bastard.' I pulled my head back and asked him if he was a policeman? 'No, I am not, I am far more important than that. I tell the police and everyone else in Carlisle what to do. I am the most important man in this town. I control everything. Now you will say thank you or else.' I was repulsed by his arrogance and his belief that everyone had to respect him because he was someone important, I wanted to show him that I too was important in my own way, so I spat in his face.

There was a brief moment of confusion, as clearly no one had ever behaved like this to him before. He jumped back, wiping my dripping saliva from his face and spitting out the residue. He was coughing and very red in the face. I stood up and put as much distance between us as possible. He was clearly shocked by what I had done. So was I. It was totally out of character. He looked at me in disgust before shaking his head in disbelief and telling me that I was a loose cannon and that when I returned he would knock sense into me and make me suffer. I asked him who he was again. He told me that he was my 'worst enemy', that I would always be under his watchful eye and that revenge would be his. Stubbornly, I told him that he could never be my worst enemy since that title belonged to Jack and that, in my opinion, anyone who wouldn't tell me their name was a coward. I was stunned by what I was saying. It dawned on me that I had removed myself from the atrocities occurring around me and moved into Batman mode.

The man was speechless. He moved to slap me, but I moved out of his reach. Finally, he lost control and shouted at me to get out, pointing to the curtain behind me. I skipped through this and realised I had not completely escaped. I still had no clothes on, and I found myself standing in the middle of the room. All eyes were on me, and again I was nothing more than a frightened little boy. A man picked me up and carried me to an inflatable paddling pool, where several children sat quietly. He threw me in and told me to stay there. The water in the pool was disgusting. It smelled of sex and filth. Those of us sitting in there cared little about the smell, though; we were thankful to still be alive.

I never did find out the identity of the 'Willo the Wisp' man. I never saw him again, so if he was ever there again, I was kept away from him. Jack never once mentioned the incident to me, nor did anyone else. Whether the man felt shamed or appalled by my retaliation, I do not know. However, it seems that he deemed me one to be avoided. I can see his pathetic frame and weaselly face as vividly as ever to this day. One day, it would be nice to confront him, especially in a court of law. From what he said, he may well have been part of the criminal justice system himself. I will never know. It was obvious from everything I was told that many of the people who frequented the model-railway club were not everyday working-class people, nor were they there for the love of toy trains. Many were affluent, the upper classes and figures of authority; they used the place as a cover for their crimes.

What better place to have a house of filth? The building was deep inside a secure RAF unit, with guarded fences that stood ten feet tall, on top of which sat three rows of barbed wire. It wasn't the kind of place that any member of the public could access; you had to have Ministry of

The Cupboard Under the Stairs

Defence security screening and clearance at a high level to gain access to the unit, and passes and a purpose for visiting. This is another reason why I believe the vast majority of those involved were from the upper levels of society.

Jack had access to all areas of RAF 14MU. Our house was filled with MoD property that he had stolen, everything from nuts and bolts to complete sets of spanners and toolkits, all bearing the crow's foot. He treated the electrical workshops on the base as his own free places to shop. He would tell John how he entered these with keys in the evenings or when he was on night shift and take whatever he wanted, stealing from the Government. Over the years, he must have had tens of thousands of pounds' worth of equipment from the MoD. He stole radio receivers and transmitters. Our cupboards and drawers were overflowing with nicked MoD property. Jack, you see, believed he was above the law; his position and influence in the Masonic community allowed him freedom to do as he wished. What better position of power could he hold? I believe he frequently abused his role as a police officer and his position as a member of the Masonic brethren.

After that railway club initiation, Jack didn't always take me there. More often than not, I would be collected by some unnamed stranger in a car and returned home a couple of hours later. Each time, I was one of a number of children who were abused in various ways before finally being raped. Different deviants wanted different things from us. One man liked to slap bottoms and see his handprint left on the skin. Another man wanted us to sit on his knee, where he bounced us up and down as he told dirty stories. A woman, whom I knew to be a police officer, enjoyed being stroked on her private areas by children. These were the lesser categories of deviant behaviour.

Sadly, more often than not, the abuse involved oral sex or full-blown rape.

Over the few years I attended the railway club, my bond with Lindsay grew stronger. We never openly discussed what was happening or how it made us feel. It was very much an innocent, childlike relationship, more about what wasn't said between us than anything that ever was. My brother John apart, Lindsay was the only person in the world who I could look at and instinctively know what she was thinking. She was strong, much stronger than me, yet she had a vulnerability about her that made me want to protect her, take her from the grasp of these evil people who were defiling us at every opportunity. We somehow seemed to withdraw ourselves from all that was happening around us at the railway club and mentally connect. Yet despite my affection towards her, I could never openly display or discuss with anyone any positive feelings I had for her, because if it ever got out that we were friends or had formed a bond, then we would both be punished.

One of the paedophiles who attended the model-railway club was a bald-headed Scottish man who had a sick and disgusting penchant for bottoms. He would lay himself on a sleeping bag and we would be sat on a four-legged stool minus its seat above his face. Then this disgusting individual would touch, lick and kiss our bottoms. Very often, the shock and pain of this caused the abused little boy or girl to scream out. This man was extremely repulsive. The way he looked, talked and the foul noises he made as he satiated his desires were sickening.

He would dress in different attire but mainly wore a uniform. I had no understanding of what any of this was about. I had seen the emblem on his uniform many times on some of the paraphernalia Jack kept and believed it to be something to do with war and soldiers. One day at school, I recognised the uniform and the badges as one of the teachers discussed the Second World War and showed us images in a book. My excited outburst caused shock in the class: 'Miss, miss, I know what these are. They're British soldiers, I've seen the badges on the uniforms the soldiers wear.'

The teacher's eyes opened wide and I instantly recognised that this wasn't a good reaction. 'What do you mean, you've seen these badges on uniforms British soldiers wear?' she asked. I explained that some people my father knew wore them and I had seen things he had with the badge on. 'That is the German swastika,' she said. 'You've probably seen it in a book and got confused.' I was shocked to learn what the badge was and felt unnerved that Nazi soldiers still existed in Cumbria.

The first opportunity I had, I asked John about the swastika and the German army. We had various discussions about the subject and he told me about the stories of atrocities some of these soldiers were said to have committed on innocent babies and children. He also told me about Adolf Hitler and his apparent fascination for his partners to defecate on his chest. He said there were stories that his girlfriend Eva Braun would defecate on a glass table as he lay beneath it and watched. When he saw the look of concern on my face, he added that it was only what people had said Hitler had done and I shouldn't worry about it because there were no Nazis about today. Then it was my turn to shock John. I told him about the Scottish man at the railway club and how some of the things that Jack owned, metal and cloth badges, had the swastika on them. John assured me that we were not German and had no relatives who were German, so the whole thing seemed mysterious to me.

John was convinced that Jack was very much influenced by the Devil and, in true Sherlock Holmes style, he began to piece together various bits of evidence that, to this day, seem to me compelling. For a start, there were plenty of 'dark arts' materials in the house and nothing at all of any religious significance. The Ouija board was often used by Jack and others he invited round. He would tell us it was nothing but a card table, but John recognised it for what it really was. Jack enjoyed telling us ghost stories and frightening tales about the Devil and his desire to hurt and abuse children, and he had plenty of books that included demonic images and showed torture and pain.

I never saw Mam involved with anything like that. In fact, it was she who insisted that I attend Sunday school and join the Cub Scouts, though I cannot recall one instance when either she or Jack attended church or showed any such inclination. I should also add that at no time did I ever see Jack dressed in a Nazi uniform; the oddest thing he wore was his Masonic uniform, and that simply made us children giggle. I still think something is fundamentally wrong about men needing to wear aprons and white gloves to show they are part of a body of people who can supposedly do no wrong.

I had no idea at the time how these different aspects of my upbringing were negatively affecting my life and personality. Looking back, I can see that I constantly questioned and had in fact become cynical about authority figures. Every so often, as a child, I displayed a need to strike out, not physically but verbally, rejecting instructions and orders and expressing myself in a way that was clearly not acceptable to those in authority. The next time I attended the model-railway club, I felt a curious rage burning deep inside me. I was sick of seeing other children being hurt and suffering, and, as had previously been the case with 'Willo the Wisp', I defied an adult.

At the end of several minutes of abuse by the Scotsman dressed in a Nazi uniform, I stood up and looked down at his pathetic form lying on the floor. I had rehearsed the moment over and over in my mind. I stooped down and, instead of thanking him, I said, 'The Führer is dead, Batman lives.' The man was horrified and shouted out, 'What?' He then tried to get up and grab hold of me, but as he lifted his upper body, his head struck the wooden leg of the stool and he fell down as though he had been shot. He was wailing and crying like a baby. The incident caused mayhem, resulting in me getting a smacked bottom and called a disgusting and horrible child who deserved to suffer and be hurt.

Chapter 15

A cry for help

My situation in the house with Jack deteriorated. The level of abuse escalated as I was forced to do more degrading and foul things. One of the things I began to notice was Jack's obsession with talking about the Devil and evil in the build-up to abusing and raping me. I knew he was trying to frighten me into submission and into keeping quiet about what he was doing, yet I somehow felt that the comments were not always for my hearing. I believe he genuinely felt he had an association with the Devil and was sexually aroused by the idea of practising black arts.

I felt like a guinea pig in some kind of everlasting experiment. My instincts for self-protection became heightened and I applied new methods to detach myself from my situation. Batman was a major part of my life and I was always able to take refuge in thoughts of him. The cupboard under the stairs, while still my idea of hell, was slightly less intimidating because of the secret I had with my brother, who had created our pseudo-Batcave within it. Not another living soul was aware of it; it was a good, positive secret, just as Bruce Wayne had his own important secrets in Batman.

John had helped teach me how to think about different, good things when forced into sex with Jack or anyone else. When I was beaten, it hurt physically, of course; however, the cruel words that accompanied such batterings were wiped out as I imagined myself being Batman embroiled in a fight with a villain. The most difficult thing to deal with by far was the aftermath of the abuse. After he raped me, all that remained was me and my own thoughts. It's difficult to describe how terrible and disgusting being raped can make you feel. The vulnerability, guilt, fear, lack of self-esteem and confidence are feelings that merge with the recollections of what happened. The shame I felt could never be recounted in words. It was absolute devastation, and no amount of talk, help or counselling will ever eradicate the feeling of self-disgust.

As a child, I was becoming socially inept. Sure, I could talk, but trying to communicate my feelings to someone else was impossible. What was more, I felt completely unable to describe what was happening to me to anyone who might be able to help. Fear of ridicule and of being blamed for the abuse would kick in and cause me to withdraw. Jack was a policeman, he was a Freemason, he was an adult. He held all the aces; I had nothing. I was a naughty little boy who no one loved or liked and who was forever being dismissed or punished by grown-ups.

I realised how much Jack despised me one afternoon when I was alone in the house with him. It was the school holidays – I believe the year was 1968 – and Jack was off work, so I was held captive in the cupboard for much of the time. I would be released shortly before Mam would come home from work, then it was time for tea and then bed. On the day in question, Jack stripped me naked and slapped my bottom until it was red raw. I became so weak that I couldn't stand. My legs collapsed beneath me. He found this funny and decided to call me 'dog boy'. He made me crawl around on my hands and knees and generally act like a canine. This treatment continued for so long that I suffered carpet burns to my knees and the heels of my hands started to bleed. I pleaded with him to let me rest, but he was adamant that, as I couldn't stand up like a human being, I would have to act like a dog all day.

Eventually, I fell to the floor. My knees were so painful that I couldn't bear any further pressure on them. Jack had an answer to this. He found a leather dog collar, put it around my neck and attached a lead to it. He literally dragged me round the room on my back, banging me into furniture and never giving me a moment's respite. After a time, my shoulders were bleeding and my back began to sting. It was only then that he stopped and made me bark and beg like a dog. I was sobbing and in pain, I just wanted it to be over, so I did my best to please him. I barked and sat up on my knees like a dog begging. He slapped me hard across the face and called me an idiot before dragging me to the cupboard and locking me in there.

In the cupboard, I was in wretched pain. The weeping burns stung. I could barely move without feeling some pain and desperately wanted out of my prison. I banged on the door and shouted for Jack to help me. Typically, my cries went unheeded. I was eventually released before Mam got home and dumped into a bath of freezing-cold water. Jack instructed me to keep my mouth shut and not say anything to Mam, otherwise he would force me to do it again that night. As usual, he ended the bath by forcing my head under the water and holding it there until I was gasping for air, allowing me up, then forcing me back under again. The second time I went under, I put up no fight as a numb feeling crept into my head and everything went black.

I woke up in bed. My body was covered in cuts and burns; every area of my skin felt like it was on fire. I called out for Mam and was pleased to hear her shout out, 'I'm coming now, Paul, hang on.' Jack had been called into work. He had told Mam that I had been running in the garden and had tripped on the concrete path, cutting myself in the fall. I looked at her in disbelief. Again, I felt my heart sink as I realised anew that I really was alone in my life.

I'm not saying that my mam didn't care, because I knew she did, but sometimes I needed to feel loved and wanted a cuddle, to feel believed and not have all the bad things that happened to me ignored because of Jack's constant lies. I was grateful that she tended to my cuts and bruises and gave me the space to recover in my bed, but the best remedy would have been to hear her say, 'We're leaving him now.' Sadly, those were words that she would never be strong enough to utter, though I am certain the thought must have crossed her mind on a daily basis.

I was seeing less and less of John. When he wasn't at school, he was out much of the time, and he stayed over at friends' houses whenever the opportunity arose. I was envious of his freedom. He would escape altogether soon, and he had his whole life ahead of him without the torture, pain and abuse Jack inflicted on me. He was lucky. My own attempts to protect myself had to be flexible. I decided that I would be best trying to stay close to Mam and accompany her wherever she went. This plan was destined to failure from the outset; she was working five days a week.

They say that people often take extreme action when under stress, and that certainly was the case for me. To deter Jack from touching my bottom and raping me, I would deliberately poo my pants and not clean myself up. For a while, it worked. He would slip his hands down the back of my trousers and inside my underpants and find his fingers covered in excrement, causing him to remove his hand and hurl abuse at me. He became so incensed by this behaviour that he wrote a letter to the school, advising the teachers that I had a propensity to shit my pants and they should be aware of this because of the hygiene issues. I was ashamed of what I was doing, but I didn't regret it. It's not a nice or easy thing to confess to, however, when needs must. It worked only for a brief time, but it was enough to make Jack think twice about raping me whenever he felt like it. What also resulted, though, was beatings and extended periods in the cupboard under the stairs. The difference now was that I would have to sit in my own excrement-filled underpants in the cupboard, which was both uncomfortable and smelled rotten.

I hated what I had become. There seemed no escape from the various tortures and punishments that would be meted out by Jack simply because he felt like it. My world collapsed one afternoon when Mam revealed that she was going away for a few days to see my auntie, who was having an operation in St James's Hospital, Newcastle. I begged to go with her, but the answer was no. I felt as though I was being abandoned, left alone with Jack, without any support or help. I was at the end of my tether and couldn't cope with any more of his advances. I needed him to stop, but no one seemed to be prepared to listen.

I felt angry and frustrated by my predicament, so I took hold of a pair of scissors, stood on a chair in front of a mirror and began to chop away at my hair, cutting off large clumps of the stuff and gouging out lumps of scalp. I saw the blood emerge through my hair and felt it running down my face, at first in small drops, then in a steady stream. I calmly sat down on the sofa and waited. My mam screamed when she saw what I had done and quickly moved me to the kitchen sink, where she stuck my head under the cold-water tap and kept it there until the flow of blood was stemmed. She couldn't understand why I had done it, why I would want to disfigure myself so badly, albeit temporarily. I told her it was because I hated Jack and didn't want to be left alone with him any more.

My cry for help failed. Other than a sore scalp and a good hiding off Jack, I achieved nothing. Mam still went to Newcastle to see her sister. Unfortunately, my appearance gave Jack a reason not to let me out, to keep me hidden away. He said I looked grotesque and that I would frighten people if they saw me, therefore I had to stay in the cupboard under the stairs until I recognised how ugly I was. He also said that I couldn't do myself any harm locked in there with the Devil watching my every move. I spent a full 24 hours locked in the cupboard. At least I had the Bat-Torch and I found biscuits and sweets left by John. When it came to going to the toilet, I was able to wee onto some old towels and rags that had been thrown in there, which soaked up the wet and didn't leave too much evidence of what I had done, other than the acrid smell. I was still very nervous of the insects I had seen in the cupboard and would shine the light of the torch around every now and again to check for spiders. I couldn't sleep and hardly rested at all. However, things did get a little more bearable once I knew Jack had gone to bed.

On my release, I went upstairs and kept out of his way. I was starving hungry and felt grubby and dirty, but there was no way I was going near the bathroom to wash when Jack was about. I managed to find John's secret stash of biscuits and crisps in our bedroom and helped myself to the bare minimum. John stayed away the entire time Mam was in Newcastle, and even when she came back he made cameo appearances only. He was growing up fast, and doing things his way. He had secretly started to smoke and I knew he was drinking lager. It was as though overnight he became an adult and I remained the little brother, a little boy who really had no place in his hectic daily schedule.

I was angry that Mam had left me in that house with Jack and that my efforts to shock her into taking me with her had been dismissed as an idiotic prank, nothing more than selfish attention-seeking because I hadn't got my own way. That was how I heard them describe it to other adults. Without John's help and support, I found myself sliding down the scale of despair. As he came home less often, the supplies in the Batcave were no longer replenished and the batteries in the Bat-Torch soon ran out. My days and nights spent in the cupboard under the stairs returned to being horrific nightmares. My imagination ran riot. I felt abandoned and helpless to defend myself, and I began to have morbid thoughts.

I decided to try and kill myself. It's a pretty drastic decision for anyone to make, let alone a child, but I was desperate and that seemed the only escape from my hell. Thankfully, because I was only a child, I didn't actually know how to commit suicide, and I opted to kill myself by shoving tiny pebbles up my nose to stop myself breathing. I sat and forced a long, reasonably sized pebble up my nostril. Once the stone had got to a certain point, I felt blood burst from my nose. The pressure in my head increased and I began to feel very dizzy. After a few moments, I collapsed unconscious at the top of the stairs, tumbling down the steps and landing in a crumpled heap at the bottom. I awoke in the back of a neighbour's car, my face covered by a white towel, which was held across my nose. I saw Mam. She looked worried, and in a calming voice she told me she was taking me to the doctor to get the obstruction removed from my nose. I felt tired and I was drifting in and out of consciousness.

At the doctor's surgery I was awakened and sat in a

chair. The doctor asked me to stop shaking and said I looked exhausted. He asked Mam if I was sleeping all right. She told him I was, which she knew wasn't true. It took several minutes, but he finally dislodged the pebble with a pair of tweezers. The pressure inside my head eased and I began to feel sick. The doctor asked me why I had felt it necessary to push an object up my nose and why I had chopped off my hair. I looked blankly at him, contemplating telling him about the agonies I was suffering. Then I remembered Mam was in the room. I looked over at her and knew she wouldn't want me to reveal the family's secrets. I started to cry.

The doctor saw that I needed to talk and asked if I wanted to speak to him alone. This was it, my big moment, a chance to tell someone what Jack was doing to us. I nodded yes. The doctor asked my mam if she minded leaving us for a few moments while he examined me further. She got up and left the room, and I blurted out some of the dreadful things that Jack had done to me, John and Mam, including the rapes. As soon as I told him, the doctor became agitated. He called me a liar and told me how wrong it was to make such things up. He said that Jack was a policeman and would never do such things, certainly not to his own children. He jumped to his feet, grabbed hold of my arm and marched me to the door, where he called my mother back in and told her everything I had said. She was outraged and reprimanded me, telling me in front of the doctor that she would tell Jack about it when he got home.

To this day, I will never truly understand why, but my mother took me home and told Jack precisely what I said to the doctor. Naturally, I was beaten and locked in the cupboard as punishment. When I was removed from there, Jack raped me and reiterated his mantra that no one would ever believe me and that bad boys get treated like this until they do as they are told by their parents. 'There is an easy way and a difficult way. It's your choice. You're no son of mine, otherwise you would have had a brain and you would have realised that if you do what I want then you'll get your own way in other things. I'll give you little surprises and Santa Claus will see you differently and bring you the presents you want.'

My mind flicked back to Christmas. It was filled with sadness and hatred. All I could see was John being raped on Christmas Eve, followed by my own rape the following evening and the fear of what lurked in the darkness of the cupboard under the stairs. I had no fight left in me. Mentally and physically, I was drained. So, for now, Jack had won.

I was an empty shell. I avoided conflict or discussion. I was submissive at school and with Jack and his strange companions at the railway club. My life consisted of hating school, hating life with Jack and hating the people Jack introduced me to. There was no option; I had to just get on with it. At the end of each day, I would lie in bed and wonder if tomorrow might be the last day of weakness, the day when I would find the strength to fight back against evil. I desperately wanted to find peace and live the first day of my proper life.

Chapter 16

Growing up

I despised the railway club. Every so often, different paedophiles arrived and others left, presumably changing locations as opposed to stopping their abuse of children. Eventually, there comes a stage when you've suffered so much mentally, sexually and physically, that you begin to detach yourself and to observe and notice things about the abusers themselves. These people were weak, pathetic and needy. Their mental weaknesses in particular were something I tuned into and focused on. I saw this as a potential means of helping myself and keeping strong. I felt like an assassin, on the surface acquiescing to their orders, yet waiting for the right opportunity to strike back, just as I had with the Willo the Wisp man.

One of the abusers at the club asked that I cut off some of his pubic hair with a tiny pair of scissors. He was a fat man with a huge stomach that obviously obstructed his view of his genital area. He was lying on his back and, prior to this instruction, he had demanded various obscene activities, such as licking the soles of his feet, which stank to high heaven. His fetish was getting children to act as his serfs, tending to his grotesque form and cleansing the dirt from him. He had struck me hard across the face several times when I'd refused to do what he required. This riled me and I vowed to show him that he could not treat me or any other child like he did and hope to get away with it.

So I agreed to cut his pubic hair, but not as he wanted. Instead, I grabbed clump after clump and chopped it off, leaving bald patches. He went wild and kicked out at me, catching me in the ribs and winding me. In my temper, and in self-defence, I took hold of the manicure scissors and rammed them down into his left thigh, leaving them embedded there. The scissors actually bent on impact, so the injury was not particularly bad, but my abuser reacted as though he had been shot by an elephant gun at point-blank range. I further surprised myself by not running away. I stood my ground. I told him I wanted him to call the police and report me, have me arrested and put in prison, where at least I would be safe from people like him. Also, that way I could reveal all and my abuser would have to explain why he and several others were in compromising situations with young children. Needless to say, the police were not called. I, however, was banned from the railway club for life and punished by Jack. I spent two consecutive days locked in the cupboard under the stairs, with food being thrown in to me as if I were a dangerous caged animal.

My discomfort in the cupboard was increasing. I was growing and therefore the space was more cramped than ever. On the other hand, Jack found it more difficult to throw me in; now, I was more manhandled than tossed into that place. Still, the Batcave theme helped immensely, when John remembered to replenish my rations and the batteries in the torch. He also secreted an old sheet and blanket at the back of the cupboard to help keep me warm. None of this detracted from the fear and mental torture of being imprisoned. It did, however, help make it more tolerable.

Thankfully, I was no longer required to go to the railway

club, but sadly this was replaced by other foul and damaging abuse. On 15 October 1969, when I was ten, I was taken by a police colleague of Jack's to a football match at Carlisle United. It was a Football League cup tie against First Division Chelsea, and I felt privileged to be able to see footballers like Peter Bonnetti playing in Carlisle. I was collected from Crindledyke by the man – his name was Chris – and we went to his flat on the corner of Warwick Road, where he collected his coat to wear at the game, which had an evening kick-off. He didn't seem at all threatening; in fact, all he spoke about was football, which was of course among my own interests.

It was at the game itself that things deteriorated. He stood me at the front of the paddock area, by the wooden fencing, and pushed up close behind me. I was trapped among a large crowd. He started touching my private parts through my outer clothing and rubbing himself against me. The crowd acted as an ideal cover. The pushing and jumping of the people around us gave him the opportunity to touch me up. I did everything I could to get away from his grip but couldn't. By the time the game was over and we walked back to his flat, he was talking about us both having a bath before he dropped me back at Crindledyke. I was forced to bathe with him and I was raped during the process.

What should have been a memorable event, seeing Chelsea play, turned into a night I would never forget for all the wrong reasons. When he returned me to Crindledyke, he was very touchy-feely in front of my mother and told her how we had had a great time. He handed her an envelope and asked her to give it to Jack as payment for the evening. She ignored the comment and put the package down on the sideboard, before walking Chris to the front door. While she was away, I looked inside the envelope and found several pound notes. I wondered what he meant by the term 'payment for the evening'. It was to be several years before I realised I was being pimped, rented out for sex.

By the time I left primary school and went to a secondary modern called Eden School, I had no trust whatsoever in authority. I had been told so many untruths by adults that I questioned everything that was said to me. This is hardly the basis for a good education. Unlike John, who had a grammar-school education, I struggled to attain any academic achievements, although I did hold the record for the number of times I'd received the cane. Jack took great delight in telling me how well John had done for himself and how stupid I was. 'Eden School is for the thick duffers who'll make nothing of their lives,' he kept telling me.

Jack was on friendly terms with the headmaster at the new school, a man known to the pupils as 'Old Joe'. He was also locally active in the Boy Scout movement and on the whole I found him a decent and fair man. My every move at Eden School was monitored and misdemeanours, no matter how small, would be reported to Jack. It goes without saying that my anti-authoritarian reputation preceded me and the teachers had been told to clamp down on me from the start. It wasn't long before Old Joe was wielding the cane and I was soon breaking records for punishment again. Sometimes I found myself set up as a fall guy for others, but on other occasions I was reckless or thoughtless and undoubtedly deserved to get in trouble, like the time I wrote 'penis' in the condensation on a bus window. I thought it was really funny, but when I looked up I saw the school secretary sitting in the seat directly next to the window. She reported me. Incredibly, on that occasion, I managed to talk myself out of the cane by telling the headmaster that I had been trying to spell 'peninsula' and had got it badly wrong. He admired my ingenuity and let me go with a serious admonishment. There can be no denying the fact that whenever there was trouble I seemed to be associated with it in some way.

It was a traumatic period in my life. I was physically growing up, but mentally I had the cynicism of someone much older. I trusted no one and I never allowed anyone to get close to me. Everything I did was fake, an act, not because I was naturally or deliberately deceitful, but as a result of the years of abuse and rape. I had not been able to form my own personality or identity, and, because my childhood had been cruelly taken from me, I didn't know how I should react to certain situations, especially those where someone was showing me genuine kindness. I always believed that there would be some price to pay or a sexual act to be committed.

I was asked by a number of different girls if I fancied going out with them. However, I had no idea how to behave in a relationship. I was genuinely frightened by the thought that I would have to engage in intimacy of my own volition. I always resisted such advances and, though I was attracted to various girls, I didn't allow my relationships with them to go beyond friendship. There was even a time when I considered whether it would be easier, because of the years of sexual abuse committed primarily by men, to enter into homosexual relationships. I realised, though, that I was not attracted to other boys at all, whereas I was interested in some girls and women.

At Crindledyke, John had gone, moved out and away. The abuse took a different turn as Jack continued to introduce me to some of his colleagues, mainly men. Over a period of years, Jack would take me to visit these people at their homes across the Carlisle region. The first meeting was always an ice-breaker; nothing untoward would happen. Later, I would be invited back on the pretext of carrying out some odd job for the person. Once there and alone with the individual, I would be forced to carry out a variety of sexual acts. These paedophiles were generally sadistically abusive, and I would be strapped to beds or chairs and ultimately raped. These people often used drugs to relax and sometimes made me use them too.

I was just 11 years old when I was forced to smoke marijuana by one of these people. I remember the horrible taste, which made me feel sick. My head began to spin and I lost awareness of where I was and what was happening. When I eventually came round, I was lying on a bed and my back was stinging. When the paedophile appeared, he was wearing a black cloak and a mask covered his face. In his hand was a goblet of wine, which I was told to drink. He told me that my back was sore because I had been whipped, as I needed to understand the pleasure of pain. When he left the room, I poured away the wine, got dressed and asked him to let me go home. I was told to wait outside because Jack was coming for me. I was handed a sealed envelope and told not to open it and to hand it to Jack as soon he arrived.

Such encounters occurred about twice a week over a period of years. Each time, the individual would tell me he or she knew Jack through the police or the courts and solicitors' offices or through his 'club' (a term he used for the local Masonic lodge). I had no idea who these people were, and the journeys to and from their houses and other locations were unfamiliar to me, with Jack taking different routes each time to further add to my confusion.

Things were to get even more disorientating when once I was dropped off at a house and was greeted by an attractive young woman. I was convinced that this must be a mistake, that Jack had dropped me off at the wrong house. I had never been introduced to this woman before, so I was very apologetic and said I must have come to the wrong house. However, she asked me, 'Are you Paul?', so I knew I had to be in the right place. I felt panicked.

I was invited in, given a glass of orange juice and told to come upstairs once I had drunk the juice and washed my hands. Male paedophiles had usually been rough with me, especially once the sexual assaults had begun. I thought that, because she was a woman, it might at least be less violent. To an extent, that was true, but it was as painful and humiliating as the other experiences.

Upstairs, I was told to remove my clothes and climb onto the single bed. Despite the regularity of the abuse I endured, I never became comfortable undressing in front of other people, especially adults, as I hated that seedy, lustful look that appeared in their eyes. I climbed onto the bed and lay on my back as instructed. The woman bound my hands and feet to the corners of the bed and left me there. She returned a few minutes later wearing nothing but an open, loose-fitting gown. She told me she was a white witch and not to be scared as she wasn't going to hurt me but help me enjoy being with her. I didn't know what to expect and was surprised when she started to rub an ointment on my private parts. It had a medical sort of smell and stung. I couldn't see what she was doing, but she worked in the ointment for some time. My lower body was tingling and I felt strangely numb. I hated being abused, yet it looked from my state as if I was enjoying it.

The woman climbed on top of me and for the first time in my life I engaged in full sexual intercourse with a woman. It seemed to go on for ever. My eyes were shut tightly and in my mind I again became Batman fighting his foes. The one problem I had was that I could never fight a woman, let alone believe a woman as pretty as this could be truly evil. I felt a strange sensation happening inside me. It was as though I had exploded inside her. For a moment, I thought I had upset her. Then I saw how pleased she was with me. She climbed off and knelt by the bed, stroking me, and the warm exploding sensations continued over and over again until it began to hurt. I asked her to stop, but she continued rubbing her hand up and down until blood emerged from my penis. The pain was like a thousand red-hot pins had been inserted inside my private parts. I wanted to hold it myself, to protect it, but my hands were still bound. I was left in that state for several minutes before being released and told to take a bath. Once in the bathroom, I bent over the toilet and was sick. There was no place to hide; the evil was not only in men but in women also. I looked at myself in the mirror and saw a blank, expressionless and lonely face peering back. Everything was gone, my privacy and innocence destroyed. There was no one to trust.

Knowing that Jack was renting me reinforced what type of person he was. In the disgusting world of sex abuse and paedophilia, there are no moral boundaries; selfish adults take advantage of children and destroy their lives. I was like thousands of children in Britain: alone and viewed as nothing more than a commodity, moved around the various houses where these people carried out their criminal activities.

I always wanted to know what it was that made me so different from other children. What was it that meant that I was abused while other children led happy lives? One question I asked of all my abusers was whether they had a family or children of their own. In almost every case, they confirmed that they did. I would follow this up by asking what they looked like. The vast majority produced a photograph. The children looked no different from me, except that they seemed happy and contented. This only added to my confusion. What I could not understand as a child was that the abuse I suffered was not my fault.

I often wondered how Jack had so many contacts with

the same sick interest. I wasn't foolish enough to believe that all policemen and public figures were involved in child abuse. I hate to say it, but over the years I became a bit more 'streetwise' to such deviant adults. I got to know their modus operandi and what made them tick and how to avoid the triggers that ignited their abhorrent desires. I had ways in which I could extract information from them. I wasn't interested in them, their occupations or lifestyles or anything of that sort. My need was to find out why Jack, my own parent, despised me so much and why he acted the way he did towards our family. There was no way I could ever approach Jack and quiz him on his behaviour, so I had to rely on others to provide information.

I was told by John that Jack made initial contact and communicated with many of these people through his radio receiver and transmitter. He had built this from stolen MoD parts. He was what was referred to back then as a 'radio ham'. It wasn't a CB; it was far superior to and much more secure than that. During the hours he spent in the kitchen 'fiddling' (as he called it) on his radio receiver and transmitter, he would identify potential clients to whom I, and possibly others, could be sold for sex. Those involved had to be security conscious and would be vetted by Jack before any business was done. It goes without saying that most people who delved into such matters were not the archetypal paedophile portrayed in the media. These people were clever, intelligent, devious; they hid behind a wall of social status; in many cases, they were people with influence and an element of power, the so-called paragons of virtue on which society relies.

I never did find the answers I wanted, and I now know that I never will, because they don't exist. Jack would never be able to tell me why he treated me like he did, why he raped Mam, John and me. He would never tell me what it was that made me so bad, deserving of the torture he inflicted on me as a little boy, why he never showed any real love towards me. These are the questions that torture the minds of abused children across the world. I call it the 'not knowing why' factor.

Chapter 17

Standing up for myself

I entered puberty when I was 11. Like all youngsters, I was confused by the changes, and I did my best to hide my private body parts in the school showers and when we were changing for games sessions. There were always some kids who would gleefully run around the showers naked, totally naive to the very real dangers that lurked in the minds of some adults, including some schoolteachers.

I was growing bigger all the time and had become altogether stronger, partly due to my love of running and playing football. I excelled at both during this time and represented my school and the county at various events. I hoped this success would provide me with a chance to improve my life and behaviour. While I was not as outspoken or naughty as my reputation suggested, I knew myself that I asked far too many questions of authority. I now realise that ultimately these questions were never going be answered, as honest responses would expose weaknesses either in individuals or in the system. It wasn't my aim to be disruptive; I always believed I was simply seeking explanations about how rules were formulated and decisions made by those in authority. I can see now that my need to do this related to my past, and I can also see how my behaviour could have been seen as belligerent.

Standing up for myself

By the age of 12, I was getting to the stage where I felt it necessary to respond to the abusive behaviour of others. It didn't matter whether it was between children or an adult bullying a child, if I saw someone suffering unnecessarily, I would step in and speak out against the aggressor.

One teacher at Eden School did not hide his animosity towards me. Mr Owlerton was a weasel of a man, scrawny-looking and with a goatee beard to hide his elongated chin. He said I was unruly and awkward and refused to do as I was told. The only way he could deal with me was by continually punishing me, sending me to see Old Joe for the cane. On one occasion, the teacher told me he 'despised' me. I felt something snap inside. I not only challenged him verbally, I physically squared up to him and offered to meet him outside after school to sort things out. The blood drained from his face and he took a step back. For a fleeting moment, he was scared. I recognised the fear in his eyes. Ultimately, his response was again to send me to the headmaster for the cane. It was a key moment in my life, since it proved to me that I now had a physical presence that, if used properly, could have a positive influence. The fact that Batman also used his strength and skills to fight evil was not lost on me. I accepted the punishment, though, and apologised to the headmaster and the teacher.

A few days later, I returned home from school to find Jack beating my mam. It was a shocking scene and I will never forget seeing her blood-covered face and hearing her whimpers as I walked into the front room. Jack was holding her by the throat, his face bright red with rage. It was enough to trigger a response in me that I would never have believed I was capable of. I felt 12 years of anger and hatred surface and explode in my mind. My fists were clenched and I was enraged. I walked to the door of the cupboard under the stairs and kicked it as hard as I could. It was a symbolic gesture, although no doubt it was wasted on Jack. He released his grip on Mam and walked towards me. I took a few steps towards him, and there was a tiny part of me that recognised that this was the right time. Just as John had confronted Jack all those years ago, and forced an end to the years of abuse he had endured, I too was now on the verge of my own physical and mental battle with him.

Jack seized on my moment of hesitation. He took hold of me by the throat and pushed me up against the wall. He was throttling me and dismissively referring to me as 'boy'. I looked beyond him and saw Mam. She was hysterical and telling Jack to put me down. It was clear that he was out of control, that he was losing his power and this was his battle to regain it and to keep me in my place. The spittle was shooting out of his mouth as he reminded me, 'You are an unwanted little cunt. Look at you! You are a useless piece of shit that no one wants. Your mother hates you, I hate you and your brother hated you. That's why he left home, not because of me but because of you, because you are such a little cunt.'

His words no longer hurt me. I was struggling with the pain his grip was causing to my throat. Part of me wanted to drop to the floor and beg for his mercy, but I had made a stand and it was now up to me which option I took. It seemed to go on for an eternity. My mind was racing at a million miles an hour. If I gave in to him, my life would be over; I might never again find the strength to challenge him and there would be no future for me. The rage resurfaced in me, and again I felt strong. I lifted my right hand, put it under his chin and pushed his head back. At the same time, I lifted my clenched left fist and, as menacingly as I could, showed it to him.

The words that came out of my mouth hardly seemed

to be my own. 'Put me down right now or I swear I will kill you. What are you going to do, Jack? Punch me, kick me, batter me, rape me, sell me to your pervy mates? No, you are not. You can't hurt me any more, Jack. No one can. It's over. You will never hurt me again. None of you will. And if I can prevent it, you'll not hurt Mam or John again either.'

He took a step back and released his grip. I saw in his face the realisation that he had pushed me so far that I was capable of anything. I desperately wanted to kill him and the thought of getting a knife from the kitchen and plunging it into his heart crossed my mind. I looked at Mam. She was shocked, but the look in her eyes told me she was grateful and approved of what I had done.

Jack wasn't about to let it end there. 'You may be too fucking big to go in that cupboard, but this is still my house and you will do as you are fucking told. Now get upstairs and pack your things. I don't want you here any more. I never wanted you. The little boy who wasn't wanted. Now fuck off out of my sight and my house.' I wanted him to hit me so that I had a reason to give him the battering he deserved, or at least try to. I taunted him by laughing at his outburst. He must have been seething inside, but he resisted the temptation to strike me. To emphasise his complete loss of control, I walked away from him and upstairs as slowly as I could.

In my bedroom, I packed a sleeping bag and a rucksack. I came downstairs and left the house by the front door, without entering the living room or saying goodbye. I walked seven miles to my auntie's home. I told her how horrible Jack was and asked if I could stay with her for a few nights until I found somewhere else. She agreed, and so began the first day of my new life. I missed school for a couple of days. Instead, I walked the streets of Carlisle in the hope of getting my thoughts straight and putting together a plan of action. I eventually ended up at the council offices, where I asked to speak to social services about my situation.

I was ushered into a side room and told to wait. After about half an hour, a grey-suited middle-aged man joined me and took down my personal details. I became angry with him because he kept asking for my home address, no matter how many times I told him I had no fixed abode. It was obviously not the response he wanted to hear. I went on to tell him that since an early age I had been sexually abused by Jack and countless other people. He was clearly flustered by this and fell silent for a few moments. He just stared at the form in front of him and shuffled uncomfortably in his seat. I asked him if he'd heard what I'd said. Again, there was no response. He was fidgety and wouldn't make eye contact with me. Tapping his chin with his fingers, he seemed deep in thought. Then, to my amazement, he leaned across the table that separated us and said to me, 'You are lying to me. A police officer and father would never do such a thing to his own flesh and blood.' I called him an imbecile for not listening to anything I had said and for not taking appropriate action to help me.

By now, he was standing up and couldn't wait to get out of the room. He told me that it was nothing to do with him and that I should go to Rickergate to report the matter to Carlisle police, as it was their job to deal with such things, that it wasn't his or social services' problem. He added that he didn't believe me because I'd not reported it sooner. I asked him if he really thought the police would believe me, especially as several of my abusers had been police officers. He shook his head from side to side before giving the crushing response I had always half expected and had hoped I would never hear: 'No, of course they won't believe you. They'll probably lock you up in a loony bin or some children's home. No reasonable person would ever believe such a ridiculous tale about the police.'

I wanted to run, but there was nowhere to go. This was pretty much the end of the line for me. I begged him to believe me and help me. In a moment of desperate hope, I almost believed he would want to help me in the end. Reassuringly, he told me to stay where I was and he would go and make a few telephone calls to see if he could find me somewhere to stay. It was little more than a sneaky trick. The man returned a good three-quarters of an hour later with Jack. I tried to run past them both, but there was no chance of me getting through the doorway in which they both stood. Between them, they manhandled me to the floor, and I was forced to return to Crindledyke. In the confusion, I heard the man call Jack by his Christian name. They knew each other!

Jack was agitated and clearly very embarrassed by the situation. Not, I don't think, because he was particularly worried about being considered a good parent; it was only his position as a police officer that concerned him. He told me I wasn't to pull a stunt like that again and that if I agreed not to he would let me stay at Crindledyke until I was old enough to look after myself and find somewhere else to live. He went on to tell me that my auntie was very angry with me for going to her for help, since she hated me too. He made it very clear that I was not to have any contact with anyone in the family. He said that no one wanted anything to do with me.

I felt betrayed and abandoned. Social services had ignored my pleas; the police were accomplices to the abuse; my own doctor had told me he didn't believe me. It seemed that whichever way I turned, no one wanted to know about what had happened to me. Jack was right: he would always have the upper hand and retain control. It would be me who would suffer, not anyone else.

The Cupboard Under the Stairs

I didn't want to live in that house. It was a place filled not only with awful memories but also with constant physical reminders of the horrors I'd endured, in the shape of Jack and the cupboard under the stairs. Every moment I spent in the house I was aware of that black space, which filled me with fear and reminded me how vulnerable I was. The one positive aspect of my life was that I now felt I had some control over my own destiny. I was 15, old enough to stay out of the house whenever Jack was around, and I could earn small sums of money by doing some part-time evening work in pubs and supermarkets, washing dishes and stacking shelves.

My time at secondary school continued to be difficult. I had an inability to conform and, naturally enough, I was unable to trust teachers and tended not to believe anything any of them said. I did my best to put up with the often unorthodox ways of various teachers, but I was beginning to find that my ability to accept unnecessary criticism in silence was disappearing. I knew that no teacher had the right to bully me and I felt I had to defend my own corner.

One of the first real confrontations I had was with the French teacher. He was an odd-looking bloke, with the facial features of Marty Feldman, and, presumably to give himself a Gallic appearance, he had grown a bushy, drooping moustache. I hated French lessons and couldn't understand why, in Carlisle, we would need to learn the language, so I paid little attention to the scrawled ramblings that the teacher chalked across the blackboard. During a lesson one morning, I was chatting to some of the girls; a bit of flirting seemed far more interesting and useful to me. The next thing I knew, the wooden blackboard rubber slammed painfully into the side of my head, momentarily dazing me. Everything was a blur, and I remember a girl screaming because the impact of wood on skull made a sickening noise.

Standing up for myself

I looked up and saw the teacher staring at me from the front of the class. He was about 20 ft from me and had a look of shock on his face. Everyone was looking at me in complete disbelief. I felt my head and saw blood on my fingers. I reacted badly. I stood up and, with full force, threw the blackboard rubber back from whence it had come. It missed its intended target and smashed against the wall behind him. He overreacted hugely, running from the room as though in fear for his life.

I knew Old Joe wouldn't accept such behaviour and that I was going to be in big trouble, so, to save time, I marched myself down to the headmaster's office and asked to see him. When I explained what had happened, he told me that teachers were not supposed to throw blackboard rubbers or anything at all at children. I was told that he would look into it and, for now, I was to return to class and come back to see him at lunchtime.

When I got back to the classroom, the teacher had returned and the lesson had resumed. As I walked in, he demanded that I wait outside until he came to speak to me. I closed the door and waited in the corridor until eventually he came out. Squeezing my face in his hand, he forced me backwards into a corner and angrily told me that he would break both my arms if I ever did anything like that again. I pushed him back and extricated my face from his hand. At the same time, I grabbed hold of his tie, pulled him down to my face and reminded him that he was the teacher and I, for my sins, was still a child, so it wouldn't be the right sort of thing for him to do. He stood upright and instructed me to go to the headmaster's office at once. I laughed and told him I already had and that I had reported him.

Ultimately, I got the cane, six of the best on each hand, and he got a rollicking for losing his temper and inflicting an injury on me. We were made to apologise to each other and I was told to 'act like an adult' and stop goading him!

On another occasion, the class was given a pet budgerigar to care for. I suppose it was meant to teach us about responsibility and caring for others. I would often let it out of its cage prior to a lesson, and this bird became a real nuisance. It would fly down and sit on desks during classes and cause much distraction all round. It would turn into pure farce when whatever teacher we had demanded that it be caught and returned to its cage, the whole classroom transforming into a scene of absolute chaos as children jumped on chairs or ran around trying to corner the terrified bird.

I couldn't stand the thing and made no secret of the fact that I didn't like it at all, other than for its ability to stop the teachers from teaching when it was loose from its cage. On arrival at school one morning, I was frogmarched directly to the headmaster's office, where I was caned without any explanation, on my hands, bottom and the backs of my knees. It was the worst caning I had ever experienced, all the more so because I hadn't done anything wrong. I actually passed out with the pain and came round lying on a bench outside the headmaster's window in the grounds. The deputy headmaster was with me. He was a man whom I feared; he had a dreadful reputation and always looked angry. He asked me what I had done to the school budgie. I told him I hadn't done anything to it. I was then informed that someone had wrapped it in Sellotape and stuck it to its perch overnight. The poor thing had died hanging upside down and unable to move. It had probably died of fright. I was appalled and felt sorry for the creature. Whoever it was who had done that was cruel and heartless. I told the deputy that I would find out who it was and tell him. He reminded me that many of the staff believed I was the culprit.

Thankfully, I was able to prove my innocence when

another teacher confirmed that when I had left school the bird had still been OK and flying around. She then accused another pupil, who admitted doing it because the budgie had shat on his leather jacket. I got no apology for the wrongful accusation and punishment. I was told to accept it and move on. As far as the teachers were concerned, I did forget it. But the reality was somewhat different. I had taken a terrible caning because of someone else and that person would have to pay. I gave him a good hiding (during a fight that was instigated by him) and left him bruised and beaten.

Mr Owlerton and I continued to clash. It wasn't just because of my reputation that he disliked me so much. I had caught him spying on the girls' changing-rooms. I asked him what he thought he was doing and he pretended to be looking for some of his papers. It was obvious he was letching, and I made it clear I knew. My card was marked with him thereafter, but I actually made a fool of him when I caught him sharing a cigarette with a fifth-form girl. I took great pleasure in letting everyone know what he was up to and what a prick I thought he was.

It came to a head one morning when I told him I hated his classes. He looked at me straight in the eyes, grabbed hold of my hand and pinched into the skin with his fingernails, telling me that he hated me and how much he wanted to see me expelled. He held my hand in a vice-like grip and I wanted to scream out but didn't want to give him the satisfaction. So, with my free hand, I pulled at his goatee beard. He lost his grip on my hand and stepped back, telling me that one day, outside of school, he would sort me out. I laughed at the suggestion. It was with some satisfaction that, many years later, after I'd left and our paths crossed again, I reminded him of his comment. The outcome was predictable: he pretended he didn't know who I was and literally ran away.

At Crindledyke, things were hardly comfortable. Jack took to ignoring my presence. In itself, this was of course no bad thing, but it did tend to influence how my mam behaved to me when he was around; she was much less attentive. As I grew older, it became clearer and clearer that my mam lived in fear of Jack. His moods were so unpredictable that it must have been a full-time job for her trying to assess what she could say and do without provoking a violent response. The lengths he went to to control her were ridiculous. For many years, there was no telephone in the house, and when one was eventually installed, she wasn't allowed to answer it or use it without his approval, his being there or listening in on the conversation. The only social life she had was at the police officers' wives club, a place where she wouldn't dare speak out against him for fear of it being repeated back to him.

I recall a blazing row between the pair of them when my mam objected to Jack buying another scooter. Instead, she wanted him to get a car so they could enjoy days out and she could have a bit more freedom to escape Crindledyke. Jack eventually agreed to this, but he went out and purchased the most embarrassing and useless vehicle he could find, a Reliant Robin. He got it cheap from a Masonic friend who was a car salesman for Reliant in Carlisle. My mam hated that car and would only be seen in it when it was absolutely necessary. The situation undoubtedly pleased Jack, since it meant he would be the only one using it, as my mam didn't want to learn how to drive in a three-wheeler.

Around the same time, Jack did something totally out of character. For some inexplicable reason, he bought a dog, a Border Collie puppy that was given the name Roy. When he first arrived at Crindledyke, he was a beautiful dog, friendly and approachable. Within a few months,

Jack had turned him into a pseudo-guard dog that answered only to his command. At one stage, Jack took to sitting in the dark with Roy and tormenting him with a torch, using his fingers in the light to make shapes that appeared to be crawling along the floor towards the dog. Poor Roy eventually got spooked by these shadows and chased them round in an attempt to fend them off. Jack loved it and did it more and more until Roy couldn't take it any longer and would begin to cry and whine. This continued for weeks on end, after which Roy had become so paranoid about the shadows that he continually looked for them night and day.

Another of Jack's favourite tricks with Roy was to take him out in the Reliant Robin, then put him out on a country road and drive off, causing Roy to race after the car. Jack would go faster and faster until the dog could run no more and stopped through exhaustion. He would then return to him in the car, collect him and take him home. A neighbour who saw this told him it was cruel to treat a dog like that. Jack pretended it was a one-off and played dumb to the suggestion of cruelty.

Having broken his spirit, Jack taught Roy to sit on guard on the top step at the front of the house. At first, he was chained to the door frame, with Jack standing behind him and winding him up as anyone came close or even walked past the end of the cul-de-sac. Whenever a person, a car or another vehicle approached, Roy would be commanded to 'see them off'. The more he barked and snarled, the greater the praise he received from Jack. Eventually, the dog's only objective in life was to be aggressive towards anything that came near him. It got to the stage where I wouldn't go near Roy if he was on the front step. Several times, he made to bite me on the say-so of his master.

Cruelty to animals wasn't something new to Jack. When I was younger, probably about eight or nine years old, I had been bought a pet hamster for my birthday by my brother John. We went to the pet shop in Carlisle and I chose it and decided to call it Whiskey, as it had long whiskers. I would sit playing with Whiskey, letting him chase through my hands, or I'd watch him running round the wheel in his cage. Then one day Whiskey wasn't in his cage when I went to get him out. Jack said he must have escaped. I searched high and low for several hours, but there was no sign of him. I couldn't understand how he could have escaped from a sealed cage. It was winter, and if he had made a bid for freedom and actually made it outdoors, the cold would have killed him. I was attached to the little thing and was inconsolable, blaming myself. What if I hadn't secured his cage properly and was therefore responsible for his death?

Several years later, I suffered a reminder of how cold, calculating and manipulative Jack could be. I intervened in yet another row between him and my mam, telling him to stop hitting her. He was enraged by whatever it was he thought she had done and ignored me. I wasn't going to back down, so I went to find a weapon with which I could threaten Jack. The first thing I found was a hammer, so I grabbed it and returned to confront him.

This time, he acknowledged my presence and left off hitting Mam. I had the hammer in my hand and, while I hadn't threatened to use it, he stopped his pathetic tantrum. The cessation of the beating allowed my mam to run upstairs and lock herself in the bathroom. Meanwhile, I remained downstairs with Jack. He sat himself down in his armchair, lit up a cigarette and laughed at me. 'How ironic you picked up that hammer. What were you going to do, hit me over the head with it?' I made no comment, just looked back at him. He had a sickening smile on his face and was clearly enjoying the moment. 'The reason I ask whether you intended to hit me over the head with it is because I can vouch for how powerful a blow it delivers. I smashed open your hamster's skull with that hammer. It bit me once too often, so I got rid of it.' I felt sick and dropped the hammer on the floor before going up to my room to cry. As I walked past Jack, he sniggered and commented, 'It's only a fucking hamster. Hardly worth getting upset about. I was protecting us all – vicious bloody thing would have killed us in our sleep if it had got loose.'

There can be no denying that the killing of my hamster, no matter how unimportant it may seem in the greater scheme of things, had a huge impact on me. I loved Whiskey, cared for him and bonded with him. Jack removed him from me just because he could. One thing he couldn't do was have any control over Whiskey himself. If, as he claimed, the creature bit him each time he went near it, then he would have seen it as an insult, a defeat by a helpless animal that had to be corrected in Jack's favour. I was appalled that anyone could be so cruel towards a tiny pet. Maybe it was more about upsetting me than anything else. In any case, my hatred for Jack was deepened by this discovery, as was my fear of him, as it reinforced my sense of his brutality and immorality. The fact that 40-plus years after the event I continue to feel hurt and animosity about this callous act speaks of the horrific impression it made on me.

The cruelty he inflicted on Roy the dog was inevitable, I can see now. As I knew too well, any living thing under Jack's power was always going to suffer. When Roy died many years later, my mam told me that Jack was saddened by the loss. She said he was more upset about the dog's demise than he was about losing, through death or otherwise, members of his family.

Chapter 18

I'm on my way

As I entered my teenage years, I began to find the freedom
to spread my wings a little more. I was regarded as one of
the best footballers in the whole school, and at the age of
13 I was representing the Under-15 and Under-16 teams.
I had the height, although not the weight, to compete
physically with older kids. My greatest assets were my
dribbling ability and skill at crossing the ball, so I was
played as a left-winger and, if I say so myself, was very
successful.

Being good at sport meant that I was noticed by the
girls, and it wasn't too long before I was flirting with the
better-looking ones and enjoying their attention. Naturally,
this led to 'out of school' activities. I met up with one girl
in particular and we became boyfriend and girlfriend. It
was little more than cuddling and snogging (as we called
it), and I was happy to keep it that way, as I still wasn't
certain how I would respond to any kind of sexual
behaviour.

One Saturday morning, when Jack was at work and my
mam was out shopping for the day, I invited the girl over
to Crindledyke. One thing led to another and soon we
were in my bedroom and in a clinch on my bed when she
suddenly let out a scream and pushed me away. I asked
her what was wrong and found myself automatically

apologising for whatever it was that had frightened her. She was sitting up on the bed, looking over my shoulder and pointing towards the door. She mumbled, 'There was someone there watching us, a man.' My mind went into turmoil and my stomach turned as I imagined she had seen Brookie. I stood up and went to the door, which, to my surprise, was ajar. I knew I had closed it properly, so someone must have been in the room. I panicked as I wondered if it was my mam. The last thing I wanted was her to find me in an amorous situation in the house. As I walked out onto the landing, the smell of stale cigarettes and cheap aftershave hit me: it had been Jack.

I was angry that he would have the audacity to watch me in such a private moment; then I reminded myself that he was a sexual pervert with no morals. I heard a car start up and when I looked out the kitchen window I saw a police car pull away from the front of the house. In the driver's seat was Jack. It was going to be difficult trying to explain to my girlfriend that it was my father who was the peeping Tom. By the time I returned upstairs, she was dressed and wanted to leave. I tried to brush the episode off by saying that she might have seen a shadow or some trick of the light. This clearly wasn't what she wanted to hear. I was annoyed with myself because, once again, I was lying and protecting Jack rather than saying he was a sexual deviant. Her brusque manner and desire to leave left me in no doubt that our relationship was over. I walked her to the bus stop, where she promptly confirmed the fact that it was over, saying that as long as she lived she would never come near Crindledyke again because it was full of weirdos. I took offence at this and told her that in that case she should come back as she would fit in very well. In return, I received a hard slap across the face and was called a bastard.

The situation reinforced my belief that Jack could never

be trusted. However, I was only 13 and couldn't say anything about it. After all, I wasn't supposed to be in the house alone with a girl in the first place.

It wasn't too long before I was on friendly terms with a girl who lived in the area. Funnily enough, John, my brother, had at one time been involved with her older sister. Their relationship had suddenly faltered and come to nothing, but, to me, it showed we had the same kind of taste. From my perspective, the relationship was more a friendship than a serious emotional attachment. We would sort of hang out together, drink the odd can of Tennent's lager and talk about all kinds of things, including skirting around the subject of sex, which was politely referred to using the phrase 'having it off'.

One evening after school, Jack told me that the girl had been round and asked me to go to her house after I'd eaten my tea, as she needed to speak to me urgently. I was surprised, as I thought she'd gone to the cinema with her sister that evening. I discreetly smartened myself up and didn't delay in making my way to her house. It was an unexpected bonus being able to get away from Jack for the night. When I knocked on the front door, I was greeted by her mother, who was much younger than I'd expected and no less pretty than her daughter. I was led into the front room and made to feel very at ease and given a soft drink. There was no sign of my girlfriend, so I politely sat and talked to her mum, who had an uncanny ability to make me laugh. She told me she practised black magic and that she was a witch of some kind. It seemed ridiculously far-fetched and I thought she was playing some kind of practical joke on me to see how I reacted. After a good half-hour of teasing me about black magic, her pact with Satan and the people she had under her power and controlled for her own purposes (which would have made me uncomfortable under different circumstances, but she seemed so nice and normal that I didn't see her as a threat), she asked me if I'd mind helping her move a chest of drawers in her bedroom, as it was too heavy for her to manage on her own. She added that her husband was away for a few weeks, so it was useful to have a man about who could help her. Innocently, I agreed.

She went upstairs, telling me to wait where I was until she cleared some space in the bedroom. After a few minutes, she called me up. On walking in, I felt my heart falter. The woman was standing by her bed dressed only in a basque and stockings. She smiled and seductively beckoned me towards her. I was shocked and wanted to run, yet something made me stay. Part of me wanted to confront and deal with the situation in a proper way; running wouldn't answer any of the questions I had or help me to understand what made adults act so abhorrently. So I stayed. I was seduced, and while it could never be right for a grown woman to have sex with a 13-year-old boy, I didn't fight or offer much in the way of resistance. I was wholly submissive. I didn't feel strong enough to fend her off. It would be wrong to suggest that I enjoyed it. I tried it to use it to my own benefit and asked many questions throughout. Few, if any, were answered as I was bullied and intimidated into satiating her desires.

This continued twice weekly for a period of around six weeks. Each time, the pleasantries were fewer. She slapped me and forced me to 'perform' to her satisfaction. It was rape, and once again I began to hate myself for allowing myself to be abused. The woman told me that I should never mention what was happening to anyone, otherwise she would accuse me of rape. I told her that I wouldn't tell a soul. I explained that I couldn't continue any kind of relationship with her daughter, as the deception was too great a burden for me to handle. She agreed and told me that the relationship was never going to come to anything anyway, because a girl like her daughter was far too good for a weird reject of a boy like me.

The self-esteem and confidence I'd built up since I'd confronted Jack was all but thrashed out of me by this woman. Mentally and physically, she punished me. I became distressed by the situation and couldn't sleep at night. I imagined being accused of rape and locked away in a tiny cell for something I hadn't done. The cupboard under the stairs had been my prison for too long and now this woman could threaten to put me in a similar place. My nervous state escalated the more I thought about it. My education was suffering as my mind was always elsewhere, which was the last thing I needed given the attitude most of the teachers at school had towards me.

My life was in tatters and there was nowhere for me to turn. I considered killing myself, but there was no easy way to achieve that. I visited a local church in an attempt to find a solution; no answers were forthcoming. I talked it through with John. He just told me to get out and away from home as soon I was legally able to do so. Night after night, the worry of it all consumed me, eating away like a cancer at my every thought. Everything Jack had said to me was coming true: no one would believe me; adults disliked me because I was a horrible child.

Then I saw Jack at the woman's house. She was handing him a wad of notes. I was incensed. Clearly, they knew each other a lot better than I had realised. I was frightened as it began to dawn on me that Jack was still influencing proceedings. I didn't know what to do. If I confronted Jack, he would deny everything and might tell the woman to go ahead and accuse me of rape. Instead, I waited until he had left and went to demand an explanation from my abuser. I wish I hadn't done it, because what she said didn't offer me any sense of resolution, it only hurt me.

'You came highly recommended. Don't worry, your father knows all about it. He says it's all right for me to use you as long as I pay, and I've been paying him very well, so it's all above board. Nothing wrong or seedy about it. I feel fortunate to be able to say I shared my bed with you and with your brother. I like to think I have helped in your development, and one day you'll thank me for it, I'm certain you will. I haven't done anything wrong. You wanted it. You didn't fight me off or tell me to stop. They call people like you child prostitutes. I'm certain you'll have lots of business in the future. As a child, you have consented to sex, but it's illegal for me to pay you any money for doing it, so that's why I arranged it all through your father. Your father is into black magic too. One day you'll understand how much it can help.'

I felt numb and ashamed. I had been duped by this woman and at the same time Jack had got one over on me. At no time did I ever consider myself to be a prostitute. The sexual acts I was involved in were forced on me by adults, always without my consent. I hated the woman for deceiving me and for calling me a prostitute. I should have just walked away, but I told her she was nothing but an old witch and to fuck off if she thought she would ever get near me again. She smiled at me, and said, 'Money talks to little whores like you. When you're old enough and you get the smell of hard cash for hawking your body to the highest bidder, you'll come running for more. Now get off my doorstep and make your way home by the gutter before I place a hex on you, freak child.'

That woman's comments stung. At the time, she represented other people, the human race, and what she said chimed with what Jack often told me: no one respected me; I was there to be used and abused by others.

I slowly turned away from the house and walked out

into the countryside. It was daylight when I set off, but night had set in by the time I came to my senses. I had walked through back lanes and roads to Gretna. I hadn't walked that way deliberately, I'd just needed to get away.

For a teenage boy from my area, Gretna was bandit territory. While we didn't have the kind of inner-city gangs you get today, there existed fierce rivalry between certain districts and groups. Gretna was regarded as a no-go area for a lad with an English accent. In Central Avenue, a group of lads loitering outside the local chip shop started to hurl abuse at me. They recognised that I was a stranger and were clearly keen to find out where I was from. Realising the danger I had placed myself in, I ignored the shouts and began to walk back towards the border.

I didn't look back, but it was clear from the noise that my behaviour was whipping the gang into a frenzy, and soon they were running after me, chasing me through a housing estate as I attempted to get out of their territory. The streets were filled with bungalows with low hedges or fencing, offering me little in the way of protection or a place to hide. My heart was pounding as I ran down an alley between two sets of bungalows. I was confronted by a dead end. I turned to get out and saw the gang blocking the only exit. I was trapped. Few words were spoken as the gang moved to batter me. I fought my corner and managed to land a few decent punches but was soon overwhelmed. There were many of them, all wanting to kick my head in. It was all over in a few minutes. I hit the ground and curled up into a ball, protecting my head with my arms.

I waited until I was certain the gang had gone before uncurling myself and making an effort to stand. I couldn't do it. My legs felt like they had been through the blades of a combine harvester and my head was spinning. On my hands and knees, I vomited before collapsing back onto the ground. Sitting with my head in my hands, I became aware that someone else was there. I wasn't able to defend myself any more, so I waited for the boot to make contact with my face.

There was no boot, no further pain: a girl was kneeling before me, the prettiest and kindest girl I had ever seen or known. Helping me to my feet, she walked beside me and guided me to her home, where she cleaned up my face and generally helped make me feel better. She advised me not to go to the police, since they would do nothing about it, as one of the gang who had given me the kicking was a policeman's son. This was Scotland and therefore the police force was totally different from the one Jack served in across the border. I explained that I wouldn't be going to the police, but I would be coming back to exact revenge on my attackers. I would pick them off one by one.

As I looked into her eyes, I saw compassion and warmth, and felt somewhat stupid for trying to play the Clint Eastwood hard man in front of her when she was trying to help me and give me good advice. I broke down and began to cry, at which point she put her arms around me and gave me the most reassuring hug I had ever had from anyone other than John. The clinch didn't last long, as she had to get me out of the house before her mother came home from the bingo. I was grateful to the girl and didn't want to cause her any problems, so I thanked her for her help and was soon back out in the fresh night air.

Every part of my body ached and my face was stinging from the disinfectant she had used to clean my wounds. As I walked the seven miles back to Crindledyke, I couldn't stop thinking about the girl who had helped me. I felt foolish that I hadn't asked her name and had made no effort to find out anything about her. She had seen me at my worst, beaten and crushed and in tears, yet I had felt no embarrassment or shame with her.

The Cupboard Under the Stairs

By the time I got home, the house was in darkness; Jack and my mam were in bed. I crept in and went straight to my room. I caught a glimpse of myself in the mirror as I undressed. My face looked as though it had been stung by a thousand wasps. Lumps, cuts and bruises were everywhere, and my top lip was inflated like a football. Again, I considered the angel who had helped me. I told myself I was deluded to think she would see anything in someone like me. In my current state, I was the weird freak Jack and others said I was. If trouble was abroad, then it was sure to find me.

As I stared at my battered reflection in the mirror, I began to dream of a better life, one where I would get the girl and be able to commit to a normal relationship with no fears or worries, one where I could trust people and be blissfully unaware of the deviants and perverts who exist in all walks of life. For the moment, I was most concerned about not getting the girl. I wanted to at least get to know her name. I had no idea how I was going to achieve it, but I was certain that I wanted to find her, and that feeling alone was new and exciting to me.

The strangest aspect of the beating was the aftermath: there wasn't one. Neither Jack nor my mam ever commented on my battered appearance, and none of the teachers at school asked how I had come by the injuries. The only people who did discuss it were my peers. They saw the cuts and bruises as battle scars that proved I was something of a scrapper. Unfortunately, this attracted idiots and people who thought I wanted nothing more than further confrontation. Whenever I had to deal with someone who fancied a fight, I would do my utmost to talk them down or walk away. Sadly, with an attitude like that can come a reputation for cowardice, which I wasn't prepared to earn myself.

I'm sad to say that I did get involved in far too many

scraps. Some I won, many I lost. There wasn't generally any real animosity behind these scraps; they were usually organised by boys who would convey made-up messages to two parties, baiting them to fight each other. One such agitator (or coward) was Kirky, the ginger-haired kid who I'd met in the back field as a small child. He relished arranging fights and witnessing them from a safe distance, but never once did he get involved in one himself. Like I say, he was nothing but a coward.

My reputation as a scrapper was enhanced by my use of the head-butt. In a fight, I would get my opponent on the ground, then seize him by the ears and butt him on the forehead, generally causing immediate submission. Kirky brought this into question one day, claiming that I was cheating by using it. He called me a coward and a cheat, so I offered him the chance to fight me. He enthusiastically declined and we moved in different social circles thereafter. I never, ever went in search of a fight; they seemed to come looking for me, which meant that I attracted very few real friends, since those who did hang around with me ran the risk of getting tarred with the same reputation.

I was aware that my life was going down a route I didn't want to travel. I yearned for normality, peace and quiet, not to be bothered, not to be stereotyped. I wanted to be anonymous. For weeks, I thought about the girl from Gretna. I couldn't get her out of my mind. Then, one day at school, I overheard a girl talking about her older friend who lived in Gretna and went dancing at Wigan at weekends. The girl was a fantastic dancer, apparently, and had no interest in dating boys, only in music and dancing. I asked what the girl looked like and, sure enough, the description matched. Somehow, I plucked up the courage to ask the girl at school to find out if her friend had been the one who'd helped me.

The Cupboard Under the Stairs

It took several weeks, but finally the answer I had been waiting for came back to me: it was her and she wanted to meet me. In fact, I had no option but to meet her, since she was going to be waiting at the bus station that very evening. This was the situation I had dreamed of countless times; now that it was to be a reality, it caused me nothing but panic. I played out every scenario in my head. What if I got off the bus and she looked at me and was repulsed or laughed at me for being a wimp? There would be no hiding-place for me. I had wanted our meeting to be discreet, but the busy surroundings of a bus station seemed less than romantic or private to me.

The rest of the school day flew by and soon I was on the bus on my way into Carlisle. I was nervous and would have done anything to put it off. As the bus pulled into the station, I saw her standing by a wall. My heart skipped a beat. She was even more beautiful than I had remembered. I had rehearsed what I was going to say to her and wanted to act in a cool and collected manner, not too eager or excited.

As I stepped off the bus, she moved towards me and said my name. 'Paul? Is that you, Paul?' I was a gibbering wreck and got all tongue-tied. I nodded yes and went to shake her hand, at which point she pressed forward and gave me a kiss on the cheek. I was so thrilled I couldn't speak. She smiled and said, 'Well, you're much more handsome than the last time I saw you.' I have no idea what came over me, but I grabbed hold of her, gave her a big hug and began to cry. She took hold of my hand and led me away. 'Let's go for a coffee where we can talk in private, shall we?' she said.

To my amazement, she told me she hadn't been able to stop thinking about me and how nervous she had been waiting for me at the bus station. We talked for what seemed an eternity, until we realised that we had to leave because the café was closing. We had a little more time together, though, as she had to catch the same bus home as I did. It passed through Crindledyke on the way to Gretna. I was so happy. This one person made me feel special, important and worthy of being alive. As I stood up to get off the bus, we kissed and I melted.

The following evening we met again. She was one year older than me and much more streetwise. I allowed her to take the lead and each time we kissed or she held my hand I felt like I could take on the world. Suddenly, Jack seemed less significant in my life, perhaps because I was at last being allowed to develop naturally, through my own choices and needs. It was very much an emotional relationship, as opposed to a physical one; we did nothing but kiss or hold hands and talk. She introduced me to the world of Northern soul music and told me about the dancing at Wigan Casino. She said we would go to Wigan together and she would teach me to dance.

Then, one evening, she didn't meet me at our usual café. I waited for more than an hour, but she didn't arrive. Worried, I used a phone box to call her home to check that she was all right. I was surprised when she answered the call. It was clear that she didn't want to talk to me. My inexperience with relationships showed as I persisted in asking her if we were still going out together. Eventually, she said, 'No, we're finished. I don't want to go out with you. I hate you,' before putting the phone down on me.

I hadn't a clue what I had done to deserve being stood up and dumped. I was glad of the relative privacy provided by the phone box. Once again, I felt vulnerable and weak. The curious thing was, I couldn't cry. I felt empty, confused and hurt, but there was an air of inevitability about it all. My life had been one unhappy event; at least now I had some understanding of the value and power of a proper emotional attachment. I felt that this had been cruelly and inexplicably ripped from me, but at least I had the memories. I guessed I must have acted strangely in some way for her to suddenly dump me as she had. Past experience had taught me not to go in search of answers, since they often brought only more pain.

One good thing was that I had a new interest in my life: music and dancing. The music scene in the north of England was diverse. There were as many fans of heavy metal as there were of the Bay City Rollers or Showaddywaddy. Northern soul, however, was more of an underground scene. I became hooked on Northern soul and avidly read magazines that discussed the culture, finding out about everything from the clothes to the venues and the legendary all-nighters at Wigan Casino. The club was for people over the age of 18 and you had to apply by post for a membership card. I was just 15 when I applied, but I made out that I was old enough and was accepted as a member.

I made my first trip to Wigan Casino shortly after that, and from then on I visited virtually every weekend until its closure in 1981. It rivalled my love of and pleasure in watching Leeds United. Every penny I earned went towards subsidising those two pleasures, which also got me away from Jack and that house on Crindledyke Estate. I took the train to Wigan, which took less than a couple of hours. The excitement and anticipation of that very first visit remains vivid when I recall it today. I didn't really know what to expect, but once I got there I felt I was among kindred spirits. Hundreds of people had gathered to enjoy and express themselves through dancing and music. Newcomers were welcomed like old friends. Spins, splits, twists, back flops, front flops, hand-clapping and shuffling were all in the mix during every record. Some people were incredible on the dance floor; others simply did their best. Either way, everyone had a permanent smile on their face.

The Casino building itself was nothing special, an old dance hall. It had a stage with a piano, an upper gallery and a wooden dance floor that seemed to move along with the music and gyrating bodies. There was no alcohol sold, only soft drinks; there were, however, plenty of other substances available. It wasn't a place that was full of drug addicts or serious dealers. It was mostly people taking amphetamines recreationally or to help them dance all night. The drugs were typically sold in cloak-and-dagger circumstances, handed over in the toilets or in the darkness beneath the gallery, always out of sight of the management and staff.

It took me some time to pluck up the courage to get on the dance floor and start to move, but once I was into it there was no holding me back. I was swinging my arms, kicking my legs and sliding around the talcum-powder-covered floor with the best of them. I loved it. Being able to express myself without criticism or judgement was wonderful, if a little tiring. I danced non-stop for about an hour before feeling my body start to tire out.

As I stepped off the dance floor, I was greeted by a familiar face: it was my ex-girlfriend. She was enthusiastically applauding me, and gave me a hug. 'You're alive! You can dance!' she screamed, as though we were still best of friends. She grabbed me by the hand and led me to the side of the hall, to a place beneath the gallery. 'I have missed you so much. I was devastated when I found out about you moving away. I thought it was only fair to end it straight away. I wouldn't have been able to cope, knowing I was going to lose you.'

I was astounded by this statement and responded, 'Moving away? I never was moving away. Who told you that? Where have you got that from? It's a lie.'

I saw doubt creep across her face. 'My dad knows your father. They go to the same club or something. I think my dad asked yours if you were related and that's when it came out about you moving away, because of your terminal illness. Your father said that you were in denial and would never admit it. He asked my dad to tell me to end it for your sake. That's what I was forced into doing by my dad. I'm so sorry, Paul.'

Instinct took over and I grabbed hold of her and kissed her, squeezing her body as I did. I whispered in her ear that I wasn't going anywhere, let alone going to die. I told her that my father was a controlling liar who didn't want to see me happy. She seemed spooked by the whole thing and changed the subject back to the dancing and the music. It was never on the agenda that we could be an item again, I realised that, but there was clearly still a spark between us.

She asked me if I wanted to get back out and dance with her. I explained how tired I felt and she introduced me to a man who gave me a pill to take. This was amphetamine, known at the Casino as an 'upper', a stimulant. After about 20 minutes it energised your whole body, providing a real lift. The effects lasted about six hours, perfect timing for Casino all-nighters. 'Speed', as it's better known, helped enhance my performance on the dance floor. Gyrating around the wooden floor was exhausting, and the majority of the better dancers I knew took speed to help keep them going and for no other reason. For me, it also helped put me in a place I enjoyed. The collective uniqueness of everyone who attended – we were a culture to ourselves: the music, the dancing and the common purpose to enjoy ourselves without harming anyone else – was something I loved. The drugs helped me forget that I was, in so many ways, different from everyone else. Occasionally, if I wanted to blow away all of my bad memories, I would take two pills. This could be extremely dangerous, as speed is addictive and the 'rush' does affect the heart. We all had particular dealers we would buy amphetamines from. I only bought from those I knew to be safe. There were rogue dealers who introduced the occasional bad batch and stories were always circulating of people suffering as a result of taking these.

Despite what it might sound like, Wigan Casino was not really about drugs; it was simply a dance hall. The local drug squad raided the place now and then, but nothing of note was ever discovered. The people who really had a problem with the Casino were the local council, who owned the building. Incredibly, in 1978, after Wigan Casino was named the best disco in the world by the influential *Billboard* magazine, the council began to look at the terms and length of the lease. They wanted to demolish the Casino in order to extend the civic centre and they tried several times to have it closed down. Various arguments were put forward in favour of shutting down the club, including increased crime rates and the negative effects of the influx of people into the town at weekends. The truth was, relatively little trouble could be attributed to the Casino and its clientele. We were a good-humoured and well-meaning bunch. Every so often, trouble broke out in Station Road when the local yobs turned up looking for a fight. Indeed, I recollect seeing a policeman getting a right good hiding off a group of drunks only to be rescued by some of the all-nighter crowd. In 1981, the council refused to extend the lease and so closed the Casino down, before the place was razed to the ground in March 1982. Rumours were rife that the fire was deliberately caused by certain people in authority; however, nothing ever came of such speculation. For a time, it was a supermarket, then it became a car park and today a shopping mall stands on the site of the world's greatest disco.

Wigan Casino will always be close to my heart, not least because it was the place where I first experienced consensual sexual intercourse. It happened on that first night, with the girl from Gretna in the less-than-romantic location of the back seat of a car in the car park opposite the Casino building. We were both high as kites, passionate and physically demanding of each other. Sex felt hugely different when it was between two consenting people. Afterwards, we went back inside the Casino and, despite the effects of the drugs, I felt as though I had exorcised some of my ghosts. It was a one-off, and an experience I never replicated; having it away in the back of a car in the middle of Wigan is not something I'd advocate. The girl from Gretna and I never did get it together again, but I learned a lot from our brief liaison. Sadly, though, the ability to trust was not one of the things I found; the bad experiences I had had could not be erased by one good one.

My lasting memory of Wigan is the final event. Every all-nighter ended with the same three records, which became known as the 'three before eight': Jimmy Radcliffe's 'Long After Tonight Is All Over', Tobi Legend's 'Time Will Pass You By' and Dean Parrish's 'I'm On My Way'. The haunting words of the Dean Parrish single still mean much more to me than anyone will ever know. That morning was different. The DJ, Russ Winstanley, couldn't clear the hall. He handed the mike to the manager, Harry Green, who thanked everyone. The atmosphere was strange; it was almost like a wake. No one wanted to leave, knowing that this was the end. 'I'm On My Way' had been celebrated in the usual way, with lots of coordinated clapping and floor stomping, but we needed an encore. Around me, people were crying, wailing like lost and heartbroken children. The DJ played one final song – it was Frank Wilson's 'Do I Love You (Indeed I Do)' – and then it was over.

I struggled to get out of the hall because of the number of people who had sat down on the floor in tears, strangers united in grief, holding each other and saying their final farewells. I marched out of the club, straight to my car and drove to Morecambe, where, alone, I walked along the promenade and cried. It was like the passing of an old friend. No place, other than perhaps Elland Road, has provided me with such happiness. I very much loved the music, but it was the dancing and Wigan Casino that made Northern soul so special to me. I miss the place to this day and have revisited the site several times over the years. I still feel angry that the local council deliberately destroyed the phenomenon.

Chapter 19

From boy to man

Living in the house at Crindledyke continued to be difficult. I was still at school and unable to support myself. Despite my best efforts to live outside of Jack's control, he was still interfering in my life and pimping me to his friends and colleagues. I knew that my life was completely abnormal yet there was little I could do to alter it.

John had moved out long ago. His grammar-school qualifications had allowed him to get a job working towards becoming a chartered surveyor. He'd lived in various flats around Carlisle but never quite seemed able to settle. I would often visit him. I could see that, despite having escaped Jack, he hadn't found the inner peace we both desperately wanted. Trust was a major issue for John. He didn't and couldn't trust anyone, and he too had difficulty dealing with authority figures.

He was highly thought of in the offices where he worked and by all accounts he was doing really well for himself. That is, until he pressed the self-destruct button. His manager had been discussing professional qualifications with him. He had mentioned that he was a member of the same club as Jack and that Jack had asked him to keep him informed about how John was doing. He explained that, because of his relationship with Jack, he would make sure John had an easy passage to getting his qualifications and would help him in his career. John flipped. He told the manager he didn't want Jack knowing anything about him and to stuff his job, before walking out on the firm. I remember the manager visiting Jack at Crindledyke and trying to get him to get John to come back, but Jack could do nothing, as he didn't know where John was living. I was the only one privy to that information and there was no way I would tell Jack.

For a time, John disappeared. Through a friend, I found out that he was living and working in Glasgow as a cinema manager, so I wrote to him there and gave a friend's address for him to reply to. We kept in touch through weekly letters. It seemed that each time he wrote there was another girlfriend on the scene. He had a constant stream of relationships, but none of them ever seemed to work out. As with everything else in his life, John became bored with working as a cinema manager and with Glasgow. He had also got involved with some serious gamblers and there was money owed. Without warning, he resigned and returned to Carlisle, where he lived alone in rented accommodation.

John would arrange to meet up with me after school and take me drinking. Sometimes we were alone, other times we were joined by his mates. He had changed during his time in Glasgow. Now he seemed much more reckless about the way he led his life. He spoke openly about despising Jack and his wish to get even with him for what he had done to him. There was a time when he considered going to the police and reporting what had happened to us both as children. Sadly, he told me he didn't have the balls to go through with it. He thought that, as Jack had friends in high places, it was doubtful any action would be taken, and that even if it was it would simply drag everything back up, which would be very hard for us.

It was good having John back; it gave me an element of security, since I had a bolt-hole to run to when I was struggling or needed to escape. It should be said, though, that the flats John lived in tended not to be suitable for more than one person and his own situation was hardly stable. I realised that, although he was my big brother, guardian and protector, he was in a place where he needed my help and support until he got his life back on track.

At school, my life got no easier, and I continually found myself in trouble. At times it seemed that my mere presence in class wound the teachers up. It was a relief when I was out of the classroom environment, where I felt suffocated by the mundane routine and the rules. I put every ounce of interest I had into sport, and I represented the school at all levels in football. One of my greatest thrills was being told that I had been selected to represent Cumberland Schools in a competition at national level. However, I needed to be able to get to the venue where the game was being played. It was to be on a Saturday morning. A letter was sent to Jack, telling him about my selection and asking for confirmation that I could be safely transported to the venue and collected afterwards. Jack dismissed my achievement as a mistake on the county's part. He told me I would mess the whole thing up and they would see how useless I was.

He didn't respond to the letter, so my teacher asked me whether I was going to attend or not. He offered to pick me up and return me home afterwards if there was a problem with transport. The school saw it as an honour having a pupil recognised in this way; Jack just used it as a tool to further abuse me. I asked Mam if she knew someone who could take me to the venue, which was 18 miles away in Penrith. She told me that she would make sure I got there. She said not to worry, that she and Jack would be taking me. I told the teacher I would be there.

On the morning of the game, Jack was unusually happy and wore a Cheshire cat grin as he told me, 'I'm not taking you anywhere. I'm not your taxi service. I've got more important things to do, like going shopping in Carlisle. I don't want you to leave this house today. I'm expecting someone to drop a radio off for me to repair, so you need to be here to take it. No one is remotely interested in football. It's a dreadful sport, nothing but 22 men kicking a pig's bladder between wooden sticks. It's a game for idiots. I bet Billy Bremner didn't ever question his father or not do as he was told. He would have respected his father. You don't even respect yourself, let alone anyone in this family, so fuck you. You are going nowhere.'

Needless to say, I missed the game and was never again offered another opportunity to represent the county at football. At school, I had to make up an explanation as to why I hadn't turned up. This simply reinforced the opinion various teachers had of me: unreliable and reckless. Because my non-attendance was deemed to have brought shame and embarrassment on the school, I received the cane, six of the best on each hand, and a letter was sent to Jack informing him of the misdemeanour.

Jack thought it hilarious that I had received the cane and wrote back to the school to apologise and express his disgust at my poor attitude. The headmaster read out the contents to me and threw it at me after he had given me the cane. For many years afterwards, I read that letter again and again. The last paragraph in particular, reprinted below, causes me much confusion and is a painful reminder of how little I meant to him. The fact that Jack, as a parent, would put himself before his own flesh and blood is beyond my understanding. He deliberately lied to cover his own deceit and threw me to the wolves. Even now, when I think back to it, it fills me with sadness to think that I was the child he maligns with this pack of lies:

The Cupboard Under the Stairs

As you must know, Paul is a difficult child and a loner, he has a propensity to lie and make up stories to get attention. At times, both his mother and I struggle to believe a word he says, especially the things he says about his family, me in particular, who, for some reason, he is ashamed of. He had never mentioned the need of a lift to football, we received no notification or letter, he must have destroyed this before we saw it. Had we known, we would have got him there in plenty of time, in fact, I would have carried him there so he didn't miss the opportunity, what parent would ever deny a child such a chance. It concerns me that his behaviour can be so poor, at times I question whether he is a child of mine, he is certainly not the child I have raised and cared for. Should you require to administer corporal punishment to correct his ways, then please take this as my consent to do so. If you ever find him telling ridiculous tales about his home life, treat these as lies and please let me know. I feel this latest incident has deliberately been constructed to portray me in a bad light and get him attention. As a police officer I want to make sure he understands and respects discipline and responsibility, and does not taint our excellent family name or that of Eden School.

In the months that followed, Jack would enter my bedroom when I wasn't there and rifle through my belongings. He would steal or damage items he believed were important to me. On one occasion, he removed a cassette and taped his favourite John Hanson songs over it, completely destroying the original. John Hanson was not someone I cared for at all. He was one of Jack's heroes after he played the Red Shadow in the musical *The Desert Song*. In a strange twist of fate, in 2008, while I was on a Nile cruise, I spent a considerable amount of time socialising with a really genuine and nice man, a solicitor. The man, it transpired, was the son of John Hanson. He had his father's name. Thankfully, the connection didn't dawn on me until the last night of the cruise, so it didn't spoil the holiday. It did, however, reinforce the fact that no matter where I went in the world, even in Egypt, memories of Jack could resurface at any time, that there was no escaping him.

Jack also tore pages out of my books before replacing them on the shelf where he found them. My shirts would be ripped and buttons removed; my underpants had their waistbands stretched so they lost elasticity and would fall down. Worst of all, he would pee in my bed and in my school rucksack, soaking books and other items. It was all done to unnerve me and to show me he was still in control. He was an absolute pig of a person.

My hatred reached new heights after his letter to the school. It was several months before I felt strong enough to ask him about it. I produced the original letter and asked why, when he was a policeman, he had lied. 'I don't have to justify myself to you, but if you really want to know, it's what we do best: club together and put people we don't like behind bars. No matter what it takes, we get them eventually. It's called covering your options, making sure all the bases are covered so that our version of events is more believable. The easiest way to do that is to destroy the opposition's reputation. Your reputation stinks. That's because no one cares, you're not wanted by anyone. You'll have no life or future unless you stop fighting me and do as I say. Fair enough, you've ripened now, you've probably got pubic hair and I know you masturbate. I hear you in your room at night, don't deny it. You need to realise that at 15, you are no longer the fruit I desire, but I can still make things happen for you, good and bad. Your life is in my hands. It'll never be your own.'

The cold and calculating manner in which he said this left no doubt in my mind that what he said was correct: he held all the aces. He was wrong about my masturbating, though. I didn't do that; it was a product of his own sick imagination. Looking back on what he said, I wonder if he was trying to get me on side, get me to place my trust in him, by saying that he wasn't going to molest me any longer. There was no chance of that ever happening; he had destroyed my ability to trust a dozen years earlier. I continued to avoid him like the plague and never relaxed or let my guard down when he was around. The evil that emanated from within him was clear to me.

My final year in school was a difficult one. It was examination year and decisions had to be made about what subjects I was going to sit. I struggled with every subject except English. I had been thrown out of religious education because of the opinions I'd expressed about religion and in particular the accuracy of the Bible. My punishment for that was six of the best on each hand every day for two consecutive weeks, and instead of going to the lessons I had to sweep up leaves in the school grounds, which was far more rewarding than being force-fed something I didn't believe in.

The height of my academic aspirations were Certificate of Secondary Education (CSE) qualifications. These were graded from 1 to 5, 1 being the highest and 5 being a fail. I chose to take English, history, art, French, mathematics, science and geography. I had planned to do dance. However, I was the only pupil who wanted to do this as an examination subject and, although the dance teacher assured me that I was an excellent dancer, the school refused to process my request on the grounds that I didn't have a partner! I was disappointed by this decision, not least because dancing at Wigan Casino played such a major part in my life.

I was surprised when the history teacher told me that I was the best student he had in the class and that I should sit the CSE. I had produced a project on the history of Egypt and in particular the 18th Dynasty (covering the reigns of Akhenaten and Tutankhamun). This had been enthusiastically received by the teaching staff and used as an exemplar for future history projects.

Less than 24 hours after my history teacher told me I should take the exam, I was being caned for telling a nurse who was taking blood from pupils in our class to 'fuck off and sober up' because she had made three shaky and unsuccessful attempts to find the vein in my arm with a needle and was now about to try a fourth time. She was being aggressive and gripping my arm so tightly that her fingermarks were visible several hours later. She pushed me back down in my seat and told me to sit still or she would hit me. I recognised the signs from Jack's behaviour: she was drunk. I could smell the alcohol on her breath and her hands were shaking. The strange thing was that she had struggled to find the veins in the arms of other pupils and was clearly doing something seriously wrong, but nobody had noticed.

Unfortunately, I was the only one to protest, so I was the one to be punished. When I told the headmaster that I believed the nurse was drunk, he clearly thought I was just being malicious and the cane was administered. It was little wonder that my faith in the vast majority of mankind was non-existent. Each time I spoke out and expressed concerns about someone else's wrongdoing, I was punished. What the Establishment was trying to teach me was to completely ignore unethical behaviour. It was wrong, but that's the way the system, in order to protect itself, manipulates those who dare to question it.

As I moved towards the end of my school days, I was introduced to the careers officer and required to complete forms so that he could tell me what employment options were available to me that matched my skills and aspirations. Basically, I was told the armed services was my only option. I needed no qualifications to join and my sporting skills would make me a good candidate. The careers officer further advised me that the services would knock me into shape and force me to understand how insignificant my place in society was, which, given my lack of discipline, would be good for me.

The armed forces didn't appeal to me, but the pressure was well and truly placed on me to sign up. My mam told me it would help me escape from Jack and give me a fresh start, that I could rid myself of my past. My form teacher reminded me how academically challenged I was and continually told me that my life was going to amount to nothing, as I was trouble with a capital 'T'. Jack told me that if I didn't join the armed services then I would end up in some gutter somewhere, where I belonged, because I had nothing to offer. To hear such comments from those who were supposed to know me hurt, and my future looked bleak. It affected me sufficiently for me to go and seek John's advice. 'Fuck them. They don't know a thing about you, Paul. Look at me, I've had a few decent jobs. It's up to you. You either conform and do as they say – and die – or you find your inner spirit and fight.' I digested everything that was said to me and decided to fight. John's comments gave me the impetus not just to prove myself worthy of existing but to show that I was better than most at everything I wanted to do.

By the time I sat my CSE examinations, it was too late to change my overall academic knowledge and understanding, but, importantly, I did my best to attain the highest marks I could. The outcome wasn't all bad: in

English language and literature I achieved grades 1 and 2, and I got a grade 3 in my other exams, with the exception of mathematics, which I failed. I was quietly pleased with myself. My form teacher had expected me to fail most of the exams I sat. She didn't ever congratulate me. Incredibly, my results had created an opportunity for me: the headmaster called me into his office and offered me a further year at school, which I gratefully declined!

My confidence began to improve and I found myself getting involved in more relationships. Sadly, no matter how many girls I went out with, the issue of trust was always a problem, always at the forefront of my mind. No matter what people said to me, I rarely believed them. In relationships, I had ridiculously high expectations of my partners. Should a girl ever offer herself to me on a first date, she would be jettisoned as being weak and therefore unsuitable for me. I wasn't even certain what I was looking for in a girlfriend, though I did know that sex wasn't one of the primary attractions. I lost count of the number of times a girlfriend asked why I wouldn't show or return emotion. I felt that there was no solution to the issue, that there was a huge void in my emotional make-up. I was incapable of loving and trusting. No matter how hard I tried to bury my past, it was still there, affecting every part of my life and every decision I made.

As my formal school-leaving day approached, I became anxious that I had no permanent employment, so I took a week off school and hawked myself around every major employer in town, trying to sell my skills without appearing too desperate. Within a couple of days, I managed to get myself an interview at the Post Office for the position of telegram boy. I didn't say a word to anyone and impressed my interviewers sufficiently for them to give me the job. It was a fantastic position; riding around on a motorbike delivering telegrams allowed me freedom and flexibility.

Vitally, it provided me with an income so that I could put money towards finding my own place to live.

I have many good memories of my time as a telegram boy, not least the people I met when making deliveries. These included the Four Tops (who were down-to-earth and genuine and gave me free tickets to a concert), George Best (who invited me to go along to a party at a local hotel where there would be plenty of girls!) and Roy Wood of Wizzard fame (who was the nicest bloke you could ever wish to meet). The people I worked with introduced me to a whole different world. My weekends were solely for Leeds United and Wigan Casino, but soon weekday evenings were consumed by pub lock-ins, drugs, copious quantities of alcohol and an extraordinary amount of fighting.

John warned me that I had got in with a bad crowd, some of whom were regarded as the toughest and meanest in Carlisle. The name of my regular drinking place (The Dive) aptly sums up where my life was taking me. I confess that I actually enjoyed the camaraderie that group of friends provided. We looked after one another and helped one another out. Importantly, I began to understand what loyalty meant, although the consequences for anyone who didn't show loyalty were dire. I saw the seedier side of life. There were people who existed solely for their next fix or bout of drunkenness, and others who were battered senseless for daring to cross or question the group with whom I was spending more and more time. This made me a target for other gangs and groups of people. I was regularly challenged to a fight or found myself involved in a confrontation. It wasn't until I had shown that my pugilistic skills were more than just a reputation that these people backed off and left me alone.

I came to my senses when someone I knew well

committed suicide. It was a desperate tragedy and affected me all the more because the victim was the same age as me. Various rumours circulated that his death was drug- and alcohol-related, and these were very much part of my own life. My excuse for getting involved in this world was that it helped me to forget my childhood, to forget the imprisonment in the cupboard under the stairs, the rapes, the beatings, the abuse – all of which still existed no matter how high or drunk I got. They weren't so much memories but permanent scars I carried. But I didn't want to be an overdose or suicide statistic; I wanted to be what Jack and the others in his weird world had not seen me as: a person in my own right. I gently removed myself from that social circle and concentrated on me.

At work, I progressed to becoming a postman. It wasn't an easy transition. I regularly saw mail being deliberately opened and the often valuable contents stolen. I was angered by these thefts. It was a small group of established postmen who were responsible, so I did what I believed to be right and reported it to the duty sorting-office inspector.

Within 24 hours, I had my work locker searched and had been ostracised by many of those involved. One evening, after a late shift, I was beaten up and told that it was punishment for being a grass. The system closed ranks and I was soon put on permanent night shift at the railway station. This was the worst possible shift. It started at 1 a.m., involved weekend working and seriously limited my life. It was physically gruelling and I hated every moment of it. Other postmen who occasionally worked with me told me that the bosses were trying to force me to resign. It was a repeat of my childhood: to speak out against authority or a system that is failing means just one thing – punishment.

I was facing a desperate situation. For a time, I had moved out of Crindledyke, sleeping wherever I could, and always without any ties or roots. My position at the Post Office became more difficult as I was denied every opportunity at career development. Colleagues whom I had once enjoyed working with became distant or silent. Socially, I was ostracised; professionally, I was finished. I began looking for another job. The problem I faced was not having any particular skills or experience. Shoving letters through people's front doors and working unhealthy and unsociable hours was hardly going to stand me in good stead if I wanted to find a better job.

I spent hours looking for work. The problem was, at 18, I was now too old for an apprenticeship and not experienced enough for skilled work. The armed forces suddenly looked like a serious option. I could disappear among the junior ranks, become a number and have my questioning personality knocked out of me. I was so serious about this that I went along to the RAF office and discussed the matter with an officer there. It was clear that he didn't feel I had the right reasons or attitude to join, and he told me to look elsewhere, the army or the police perhaps.

The police force was something I had never considered. Those people and their cronies had been my abusers. They were more despicable in the harm they caused than the career criminals they supposedly protected the public from. Yet the more I thought about it, the more appealing it became. There was no better way to expose and break down corruption and get to the sexual deviants than to become part of the system I so mistrusted. I was slightly concerned that my ulterior motives would be exposed, that they would see that I wanted to become the enemy within, and I decided I'd have to make a real effort to disguise the animosity I felt towards those who wore the police uniform.

I applied and was invited along for an interview and to

sit an entrance examination. The interview went well, but the test was much more demanding, as many of the questions involved maths. I was told there and then that I had failed the exam. Then I was called in to see a local police superintendent two days later and provided with the answers to the test. He explained that 'someone with connections' had pulled a few strings to 'sort it' for me. I knew it was Jack and that this was his way of letting me know he could still control my life. I couldn't quite accept that he would be able to find out what I was doing, but, for the first time in my life, the system had worked to my advantage, so I elected to seize the opportunity.

Within weeks, I was at a police training college in Buckinghamshire. I kept my head down and my mouth shut, worked hard in my studies and passed all of the final examinations. I successfully passed out to become an officer of the law. I could hardly say that it was the proudest moment in my life, but it was another step towards proving myself worthwhile and able.

In a way, I hated the uniform, but at the same time I felt it offered me a kind of protection, that it was a shield behind which my fears and worries could be hidden. A huge employer like the police service offers anonymity to those who seek it. I was now part of a team and would no longer be viewed as different or distant. I could become chameleon-like and hide my social deficiencies, carried along by my more gregarious colleagues. I found the most difficult aspect of being a police officer was getting used to the way people looked at me. The animosity in people's eyes was all too clear. It seemed to me that people, the public, didn't trust or have any faith in me. It was nothing personal; it was the uniform and the role I carried out.

What this 'them and us' mentality created was cynicism towards one's fellow human beings. I saw people in a different light. There were genuine victims and people who relished being victims. My colleagues would question everyone's motives. Victims who reported crime would find themselves doubted and secretly investigated. This mistrust was what the officers thrived on; it provided them with a false sense of being special and superior. For many policemen, this attitude also helped them stick together and created a sense of camaraderie.

I took a back seat and opted to try to understand the mechanics of the police mentality before pushing myself forward. I got through my probationary period and began to specialise. For a time, I was a dog handler. Then, at the first opportunity, in 1980, I moved away from Cumbria altogether (to completely escape Jack) and managed to get myself to Leeds, where I could settle and watch football in my spare time. I was firearm-trained and often served as an armed officer on nuclear convoy escort duties. To have the power and responsibility of handling and being in control of live firearms, including a Sterling sub-machine gun, was overwhelming. I couldn't believe I had got to that stage. I would often wonder how those in charge would react if they ever found out about my less-than-orthodox past or my underlying reasons for being in the police. Who would have guessed that the naughty little abused boy in the cupboard under the stairs, the boy and man who despised the police and authority, would end up as part of the Establishment?

Relationships came and went like days of the week. In the police force at that time it was almost as if sexual relationships between male and female officers were an accepted part of staff development. I had a relationship with a female officer who had a terrible reputation, which, as it transpired, was totally unfounded. We became as close as I had got to anyone other than John. However, our career paths went in different directions and eventually we lost contact.

From boy to man

I had become much more sexually engaged and active, but only because I had learned to switch off emotionally and detach myself from the act itself. Because I never held down a relationship and flitted from partner to partner, rumours began to surface in the force that I was gay. I had wondered in the past whether my experiences of abuse by men might somehow affect my sexuality, but as I grew to understand myself more, I realised that I had no homosexual tendencies whatsoever. My own confidence in my heterosexuality didn't stop the rumours from circulating in the police, though, and even when I did hold down a relationship, there were those who questioned my motives and claimed it was an act to disguise the real me. The perception that I was gay was damaging because the force was very homophobic at the time. None of this helped me to respect my peers or my bosses, and it came as no surprise when I learned from other officers that Jack was at the root of the rumours.

Eventually, I met a girl and we did marry. To be frank, she knew next to nothing about me, certainly nothing to do with my childhood. It wasn't a partnership that was made in heaven and there were plenty of struggles and disharmony between us. Our relationship was more like two people living in the same house than a joyous marriage. We were too young and too different from each other. It was a marriage that was never going to last and perhaps one that was forced upon us by others' expectations rather than being our own choice.

The one thing I will say is that as a result of this relationship I received the greatest gifts ever: two wonderful children, who, from the moments of their births, became the sole focus of my attention and life. They were and still are everything to me. Wigan Casino was gone. Batman was a private and secret friend that I kept to myself. Leeds United were still a major passion.

But now, much more important than all that, I had children to love and raise. I wanted them to have the chances and the happy upbringing that I'd never had. I would educate and protect them, pick them up when they fell down and make sure they understood the difference between right and wrong. I wanted to be a proper caring and loving dad. Despite the emotional problems my childhood had left me with, my love for them came naturally and is wholly unconditional. The moment I held each of them in my arms, I instinctively knew I would die to protect them. Like all families, we have had our ups and downs, but we are still close and know we can rely on one another. They didn't ever let me down as children and both have grown into fine adults. I remain the proudest dad alive.

With my attention focused on my children, I let my relationship with my wife fall by the wayside, and we eventually parted. We divorced in true Mason style, acrimoniously. When I left the family home, both children asked to come with me, and my wife agreed to allow this, as she felt they would have more chance of a better life with me. They were my everything, and I tried to make the divorce and our future life together a positive journey, an adventure. It was far tougher than I thought, especially when other people tried to get involved, telling me how to raise my own children. The three of us grew together, and I like to think they experienced all they wanted throughout their childhood years.

In the police force, I was promoted and moved into other areas of work. I achieved a great deal. Yet all the time I knew I was running from my past, and I would find that some set of circumstances would remind me of it, causing me to take flight again. I hated myself for being so weak and not being able to deal with certain situations, especially those where child abuse, in any form, was involved. In sexual-abuse meetings and conferences, I would feel as though everyone knew I was hiding my past, so I became withdrawn and embarrassed. I would rarely comment or get involved in such discussions; I just wanted to be anonymous. So my career drifted on.

Chapter 20

Love and loss

When I was 24, just before Christmas 1983, I made a brief visit to Carlisle. I met up with John in the St Nicholas Arms pub on London Road, and together we celebrated the festive season, and our temporary reunion, by getting hammered. It felt good to be with him again and, for the first time when we were both adults, he genuinely opened up about his world and life. What he said was nothing new to me. He spoke of his fear that he would one day end up like Jack, a shit dad. He didn't ever want to be thought of by his children as a poor father. His children were his life, but he struggled to bond with them because he was so frightened they would find out what had happened to him as a child and that it would make him appear weak in their eyes. It was obvious to me that relationships meant little to him; he couldn't trust other adults and so changed his personality to suit all kinds of situations and types of people. Little did I know that what I was seeing in John was what I was to become, an image of my future self.

In a raffle, John won a pair of tickets for a football match later that day. Carlisle were playing Blackburn Rovers, which, in our drunken and drug-fuelled stupor, seemed an attractive option to us, especially as the tickets were free. The game itself was dreadful, two mediocre sides kicking lumps out of each other. What was happening on the terraces was far more interesting, as random fighting erupted throughout the stadium.

After the game, the violence continued, and, as we left the ground and moved through the car park behind the main stand, a man was struck on the head by a recklessly thrown piece of concrete. I saw the man who threw it, and at once made a mental note of his description and movements. He pushed his way through the crowds to flee the scene. Within a second, John was kicked to the ground and surrounded by a gang of youths, who were literally stamping on him. I jumped in and managed to take a few of his attackers out (in self-defence) and get John to his feet. In the meantime, a group of people had gathered around the man I'd seen injured by the piece of concrete and they were shouting for the police to attend. When I looked round, John had gone; he had vanished into the cold, dark night air.

I waited at the scene, as I had a description of the man the police would want and had witnessed him throwing the concrete. It was quite a wait. So much trouble had erupted in the surrounding streets that the police were stretched to their limits. Eventually, after the man was taken away by ambulance, I found an officer and told him what I had seen. He wasn't interested at all and told me to ring Carlisle police station the following week. I did, and as a result was called to give evidence at the Crown Court trial of the offender I'd described. He was later found guilty of manslaughter, as his victim had died from the injuries he'd received.

John, meanwhile, had disappeared. He hadn't gone home and was not to be found in and around the pubs I knew he went to. In a panic, I rang the hospital to make sure he hadn't collapsed or been hurt during the beating he had taken, but he wasn't to be found anywhere. He had previous for this type of behaviour. At times, he could be completely unreliable. Wrongly, I believed he would never have deliberately abandoned me, but he did. I was sure there was something behind his vanishing act that day, but if so I never did find out what it was because, typically, he wouldn't tell me.

In general, I kept away from Carlisle, since it held nothing but bad memories for me. For work reasons, I did, for a short time, move to West Cumbria, but it was a brief and less-than-interesting period of my life that deserves no discussion here.

Towards the end of the decade, I again found spiritual musical inspiration, this time in the form of the Happy Mondays, and was lucky to see them several times during their heyday. The Mondays were a rebellious lot, and in lead singer Shaun Ryder I saw the awkward honesty that questions authority and the Establishment. The music aroused passion and strength in me, and at times I felt invincible listening to their music and was able to forget how fragile life can be.

In November 1989, I was working a night shift in Bedford when I received the most devastating news of my life. A single telephone call sent my world spiralling downwards, towards all the terrible memories of my childhood. 'Sergeant Paul Mason?' the caller enquired. I confirmed my identity and realised from the tone of the woman's voice that what she had to say was extremely serious. 'Your brother, John Mason, is being admitted to our hospice here in Slough in 24 hours' time. He isn't very well and he has asked us to let you know where he is. I've tracked you down through the police. I'm sorry to tell you like this, but there is no other way.'

It was like being hit in the face with a sledgehammer. I replaced the receiver and vomited. I hadn't seen John for several years. It had been the longest period of time we'd gone without seeing each other. I knew his life had gone off the rails. Various relationships had failed and he'd acquired a criminal record. That wasn't good; it was, however, Jack's legacy. John was deeply ashamed of having stolen, but he had done it to survive, not to cause harm to anyone. I worked the rest of my shift and at 6 a.m. I set off on the 120-mile drive to Slough, arriving at the hospital shortly after 8 a.m. I was nervous, not having seen John for a couple of years, and knowing that, since he was being admitted to a hospice, whatever it was he was suffering from must be terminal.

A nurse directed me to his ward, where he was lying on a bed. His once muscular body was painfully thin and he looked jaundiced. As I neared him, he looked up and gave me a huge smile. 'Our kid! How you doing? Thanks for coming to see me.' I asked what he was doing in hospital and received an obvious yet shocking reply: 'I'm dying. What do you think I'm doing? I've got bone cancer in my spine. It's from all those fags. Don't you ever smoke, Paul. Stay off the things. They are killers, all right?'

I was given permission to take John out of the hospital for the day. It showed me how cruel and inconsiderate some people can be. I had to push John around in a wheelchair and found obstructions everywhere, bodies refusing to move and deliberately bumping into the chair, pushing it out of the way and making nasty comments about John's appearance. At first, I kept my own counsel. However, my patience snapped when a woman rudely commented on John's jaundiced look. I explained to her that he was a human being, he could see and hear and, like her, he had feelings. I pointed out that she was drastically overweight and asked where the local camping shop was, since she clearly bought her clothing there. Point made, we moved on. John found it within himself to thank me and admired the fact that I had got balls and could now stand up for myself!

I spent two excellent and memorable days in John's company. We reminisced and discussed our childhood. The subject of Jack was raised and both of us spoke of our hatred for him and how the abuse had affected us. We had the same issues: relationship problems, inability to trust, conflict with authority figures. It was cathartic finally discussing that with him. As I left him, I gave him a hug, told him he had been the best brother in the world and expressed my love and appreciation of everything he had done for me. I told him about the positive impact he had had on my life and that I could never have had a better brother or person to look after me when I was a little boy. His eyes filled with tears as he told me he loved me.

Less than 24 hours later, I got the call to say that John had passed away. His last words were: 'Tell Paul I'm sorry I have to leave. I love him.' To say I was devastated would be an understatement. I never got to say goodbye. I visited him in the parlour of repose and paid my last respects. I was inconsolable and cried for days.

John was cremated in Slough and his ashes removed to Carlisle, where, at the formal request of my mam and Jack, they were to be interred with Robert. I asked Jack to let me know when this was taking place, as I would like to be there. The call never came and when I asked why he hadn't let me know, he said, 'It's none of your fucking business, that's why. He was our son. He fucking hated you. He wouldn't have wanted you there. None of us did.' Those remarks had the desired impact and I assured Jack that one day he would regret his life and everything he had done in it.

Inwardly, I struggled to deal with John's death. No amount of tears, looking at photographs or dwelling on memories could ever bring him back, and the reality of everything he had done for me overwhelmed me. I still miss him now and not a day goes by when I don't think of him. He was a fantastic brother, a decent human being and a greatly misunderstood father.

If I felt then as if nothing worse could happen, I was wrong. Six years later, I was left truly alone. For as long as I could remember, my mam had been a heavy smoker. She was never the most active or fittest of people. This was hardly surprising. She had a very stressful and busy life, working and playing her role as a wife and mother in order to get by and to keep her family as safe as she could. I know she despised Jack and all that he stood for, yet she was too frightened to speak out or do anything about it. I had seen Jack rape and abuse her many times in my own lifetime. I firmly believe that my mam's addiction to smoking and John's were caused by what Jack did to them and the way he made them feel every minute of their lives. Cigarettes were not something I needed or wanted. I saw them as dirty and disgusting things that smelled foul and littered every room of the house when I was growing up. It was their association with Jack, more than anything, that made them so repulsive to me.

Again, it was hospital staff who conveyed the terrible news of an impending death in the family. Mam had cancer of the lung and had been admitted to hospital with days to live. As much as it hurts to say it, the call wasn't as devastating as the one I'd received about John. I loved my mam – she meant everything to me – yet there was something that kept us apart. She was associated with Jack and at times she appeared to be on his side. That was confusing because, to this day, I don't know how anyone could ever love or support Jack or anything he did.

Despite everything, within an hour of receiving the news, I was driving to Carlisle, not quite certain how I was going to handle it or deal with Jack, who I knew would try to use the situation to his advantage. When I arrived, she looked awful. She seemed so small and her features were drawn. All she could manage to eat was ice cream, and talking was a struggle. She was on a ward with other people and her condition was poor.

I sat on the bed and told her I was with her, taking hold of her hand. She moved her head to look at me and smiled through the clear plastic oxygen mask that covered much of her face. I squeezed her hand and she spoke to me, asking if Jack was about. He wasn't and I told her we were alone. 'Paul, my lovely son, I am sorry for everything that has happened. I love you dearly. Every one of my side of the family loves you dearly. I have let you down. I'm sorry that I'm leaving you with him, that bastard. The wrong one is dying, Paul. It should be him, not me. He has done this to all of us. Now it's just you and him. I'm sorry that you have to deal with it.'

That was as good a confession as I was ever going to get and I knew it. My heart was pumping like a steam train thundering through the night. I looked at my mam and saw in her honesty and love that I had never before seen. I leaned forward and kissed her on the forehead and told her I forgave her for everything and that I understood the pain and pressure she'd suffered. A few tears ran down her cheek. Finally, 34 years after my birth, I bonded with my mam and we were together.

The moment was lost when Jack appeared and told me to get off the bed and leave his wife alone. I told him she was my mother and that that meant more than being a wife, as she was a good mother. Jack was clearly scared and openly displayed his anger towards me. 'Get out of this fucking place before I kill you,' he said. 'I don't want you asking your mother any stupid questions. She hates you, so clear off.' My reaction to this was one of my better ones: I simply smiled at him in the most condescending way I could.

'Mary, Mary,' he called to my mam, causing her to look

at him. 'I have been a good husband to you, haven't I?' he asked. Mam was clearly struggling, but she lifted her oxygen mask and forced her upper body from the bed. She gave him a cold stare and replied, 'You have been a good provider. That is all.' Jack seemed disturbed by this response and reiterated to her that he had been a good husband. Mam didn't falter. Still with a blank expression on her face, she looked at him and said, 'Jack, I have said, you have been a good provider.'

On hearing this a second time, he could no longer control himself and blurted out, 'You stupid cow, I have given you and your family everything you could ever need. A house, food on the table, clothes, holidays, you have wanted for nothing, damn it. I have been a good husband and you know I have. Don't lie or pretend I haven't. It's you who has let me down more than I ever have you. Now you're going to die and leave me, with this little shit being the only thing I have left in my family. How dare you do that?'

Mam didn't flinch. 'I'm sorry, I didn't know this was all about you. Our whole life has been all about you, but it isn't going to be that way any more. As you say, you have been a good provider, and that is all I can say to you.' She then looked to me and asked, 'Do you think Jack has been a good father, Paul?' Jack didn't wait for my response. He turned on his heel and stormed out of the ward and the hospital, calling us 'stupid bastards' as he did so, showing everyone else on the ward how unkind he was to his wife in her final desperate hours of need.

Within 24 hours, Mam was moved to her own room, and thankfully I was able to see her one final time and reiterate not only my love for her but John's too. There had been something of a scene at the hospital prior to my arrival when Jack had refused to let my mother's sister in to see her to say her final farewell. Mam had always been close to her sister and, despite Jack's determined efforts to keep them apart, they were loyal to each other. It was an awful situation. When I arrived, the staff nurse told me what had happened. She said it was as though Jack was frightened to allow anyone in to talk to my mam. I was advised that he might not want to allow me access to her, so to be prepared for that.

When I got to the ward, he was on guard outside her room, with the door closed. He had the look of a haunted man. 'What do you want, coming here?' he asked. 'She doesn't want to see you. Now go away and leave us both in peace.' Not even the Devil himself was going to prevent me from saying goodbye to my mam, so I fronted up to Jack, looked him straight in the eye and quietly but firmly demanded that he get out of my way and allow me in. For a brief moment, he looked as though he was going to attack me, then he looked down at the ground and moved to one side. He told me, 'On one proviso: I'm coming in there with you.'

I walked past him and saw Mam lying in the bed. She seemed even smaller and frailer. I knelt down beside the bed and took hold of her hand and kissed it, telling her that I loved her and that John and I knew she had always done her best. She couldn't speak but managed to give my hand a slight squeeze to let me know she had heard what I'd said. I kissed her on the forehead and left the room, glancing back to see her eyes open a little then close again. A huge lump appeared in my throat and I felt very sick. I ran out of the hospital and vomited in the car park. A short time later, she slid away in her sleep.

Jack's reaction to her death was very much that of a man out of control. He drank himself into a permanent stupor and went into denial. He blamed me for being such a bad son and giving her so much grief in her life. Then he blamed the doctors for not identifying the cancer sooner. Then it was her family for not being supportive. It was everyone's fault but his own. He got little in the way of sympathy from me, though I did try to get him focused on the funeral. His response to this was to tell me that he had changed his will, and that this time I was included. I told him I didn't want anything from him, so not to bother involving me.

I said I would escort him to the various agencies to register Mam's death and would help him organise the funeral. I wanted her to be given a decent funeral, with those she loved gathered to say their farewells. Jack, on the other hand, showed his complete lack of respect when he laughingly told the registrar of deaths that his wife had 'popped her clogs and was going up the chimney in smoke'. I intervened, apologising on his behalf, at which point Jack told me to shut up and not to be so sensitive, because Mam had gone and now the parasites who dealt in death were coming to feed off his savings to get her buried. I got up and walked out of the office.

I waited outside and as Jack emerged from the building, I wanted to hit him as hard as I could, but before I could do anything, he fell to the ground. I rushed to get him to his feet and managed to sit him on a wall while he slowly pulled himself together. After a while, he was well enough to want to go for a coffee and something to eat before we made our way to the funeral parlour to discuss arrangements. As we walked through the centre of Carlisle, he again collapsed, this time in the busy main shopping area. Not one person stopped to help; some even stepped over him. I lost my temper at this and told the ghoulish crowd of onlookers that had gathered to 'fuck off or get me some help'. A shopkeeper came out and helped me get Jack onto a seat and give him some water. I was about to call an ambulance, but this seemed to cause Jack some anxiety and he said he would refuse to get in it. He agreed to go to hospital, but I had to take him there.

After a time, he was fit enough to walk back to the car and at one point was making light of the collapse. He told me that, judging by the way I'd reacted, he still pulled the strings. Inside, I was seething. At a time like this, he was still playing games with my emotions. When we got to the car, despite his protestations, I drove directly to the hospital so he could be examined. There, he thrived on the attention and sympathy, and claimed to believe he had suffered some form of heart attack. He was admitted to a ward immediately and I left him there.

I had little doubt that his illness had been feigned so that he wouldn't have to deal with any of the arrangements for Mam's funeral. With him hospitalised, that was now my responsibility. When I returned later, the duty doctor informed me that Jack had told him he didn't smoke or drink, but the samples they'd taken had shown otherwise. Even immediately after his own wife's death, he continued in his deceitful ways. I was angry with him and couldn't be bothered to discuss his emotions or his health with him. For most of my life, I had wanted him dead. Instead, John and now my mam had been taken from me. There was no justice.

Jack was released from hospital the day before the funeral, and his spiteful behaviour continued. His guilt and his fear of someone speaking out and exposing him for what he was ruled his every move. The funeral itself was dreadful. Mam's side of the family came, but it seemed that no one wanted to see or speak to Jack. I was forced to travel in the funeral car with him and barely a word was exchanged between us during the journey. On arrival at the crematorium, he ignored everyone and boldly marched into the church. I heard things openly said about him that should not have been said at a funeral;

I know he heard them too, but he chose to ignore them.

As soon as the service was over, we returned to Crindledyke, where a select few people had gathered at Jack's request. For him, this moment was all about him and no one else, let alone my deceased mother. I took him to one side (perhaps fittingly, it was outside the cupboard under the stairs) and told him that I hated him and that he should consider how his disgusting actions had destroyed a whole family. He laughed at this, so I reminded him that there was one survivor who still knew his sordid secrets and told him that while I was alive he would always have to look over his shoulder. I pressed my face to his, our noses touching, my eyes cold and my mind full of hatred. I told him, 'I despise you. Everything in my life has been a fake, even this funeral. You have messed it up. Every positive thing I've said about you has been false. I wanted a father, instead I got a twat, a worthless paedophile who couldn't even look at his own wife in death, a worthless excuse for a human being.' He spat in my face and told me there would be just one winner: him.

I walked away knowing that I was the better man. Now it really was just him and me, and, despite my hatred for him, a part of me still yearned for an apology and an explanation as to why he had abused me and despised me. To this day I have never received either.

Everything was catching up with me. There was no escaping the legacy created by Jack, and the secrets I harboured about my life were a cumbersome burden to contend with each day. I had no trust for anyone, my relationships were dreadful and I drifted from one woman to another in an attempt to prove to myself that I was worthy of being loved. The sad fact of the matter was that as soon as a woman declared her love for me that gave me the validation I needed, ultimately signalling the end of the relationship. In my latter years in the police service, I really wasn't happy. Everything about my professional life was becoming less appealing. The service was full of people with all kinds of psychological issues. Many were small people in big uniforms who enjoyed the power and control. I hated it, but I didn't know what else to do. I could feel myself slowly drowning as the tide of my past began to overwhelm me. I tried various methods to help me deal with my feelings about my childhood, even collecting Batman memorabilia in an attempt to rediscover the power of my superhero saviour. Nothing worked.

For a time, I worked as an undercover intelligence officer in the hostile world of football hooliganism, but I felt that the approach forced on us from the top down was misguided and that this was the reason why the police only ever scratched the surface of the problem. Looking back, my last months of active police service were littered with confrontations with senior police officers and those in authority. I found myself questioning the integrity of the police service in general, which it seemed to me was clearly becoming politically motivated and controlled.

On one occasion, I expressed concerns about the immoral behaviour of police officers and actually passed on high-grade intelligence concerning one particular officer who was allegedly sexually assaulting a female special constable. Nothing ever came of it because he was an established officer and 'one of the boys'; meanwhile, the woman left her voluntary role, having lost faith not only in the police system but in justice also. I'm glad to say that several years later the same officer was prosecuted for a distinctly similar offence. I can only wonder how many other victims suffered unnecessarily as a result of organisational failures to act appropriately. To give another example, a probationary constable I knew very well was bullied and intimidated by an entire shift of officers and their manager; again, when I stood up to express my concerns, I was ignored by the system and made to feel as though I was in the wrong for highlighting the matter.

One need only pick up a newspaper or listen to the news to see how corruption and unlawful behaviour remains endemic in many areas of the police service. It is very much a case of one law for the police and another for the rest. I saw police officers who had their entire careers destroyed by canteen gossip and the gang culture that is still present throughout every force. In 2007, almost a decade after I was medically retired from the police, a superintendent in the Metropolitan Police told me that the gangs of London were afraid of one particular gang: the Met. 'We are the biggest and the toughest,' he told me. The sad thing was, he actually believed it.

After sustaining injuries while on duty that would cause me to be classed as 'disabled', I was forced into a period of rehabilitation. This basically meant sitting at home and doing nothing. At least I had the children to focus on. I had suffered damage to my knees, which would never fully recover. The official line from the police was that I no longer fulfilled the criteria for being an active police officer. I couldn't kneel, bend or rely on my knees to support me. Gradually, contact with people within the force faded away and I was forgotten. I felt I'd been discarded onto the scrapheap.

Sure, I was disillusioned that my police career was over. However, I was pleased to be out of a system that was so insular and unbending in its approach that it had started to become an enemy of society. The respect communities once had for the police had disappeared. People no longer reported crimes because the police rarely dealt with them appropriately. With the loss of public support, the street intelligence systems began to dry up and so criminals escaped justice. Ultimately, the crimes of sex offenders and paedophiles were being missed, therefore thousands of children were being unnecessarily abused, and that for me was an unforgivable failure of the system.

Chapter 21

Out of the shadows

My forced retirement from the police left me contemplating my future. I was too young to stop working and, besides, the lump sum I'd received was not going to keep me and the kids for very long. Before I could decide what to do, I had to get my mindset right, allow my injuries to heal as well as possible and lead as normal a life as I could. The worst aspect was having time on my hands. That was something I had never before allowed myself. My life had always been somewhat chaotic and I'd focused on looking forwards, never daring to look back at my childhood and the abuse that had left me with such terrible scars.

Serving with the police had helped me to hide the insecurities and fears instilled in me by Jack from birth. But, to be honest, I could not look back on my career with any great fondness. It was clear that injustices did take place. Yes, police officers of all ranks lied in order to gain convictions, be it under oath in a court of law or in a written and signed statement. This was something I could never do. For me, it was about getting the right person for the crime, not simply a possible contender. I despised that aspect of the criminal justice system. There exists a belief that police officers are paragons of virtue and therefore never make wrong decisions and always serve the people with diligence and propriety. It's absolute rubbish. A good percentage are seriously flawed individuals; many are bullies who hide behind the power that the uniform and the warrant card give them. I could write a sensational full tome on such matters; however, those details are for another day and another book. I should also point out that there exist officers who are decent and professional. They are, though, a minority.

I had reached a point in my life where, having served in the British police force for a period that spanned three decades, I had time to consider my achievements and assess my skills. Sadly, I felt as if none of the skills I had acquired in the police were relevant to life in the real world. That said, I wanted to distance myself from my police career and do something quite different in any case. However, I had already had a book published, and I was fortunate that, as a writer, I was able to put pen to paper and construct a legible sentence. The decision was made: I would use my literary skills and become a full-time writer.

The downside to being a professional author is that one spends a considerable amount of time alone, reading, researching and writing. I treated myself to a state-of-the-art computer and new software and locked myself away in my study for hours on end. The days came and went, and, although my two children were a fantastic distraction, gradually the memories I was running from and which I'd thought I had escaped began to resurface. I would be sitting typing when a word, comment or image would create a flashback in my mind to scenes such as Jack raping John on Christmas Eve or the gross and indecent acts I had been forced to commit on adults and had had inflicted on me. Every day and night, in the recesses of my mind lurked the cupboard under the stairs. It's still there now and, although I know I will never physically enter that place again, its presence terrifies me.

Out of the shadows

There was not a living soul I could confide in, so, in moments of weakness, I succumbed to the powers of what I thought of as a friend who would help me forget, help ease my pain, and who was there for me whenever I called. I was misguided. My friend came in a bottle or a glass and was a demon every bit as harmful and destructive as Jack. Let me assure you, alcohol is not the solution to anything. My intake increased without my realising. It started with a few pints down the pub, followed by a few chasers to help me sleep at night. Gradually, it became more of a habit, and the more I drank, the less I noticed the effects, so I consumed more and more to keep myself in a place where my thoughts and memories were subdued.

It was only when I caught a glimpse of myself in a mirror when I was in one of my drunken states that I realised what was happening to me. I had lost focus, lost track of the days. I was unshaven, haggard and bloated. Worse still, it wasn't me that was making the decisions in my life – the alcohol was. The shock of seeing myself in such a bad way was enough to cause me to stop. I had a bath, shaved and cleaned myself up before clearing the house of every drop of alcohol. I poured it down the sink and put the bottles in a skip. I didn't want to be manipulated or guided by something or somebody else; I was going to be my own person and continue the fight to keep myself ahead of my past, which, I realised, was constantly thundering on behind me and ready to overwhelm me the moment I dropped my guard. There was no easy solution, no escape from the living hell I had suffered since I was a tiny child. This was my life and I had to deal with it. I accepted that, as a result of my childhood, my life was going to be a constant battle with the Establishment, which had continually failed me.

I had to keep myself busy, retain my dignity and find

something to focus on. The writing life I had hoped for wasn't as easy as I had envisaged, certainly not when I was under the influence of alcohol. I needed to find employment, something that I could physically cope with; my knees ruled manual labour out. I was surprised that it didn't take me long to find work. I got a job as a mushroom picker. Soul-destroying does not describe how mind-numbing and without any responsibility that work was. Picking mushrooms and putting them into baskets was all it consisted of. Few of the people who worked there had any conversation; even less had any aspirations to do anything other than pick mushrooms. I lasted four days before telling the shift manager that I couldn't do it a minute longer. To be fair, he had told me from the outset that he didn't think I had what it would take to be a mushroom picker, a comment I had laughed at; I understand now that he was right. The next time you grab a box of mushrooms from a supermarket shelf, spare a thought for the people who pick them and put them into the carton.

Despite everything, the job had made me feel valid and that I was making a contribution to society. The minute I left the mushroom farm, I went in search of something else. I had been offered bar work, but the long, irregular hours didn't appeal. Within a couple of days, I was given a two-week trial period in an upmarket sandwich bar at a railway station. My job was to help make up sandwiches and speciality coffees.

It was hellish, but I needed the money. I honestly couldn't believe how rude people could be, and they expected you to accept their arrogant behaviour. I got even with such people in many different ways, none of which need be mentioned here. I found myself the butt of much criticism and abuse because customers saw me not as an equal but as someone who was there to run around after them and please them. I began to feel alienated and it took me right back to my childhood, when I had no voice and no one cared about me or listened to me, they just abused me.

Matters came to a head one day when the manager had me mopping the shop floor. It was about 2 p.m. and we were about to close for the day. The manager had gone home and told me to lock up when I finished. I had covered the floor with cleaning agent and water and was mopping when a man dressed in an ill-fitting cheap suit walked in. Without any provocation, he kicked the mop out of my hands and pushed me down onto the wet floor, saying, 'Get out of my way, lackey. If any of that cleaning fluid gets onto my shoes or my trousers, I will sue you, serf, do you understand me?' Sitting on the wet floor, I was suddenly consumed by the overpowering smell of cheap aftershave and stale cigarettes, transporting me back to my childhood and Jack. I was struggling to get up from a kneeling position when the man grabbed his groin and pushed it towards me, saying, 'While you're down there, you can see to me.' I snapped. I got to my feet and asked where his manners were. He replied by telling me, 'If you don't get out of my face, I'll shove your mop so far up your arse it'll come out of the top of your head.' He then slapped me across the face.

When I was in the police, I would have had to take this oaf down using the minimum and legal amount of force and restrain him. Now, there were no such legal restrictions placed on me. I was a member of the public and the clown standing before me clearly wanted a fight! I stepped towards him and he slapped me again. He was breathing heavily and was clearly getting quite anxious. He ordered me to make him a coffee as he had a train to catch. Then he spat in my face before pushing me away. The rest, as they say, is history. I had him on the floor with one punch to his jaw. He was pleading with me and telling me to leave him alone otherwise I would be in deep trouble. I wanted to hit him again but resisted when I saw the state of panic he was in. He produced from his inside pocket a police warrant card and told me I was going down in more ways than one. I was shocked by the audacity of the creep and laughed as I pointed to the CCTV camera that monitored the premises.

He looked horrified. The panic in his eyes said it all. Suddenly, his attitude changed and he became apologetic, explaining that he was having a bad day and didn't mean to offend me; apparently, I was just in the wrong place at the wrong time. He begged me not to report him, as he would be sacked. I told him I was 'ex-job' and that I thought he was a prick. He agreed. I told him he was banned from the premises for life, and I was then kind enough to give him a small cup of coffee before throwing him out.

Perhaps I should have been more aware that my life was in a downward spiral. The over-indulgence in alcohol, my inability to ignore verbal abuse from customers and now my knocking a man to the floor, albeit in self-defence, were clear warning signs that all was not as it should be in my mind. Looking back, this entire period of my life was a whirlwind, a huge blur. Everything was just a little manic as I tried to come to terms with my new life and find the real me. I decided that enough was enough. I couldn't handle menial work. I had tried it, but it wasn't for me. I worked in that sandwich bar, as what my children affectionately termed 'the muffin man', for several more months, but during that time I was searching for a more challenging role.

I received an offer of a job as a clerk to a High Court judge at the Royal Courts of Justice in the Strand, London. My children were both young adults. One had left school and was working; the other was in his last years of secondary school. They were (and still are) brilliant children, the best any father could have. They weren't at all demanding and they had been resilient and strong throughout a rather unpleasant divorce and another difficult relationship breakdown. The three of us had become a tight unit, and that closeness remains to this day. The respect and unconditional love I have for them is unsurpassable.

Needless to say, when I explained that I had got a job as a clerk, they found it hysterically funny. The archetypal image of a clerk is a subservient Bob Cratchit type of character, which I most certainly am not. I explained that it wasn't a very prestigious role and my job would be to manage the judge's affairs both in court and beyond. However, it promised to offer me much more satisfaction than work as a mushroom picker or a muffin man ever could. The salary was ridiculously small, but at least it was a regular income and would help towards paying the bills and keeping us comfortable in our own home. The children agreed that I should take the position.

Everything was changing on the relationship front too. I was well known in the area as a single father and also as an author, both things that appealed to many women. I was regularly approached by women of all ages offering all kinds of relationships. I had no desire to get involved in a long-standing relationship with anyone. I had been put off by a manipulative woman who continually deceived me, and I wasn't about to allow myself to be hurt again. On breaking up with one woman, she aptly summed it up when she told me that I was the nicest person she had ever met yet also the most devoid of emotion. Since I knew I had been emotionally distant in all my relationships, I respected her honesty. I never wanted to be like that. I wanted to be able to trust, confide in and desire someone else, but I believed it just wasn't possible. I elected not to get involved with anyone until I was ready and it felt right. The women I had been involved with before seemed unstable and not at all the kind of people I wanted to be with, let alone allow near my children.

I was invited to the Royal Courts of Justice to meet with a High Court judge to see if we were suitable for each other. It was all very odd and very much like a blind date. The meeting was with a newly promoted judge. The resplendent grandeur of the judges' corridors of the Royal Courts of Justice was very much as one would imagine, with the floor lined with thick red carpet and brass fittings. The judges' chambers were oak-panelled, with floor-to-ceiling bookcases. It was all very regal and a bit surreal.

As I entered the judge's office, I could hear classical music playing in the background. It was a huge room and it took me ten or twelve steps to reach his desk. There he sat, head bowed as he concentrated on writing up some legal judgment. I had been told to call him 'sir' until he advised otherwise, so I politely introduced myself and told him about my police background. He seemed interested and asked me various questions about my children and my hobbies. He wasn't impressed by my passionate support of Leeds United but was intrigued that I was raising two children on my own with no woman in my life. He asked if I would like to be his clerk and I accepted.

I started a few weeks later, and, boy, was I thrown in at the deep end. Within days, I was asked to escort him to Buckingham Palace, where he was to be knighted. I met his wife and children and they were just as I had hoped they would be: grounded and decent people. They seemed a very loyal and good family. The trip to the palace was less than auspicious. As a clerk, I wasn't given any special treatment at the knighthood ceremony. I didn't get to meet the Queen or any royalty. I did meet the junior staff, who were very pleasant and courteous. Nonetheless, it was a bit special to be part of the event and it's something I am proud of. It's certainly a good tale to be able to tell. It was very odd, however, referring to the judge by his Christian name one minute, then as 'sir' the next!

My relationship with him seemed promising, but it never really flourished. Being answerable to him every minute of the working day wasn't something I enjoyed. Other clerks ran around after their judges like lapdogs. They had no self-respect and deferred to their judges over everything, even when they could take toilet breaks. As a bunch, I can honestly say the clerks were a bit odd. I couldn't deal with the ridiculous bureaucracy. The clerks had their own pecking order; senior clerks got better rooms or an extra potato on their plate when they went out on circuit with the judges. They even got control of the remote in the clerks' lounge. It was at best pathetic and I had more than one run-in with various colleagues, especially when they tried to bully other clerks who they didn't like.

The commute to London from the East Midlands every day was dreadful. I was effectively working a 16-hour day for a pittance. I was spending almost half my monthly salary on travel expenses. I stuck at it, but gradually the whole bureaucratic attitude of the entire court system became so demoralising that I began to question it, and I put my opinions to various judges with whom I worked.

Common sense did not exist. Everything was a matter of case law, and we all know that the law is an ass. More often than not, during various criminal trials, I would actually sit on the bench close to the presiding judge. Knowing how the system operated from two perspectives, the police and now the judiciary, I could spot a mile away when police officers giving evidence were not being honest. Part of me wanted to get involved, especially when I could see that police procedures were flawed. I saw many people in the dock who were serious career criminals and who were rightfully being tried for dreadful crimes; I saw others who were clearly terrified by the whole thing, people who had simply made mistakes but were being rigorously pursued and punished by the authorities. The vast majority of people who appear in court are there for right and proper reasons, but a small percentage are not; they are there because, as the police would say, they are 'an easy knock-off'.

The end of my time as a judge's clerk began when I was attacked on the London Underground late one evening. From the northbound platform at Tottenham Court Road, I stepped onto the train only to be confronted by a number of Chinese men, probably in their early 20s. The carriage was reasonably busy. Despite offering no provocation, I was mocked and verbally abused by the group. I made no response and stepped away from them. The next thing I knew, I was grabbed and beaten about the head and face. All I could do was shout out to the other passengers witnessing the attack to get the police. Typically, many of them simply got off at the next stop or stood and watched me being punched and kicked and having items stolen from me. Then the group took off.

I remember feeling a numbness across my face and I could see red in front of my eyes. The train driver had been alerted and came to check on my welfare. He said I needed to go to hospital, as I looked dreadful. I refused and said I just wanted to get home to Northampton. I told him that I'd be OK. The train moved off and, as I looked down at my white shirt, which was now blood-red, I realised that I had taken a serious beating. I was coughing up blood and felt a lump in my mouth. The lump was in fact two dislodged teeth. I felt dizzy and collapsed.

Out of the shadows

The next morning, I awoke in a hospital bed. I was in serious pain. I couldn't move my jaw and my eyes were nothing more than two tiny slits. I went into a panic. Not only was I in agony, but I hadn't a clue where I was. Frantically, I called out to a nurse and asked where I was. She was foreign and I couldn't understand a thing she said. I asked another and she too was foreign. I was so disorientated, I began to think I might actually be in another country. I was panicking because I needed to make contact with my children. I knew they would be worried and would want to know where I was. I wasn't even certain about what day it was, let alone anything else.

Finally, I was told I was in University College Hospital. I'd never heard of the place and asked where it was. I felt some relief when I was told it was in London. The ward staff wouldn't allow me to make a phone call. I pleaded with them, but they said I had to rest. Realistically, there was no way I could do that until I knew my children were OK and aware of my situation. I was forced to surreptitiously make the call from my mobile phone, hiding beneath the sheets. A few hours later, I was released from that awful place. My daughter arrived to collect me and take me home.

During the journey, I went into a panic because I couldn't breathe through my nose. It felt blocked and I knew something wasn't right, so as soon as I got in I made an appointment to see my doctor, who instructed me to go immediately to a local hospital in Leicester. There, at the oral and maxillofacial unit, all kinds of tests were carried out on my face and it transpired that I had fractured my skull and my eye orbits and my nose was broken in two places. So bad were the injuries that the specialist said I needed immediate reconstructive surgery and a plate inserted into my skull to prevent it splitting open.

The Cupboard Under the Stairs

The surgeon at Leicester told me that I had life-threatening injuries and should never have been allowed to leave hospital, let alone travel 130 miles in a car. The operation took around six hours. Two plates were screwed into my skull and another into my cheek and eye-orbit bone, my nose was completely reformed and the nasal cavity was reopened. I had a further five broken teeth removed from my mouth. In total, I received 60 stitches in my head and face. A specially cast face mask was made to protect the broken bones from everyday knocks and bumps that could cause further damage. The mask had to be worn at all times for a period of up to six weeks. I didn't realise it at the time, but my injuries were not only physical; there was a massive amount of mental trauma too.

The mask was a problem. It made me look something of a freak. Privately, at least at first, I loved it. Not only did it hide my horrific scars and injuries, it would act as a barrier, protection from the outside world. It took me back to my childhood days when I'd yearned for a mask like that of Batman. Now, in my 40s, I had my very own bespoke mask, and no one could see the real Paul Mason beneath it. That gave me some confidence. However, my first outing in the mask was to a local supermarket with my children. Honestly, the way people, complete strangers, stared at me was sickening. They didn't hide the fact that they were looking. One man actually said to his wife, 'Look at that weirdo in the mask.' I felt terrible and wanted to crawl away and hide. My daughter heard some of the dreadful comments and responded in an equally vitriolic manner!

After a couple of weeks, I became immune to the staring, but the comments never desisted. However, I had found a way of making people who made such damaging remarks feel less than secure. One man walking past me in a busy shopping area made a flippant and crude remark that stopped me in my tracks. I turned and walked after him. Standing in front of him, I stared coldly at him through the eyes of the mask for a full 30 seconds, until he averted his eyes, lowered his head and scuttled off without further comment. One policeman on foot patrol in Leicester city centre said to a colleague, 'Look at that nutter in the mask. He thinks he's Batman.' I remember thinking, 'If only I was.'

All of this – the Batman link, the abusive name-calling – brought back those horrible memories of my childhood. Being made to feel different and ignored was not something I'd welcomed as a child and it was awful to experience it again as an adult. When the mask finally came off six weeks later, it was a relief. My skull was given the all-clear and my face had completely healed. I had been off work throughout that time and had spent many hours contemplating all aspects of my life. I knew that I would have to return to London and was worried about travelling on the Underground.

The police carried out a full investigation into the assault and wanted to put out an appeal on *Crimewatch*. I wasn't confident enough for that to be broadcast, because I worried that the paedophiles who had abused me as a child would find out where I was. That aside, I would become known for all the wrong reasons: 'the ex-copper who got beaten up on the Underground'. I didn't want that kind of stigma attached to me. I already had enough to deal with from my childhood. The attack was apparently given coverage in London newspapers. An off-duty policeman came forward to say he had witnessed the whole assault and said he was sickened by it and thought I would be killed. He had got off the carriage and gone in search of the police, apparently, but didn't try to intervene himself because of the level of violence! The group was never caught. It didn't help that the CCTV at Tottenham

Court Road station had malfunctioned, so the attack wasn't caught on camera. It was yet another occasion when the system had let me down and there was nothing I could do about it. I just had to suffer the consequences and get on with my life.

After receiving kind telephone calls and a get-well-soon card from Lord Woolf, the then Lord Chief Justice of England and Wales, and from other members of the judiciary, I felt supported enough to return to work at the Royal Courts of Justice. The first few journeys to work were angst-filled, particularly when I was on the Underground. I found myself walking whenever possible, anything as an alternative to taking the Tube. The mental damage caused by the attack never did heal and I still don't feel safe on the London Underground.

It's a filthy and truly depressing place, full of stressed-out people, who don't enjoy being there and want to get off as soon as they can. Everyone is therefore in a rush and not at all caring of other people's needs. Good manners disappear and it can be a volatile environment. I cannot help but think of it as a place not too dissimilar to the cupboard under the stairs: dark and intimidating, a frightening place removed from the real world. Using the London Underground puts me right back in that place and all the horrors of my childhood flood back into my conscious mind. I find myself looking at people and wondering what their guilty secrets are. I feel suspicious of fellow travellers. In 2009, an NSPCC survey found that one in nine young adults interviewed had experienced sexual abuse during childhood. The real figure is likely to be even greater. Child sexual abuse is a much more common crime than the authorities will ever admit, and it is a crime worse than murder, since the victims, innocent children, have to live with the pain and the memories for life.

I couldn't and didn't want to continue putting myself through daily journeys that made me feel very insecure and frightened. Every time I entered the grimy, almost seedy world of the London Underground, I felt sick. My interest in the work at the Royal Courts of Justice disappeared as I became more and more obsessed by the journeys. One of the judges wasn't at all sympathetic and made demands on my time, expecting me at the court building by 7 a.m. and anticipating that I would still be there tending to his every need at 6 p.m. For a few days, I did as I was instructed, until I felt the strain getting to me.

One day, he demanded that I run a personal errand for him that meant I would miss my lunch break, as he expected me back in time to escort him into court. I explained that I needed a break and that I would carry out the task while he was in court later in the day. He would have none of it and acted like what I can only describe as a spoilt brat. We had words and I went for my lunch break, ignoring his rudeness. I was actually in a courtyard outside the courts and walking past his office window when he leaned out and, pointing his finger at me, said, 'You're going to suffer for this. Don't you dare turn your back on me.' I don't know what came over me, but I stopped, looked up at him and told him to 'fuck right off'.

My lunch break was, of course, ruined. I expected the worst when I returned to the offices; after all, you can't go round telling a High Court judge and a knight of the realm to 'fuck right off' and think nothing will happen. I returned half an hour later and was waiting for the 'discussion' to continue. I decided to take the bull by the horns and entered his room. To my surprise, he leapt up from his desk, ran towards me and hugged me, apologising for his behaviour and showing me a level of understanding that I would never have expected of him. I apologised for swearing at him and the matter was never mentioned again. I had shown a serious lack of respect towards one of the most powerful people in the land, and I confess I was alarmed that I was capable of it and wondered where it had come from.

I needed to suppress such attitudes, but, despite my every effort, I had no respect for anyone in authority until they consistently proved to me that they conducted themselves properly and were of value to me and society. I would not massage an ego or bow to any self-created status of superiority. This was something that I believed was new to me at the time, but, looking back, it has been there since my childhood. The spectre of Jack continued to haunt me.

One positive thing that came of my time at the Royal Courts of Justice was an introduction to someone who I was to learn to trust. I first met her when she visited my office with trial documentation. It wasn't an instantaneous attraction; it was more of a slowly simmering relationship that blossomed into something I could never have imagined. The one problem we encountered was the physical distance between our homes: 130 miles. In truth, she was everything I didn't look for in a partner: blonde, confident and often outrageous, she was devilishly daring and, to someone as emotionally damaged as I was, she was scary. It took several months before we went out on a date, and even longer before we felt confident enough to mention it to our families. Everything about this woman had initially screamed danger to me, but she was kind, loyal and caring, and for the first time in my life I genuinely began to trust someone outside my immediate family.

Chapter 22

The framework

Many years ago, there used to be a programme on the television called *The Prisoner*. In the opening scene of each episode, the prisoner (otherwise known as Number 6 and played by Patrick McGoohan), who was trapped in a place called the Village, where people lost their identities, being given numbers instead of names, would have a conversation with a mysterious, anonymous voice that projected over a Tannoy. The conversation went as follows:

Number 6: I will not make any deals with you. I've resigned. I will not be pushed, filed, stamped, indexed, briefed, debriefed or numbered. My life is my own. I resign.

Number 2: He's an individual, and they're always trying.

Number 6: Where am I?

Number 2: In the Village.

Number 6: What do you want?

Number 2: We want information.

Number 6: Whose side are you on?

Number 2: That would be telling. We want information . . . information . . . information.

Number 6: You won't get it.

> Number 2: By hook or by crook, we will.
> Number 6: Who are you?
> Number 2: The new Number 2.
> Number 6: Who is Number 1?
> Number 2: You are Number 6.
> Number 6: I am not a number. I am a free man.

That conversation always makes me think of the idiosyncratic, bureaucratic ways in which local government works. It is my opinion that the vast majority of people who work in these organisations have no desire for freedom of thought, no wish to express an opinion or make a difference to local or national society.

This is especially so of senior management. They are grey suits, nondescript sorts of people who conform to the rules. They don't care who makes the rules, as long as there are rules for them to adhere to and quote. In a local council, the senior management team worships the chief executive officer, who, generally speaking, is full of self-importance. These people tend to be egotistical autocrats who believe they are vastly superior in every way to everyone else. Essentially, from my experience, they are little more than bullies, puppets for the politicians to manipulate.

This, then, is hardly the ideal workplace for someone who tends to be a bit of a loose cannon, someone who can't stand incompetence or corrupt and improper practice, who has a life outside the framework of the local authority. Incredibly, I took the option of this career change when I was asked to apply for a position at a local council that was, in essence, a liaison role with the police and crime reduction, titled Community Safety Officer. It had many advantages. It was closer to home, it was working within an environment I knew and felt comfortable with, it was a better salary package and I knew I could do the job. A friend who was then an inspector in a police force told me I should apply and, over a few pints, gave me a rundown of what was expected and what types of questions I would be asked in the interview. Sure enough, my application won me an interview with a panel of three people – two senior council managers and a police superintendent – I managed to waffle my way through and I was offered the job.

It wasn't a blow to leave the courts. In fact, I couldn't wait to get out. It wasn't the judges but the attitude of the clerks and the whole administration from top to bottom that was wrong. Certain juicy, more high-profile cases were given to the clerks who were liked and favoured by the listing officers; it was nothing to do with the competency of the judge, it was how the clerk was viewed that mattered. I've seen clerks fighting and squabbling over case files, wrestling and pulling them from each other in order to get a case to their liking. I've also witnessed clerks telling the listing officers which cases should be allocated to which judges!

The listing officers themselves are a peculiar breed. They see themselves as powerful and influential characters. I used to challenge what I saw as the unfair way in which cases were allocated and quickly found myself being given the worst possible cases. On one occasion, a judge contacted a listing officer to ask why he was continually getting the same type of case. He was told that I volunteered him for these cases and specifically asked for them. It was a lie. The judges themselves were supremely professional, I hasten to add, and genuinely dealt with every case on its legal merits and to the best of my knowledge in a fair and proper manner.

My first day as a council grey suit was totally boring: lots of people sat at desks, looking at computer screens and appearing to be extremely busy. I was given a desk in a corner of a large open-plan office and left to my own devices. Sitting there twiddling my thumbs, I began to notice that many others weren't actually doing a great deal: answering the odd email, making a call here and there, but nothing that looked all that constructive. Bored, I decided to walk round the office, introduce myself and find out what the other people did. Were we all part of one large team or were we individuals? I needn't have bothered asking myself the question; in councils, there are no individuals, just keyboard key-pushers. They do what they have to do and no more. It's all about protecting the pension, sticking to the rules and not going out of your way to assist anyone – that way you can't be criticised for doing something wrong.

My line manager was a woman and I was hopeful that this would be a positive in my professional life. I was wrong, and it didn't take long for the friction to start. It was there from day one, to be honest. She had been one of the panel who had recruited me. On my first day in the office, she informed me that she'd wanted a different candidate and had voted against me, that I therefore had 'a lot to do' to win her over and she was going to be watching me very closely. I gave her a reassuring smile and told her I was the right choice and not to worry.

'Are you married?' she asked.

'No,' I replied.

'Oh, you must be gay then, are you?'

I asked what on earth gave her that idea and she gave a response I hadn't expected to hear. 'Well, you're a good-looking bloke, quite fanciable, actually. You wouldn't be unattached if you weren't gay. The other thing is, you have a moustache. Only gay men have moustaches. It's a sign between you all, isn't it?' I laughed. I felt flattered, I very much liked the 'good-looking' comment. Yet the 'gay' comment bothered me. Homosexuality had negative associations for me because of the sexual abuse by men I had experienced, and to a lesser extent because of the rumours that had circulated in the police service. I felt an odd juxtaposition of emotions: part of me was pleased and felt good about myself; another part felt dirty and degraded by what she'd said.

Within three months, my relationship with her had totally deteriorated. I recognised in her a vicious and selfish streak; she was an angry woman who clearly took her frustrations out on her staff. It was like being a child again. She didn't like me at all and inside something snapped. I hated myself for allowing her the freedom to treat me so badly.

Once, she called me to a meeting in her office. She had a smug look on her face as she sat behind her desk. I went to sit down and was stopped in my tracks as she said that I had to stand up until she told me I could sit down. Then she looked down at some paperwork on her desk and began to write. I stood in silence for a few moments before asking what she wanted. 'Be quiet. Don't speak to me until I ask you a question,' she said. I desperately wanted to tell her to fuck her job, but I knew that this was what she wanted, so I elected to say nothing. I watched the second hand on the wall clock making its way round the face. I stood in silence for a full 15 minutes. 'Are you going to make me stand here all day?' I asked. She didn't look up as she replied, 'Get out of here, you wanker.'

I returned to my desk feeling dejected and very much alone. It seemed that everyone had realised I was on the 'hit list' and being forced out. It was as if no one dared to be associated with me because they might be the next target. So I decided to leave. I kept it as quiet as I could, but I knew that eventually I would have to tell her. It took me four weeks to find another job, a similar role, this time not in a council but with Age Concern in Bethnal Green.

The salary was much improved and although it was back in London, it was drivable from my home, so there was no need for me to use the Underground.

I was offered the job, accepted it and gave as a reference a director at the council, circumventing my manager. It wasn't too long before I was summoned to her office, where she mocked my getting a job with Age Concern and remarked that she knew I was a failure from the moment she met me. She added, 'A job with Age Concern is about your professional limit. You are a tosser of the highest order.'

I was speechless, but not for long. 'I don't care where I work, as long as it's away from you. You are an ignorant first-class bully. You are nothing but a joke here. People won't dare say it to your face, but plenty do behind your back. I have no respect for you. Your whole attitude and demeanour is anal.' So ended my life with that council.

I loved my job with Age Concern. Bethnal Green was a fantastic place to work and the people were genuine and honest. No one was judgemental and as a team we were as one and we helped one another. For me, it was great to be part of the legendary East End and I was soon wandering the streets that had been frequented by some of the capital's most infamous residents, Jack the Ripper and the Kray twins. I was, of course, working at the other end of the spectrum from those miscreants. It was my job to provide security to and help protect the more senior residents of Bethnal Green, the vast majority of whom were genuine Eastenders, with lots of tales to tell and some wonderful anecdotes relating to everything from the war through to the Kray twins, who, by all accounts locally, were a decent pair of lads forced into a life of crime by the authorities' failure to provide for East End folk. If I had a penny for every time someone produced a photograph of themselves with one of the Kray twins, I would be a rich man.

The framework

One man who I visited regularly was a retired policeman. He told me how 'dodgy' policing was back then, how the police would get a decent salary not only from the force but from the villains also, taking certain individual crooks off the street so that others could enjoy a free rein in their territory. Evidence would be manipulated or in many cases concocted. This was the good old 1960s, when extortion gangs ruled the streets. Being told that coppers were bent hardly came as a shock to me, since I had seen more than ample evidence of it for myself in the three decades I had been involved in crime-fighting, and I knew full well that it was still happening. For obvious reasons, I had no respect for the boys and girls in blue. It has long been clear to me that certain police forces are more arrogant and liable to corruption than others. It's the same with certain ranks. Chief inspectors and above believe they are untouchable and will do anything to further their careers – and I mean anything. By far and away, for me, the Metropolitan Police of London are the worst example, mainly because my perception was formed by an incident that took place in 1969.

As a ten year old, I was forced to sleep with a man who was visiting the Carlisle area. He told me he was from London and showed me his police badge and warrant card; it was as though he felt I should be impressed. He was a 'big-time Johnny', a chief inspector, no less, with a huge ego and morals that were in the gutter. He clearly felt that if he told me his rank, it would make me grateful for him raping and abusing me. The sickening thing for me was that in his wallet he had a photograph of his wife and children. They looked happy as a family and I asked him if he ever hurt them. 'No, never. I would never hurt my children or do this to them. It takes a certain type of boy to excite me, a dirty little boy like you,' he said. It hurt me a lot. To think that anyone saw me as a dirty little boy, an object to be abused, and not as a normal child frightened me. My feelings didn't matter to him, though: he went on to rape me twice and beat me to get his kicks. That, in part, is why my opinion of the Metropolitan Police is so damning and poor.

Sadly, my time at Age Concern was all too brief. I don't like to blow my own trumpet, but I became so successful with my crime-prevention work there that I was approached and asked to work for a council partnership, this time in Kent. It was a permanent contract and not only was the salary much improved but there was a brand-new car of my choice, too. I was courted for some time by the council. I eventually agreed to go for an interview and I was ultimately offered the job. I took it and, for the first and only time in my life, I was sad to leave an employer. Age Concern in Bethnal Green was great. It will always have a special place in my heart. The staff and the local people were the most genuine I had ever encountered.

Day one at the new council was bad. It was as bereft of common sense and as disorganised as the previous one I'd worked for. For a whole week, there was no one to tell me what my role was, what was expected of me and who I was to work with. It didn't take me too long to make enemies. I questioned the corporate induction policy (there wasn't one) and was robustly admonished by the head of human resources, who was a woman who didn't like feedback. I remained at the council for three years and throughout that time there was a constant battle with that person. I saw it as my duty to remind her that I would not let her bully or intimidate me.

Then, a local news story about a paedophile ring stopped me in my tracks and pushed me to a place I did not want to go. The case concerned a father who had introduced his young son to a paedophile ring. The boy had grown up and had recently committed suicide. He left a note, which was how it had all come out. He had been the same age as me. The story of the paedophile ring weighed on my mind, and soon memories of my childhood came flooding back.

Suddenly, everything in the workplace seemed to be connected with child sexual abuse. Working closely with the police, I was being told about local crimes, including sexual assaults and rapes, all of which affected me mentally. Many police officers, when they think they are in a safe environment, such as the inner confines of a police station, are less than professional or honourable in their discussions about sexual crimes. It was all I could do to keep my own counsel when I heard the sick jokes about paedophiles and rapists. The comments were not meant to be disrespectful; they were more of a way of dealing with such horrors. But inside I felt sickened by the situation. Even in the council, the CCTV operators whom I managed often talked about the lewd sexual incidents they witnessed on camera virtually every night. Some would be rewound and watched by the staff and others, including police officers. I put a stop to this behaviour unless it was necessary for a criminal investigation; in those cases, all viewings of the tapes would be documented.

I was driving home to Essex one evening when I felt a terrible pain in my chest and a tingling sensation in my left arm. I was on the M25 and the traffic was stop–start. I managed to cope with the pain until I got home, but when I walked through the front door I literally passed out. I awoke in hospital, with countless leads and wires connected to my chest and arms. I was on a trolley and had been left in a corridor attached to a heart-monitoring machine and a drip. My partner was there and she explained what had happened.

The pain in my chest wasn't as bad now and the only symptom I was experiencing was nausea. Every now and then, a nurse appeared, checked everything, then trotted off down the corridor. After several hours, a doctor came to see me and told me I had suffered a warning shot. My heart couldn't take all the stress and work I was forcing on it. When he asked what I did as an occupation and I told him I was a council worker, he laughed and said the attack certainly couldn't have been work-induced. He allowed me to go home only because there were no beds available and told me to do nothing strenuous for four weeks and to report to my GP.

When I got home, I broke down. For the best part of my life, I had been running away from the abuse I had suffered; now it had caught up with me and I was struggling to keep it suppressed and private. I was in the bedroom when I described a tiny part of what had happened to me as a child to my partner. She was clearly stunned and, for a moment, speechless, but then, to her credit, she took me in her arms and held me in a deeply reassuring hug like those my brother John had given me when I was a child. Incredibly, I felt like that little boy again. The tears flowed down my cheeks and I sobbed without saying another word.

I desperately wanted to unburden myself and tell her about the agony I dealt with each day of my life. I couldn't do it. I realised how distressing the entire matter would be to anyone learning of it for the first time, especially someone who cared for me. I'd already told her that my father had continually raped and beaten me, locking me in the cupboard under the stairs for days on end. I left it at that. Despite her assurances that she understood and was willing to listen and not judge, I couldn't find it within myself to completely open up.

I was tired and my head felt heavy; my body was closing down in order to repair itself. I lay down on the bed and slept like I had never slept before.

Chapter 23

The fabric of society

When I awoke the next morning, I was still exhausted. Everything that had happened the previous day seemed as though it was part of a dream. The first thing to cross my mind was fear of ridicule. I had allowed my partner access to secret and private parts of my life that had never before been exposed. I felt vulnerable and scared. I wasn't certain how she would react after a night of thinking about it. I ran through different scenarios as to how I would deal with a negative response. I was even contemplating packing my belongings and running, leaving everything behind and starting afresh somewhere different. Yet, for the first time in my life, I knew that I cared for and loved someone other than my children. I didn't want to lose that, or her. But I felt sure that she must see me as weak, tainted and disgusting. I could no longer disguise my past. We both knew that from that point on things would be very different. She would be curious and want to know more in order to understand, and I had to allow her access to my private world.

I was off work for around four weeks. Within minutes of returning to that place, I felt awkward and uncomfortable. It really wasn't my world, full of nondescript people with ridiculous job titles, although I doubt any member of the public understood what they meant. I was there for one reason: it paid the bills. A career it was not.

In my first week back, I managed to upset my manager, a lawyer. He wrongly believed I was looking for a job elsewhere and one evening had stayed behind and hacked into my email, deleting much of my inbox. He had also broken into my locked desk drawers. He failed to properly log out of my email, so when I came in the next morning, I was logged in. I went through to his office to report the hacking to him, but he was out. When I looked at his computer, I was astounded to see that it was he who had logged into my email. I wasn't at all sure who to speak to. I decided it was best to deal with it head-on and speak to the manager first, give him a chance to explain his actions. To cut a long story short, he denied everything until I showed him his computer screen with my emails on there. He went bright red and tried to blame it all on me. It ended with him walking out and going home sick.

During his absence, I was called to a meeting with a director who told me that my manager was his best friend. He made various comments about me being a loose cannon and not conforming to council culture, and told me that I had to respect my superiors. I said to him that in my opinion no one in the council was superior to anyone else – we were all equals, human beings. His response wasn't what I'd expected. 'That may well be, but many of us are better connected and we look after our own first.' I asked why he was being so cryptic and what he meant by that. 'We share the same lodge. Many of your copper mates are there too, and, yes, we talk about everything, including you.'

I felt the blood drain from my face. I had forgotten the influence of the 'all-seeing eye', the Masonic message Jack had drilled into me. He had told me that the all-seeing eye would watch my every move till the day I died.

Hearing that council director utter a similar threat sickened me. I instinctively knew from the way he had made the point that it was meant to strike fear into me. I felt utter contempt for him and Masonry in general, but I wasn't about to let him see that. I said I understood what he was saying and returned to my own desk on a different floor.

As far as I was concerned, any trust or loyalty had been destroyed by both the manager and the director. I did as my job description asked and no more. I admit I made many enemies by doing what was right for the people of the borough, as opposed to what was deemed politically desirable.

One person I seriously hacked off happened to be the local Conservative Party leader. I am not a supporter of the Tory party. One evening, this person made a ridiculous statement about the poor quality of policing across the borough. I spoke up on behalf of the police. It turned out that one particular inspector was the object of the councillor's wrath, seemingly for not cancelling a speeding ticket he had received! My card was well and truly marked when I told the Tory councillor that maybe he was in the wrong lodge.

I was eventually offered another position, on double the salary at a London council. It was an unusual situation. Rarely within the local-authority framework do you get a chief executive headhunting you, yet I did. I should have smelled a rat, but I was desperate to move on. I accepted the new job without looking into it. The new position was on the far side of London, and travelling was a nightmare, especially since I had a long journey on the Underground. I hated it from day one: the secretive and sycophantic staff; the egotistical and bullying chief executive and his hangers-on, who were known as the executive management team.

Within months, I could feel myself falling apart. I had never before despised a place of work so much, and the stress and strain of the travelling and the atmosphere of mistrust that permeated the entire council began to affect me. I had received no induction and, to be honest, I hadn't a clue what I was doing. Political and professional priorities changed every day, depending on the level and type of crime occurring. I was frustrated because I could see how inept local policing was, not because of the front-line officers but because of the poor senior management. It seemed that 'the centre' (Scotland Yard) visited the borough every week because of the high crime levels and the failure to hit Home Office crime-reduction targets.

I was permanently on edge, and on a daily basis I found myself away from home for up to 16 hours. I wasn't aware of what was happening to me, as I was on autopilot. I knew my time at the council was limited, so I did everything I could to protect myself. I became 100 per cent defensive, but I was overwhelmed by the deluge of work that was forced on me. I tried to fight back but failed. I was sinking fast and could do nothing to prevent it. My confidence was shattered and I lived every day in fear of the sack. My final act was to cleanse my conscience and soul: I sent an email to an executive director outlining everything wrong I had witnessed during my brief time at the council. In doing so, I was signing my own death warrant.

As soon as I pressed send and the email was processed, I broke down. I quietly cleared my desk, because I knew I was finished. My mental state was so fragile that I didn't know what day it was or what role I was in. I said not a word to another soul and walked away. The following day, I went to my doctor, who told me that my health and mental state were poor. He warned me not to go back to the council or do any work, since it could permanently damage my health.

I was without work for six months. Although I didn't properly understand it at the time, I was incapable of holding down a job. I was forced to enter the benefits system, and that proved as woefully incompetent as everything else connected with the Establishment. I registered online for work with charities, since this seemed much more productive and I felt as though I would be able to make a positive difference. I didn't want any responsibility; I was looking for a role that required no brainpower or decision-making.

I was offered a position with a charity that worked in the field of public awareness of child sexual abuse. I was desperate to get off benefits. I found the system incredibly confusing: countless multi-page forms to fill in, medicals to attend and letters to respond to. I didn't have the mental capacity to deal with it all. One of the worst aspects of my mental breakdown was being unable to process information. I couldn't fill in the forms or understand the questions. The application form for the charity position took a full week to complete, and still it wasn't right. However, I got through to interview and that gave me something of a lift.

It took three interviews before I was formally offered the position, not because the process was particularly rigorous but because I was all over the place mentally. I thought I was OK, but I wasn't. I hadn't actually expected to get an interview. However, with only three people being interviewed and two of those withdrawing, I was the sole choice. Even then, it wasn't straightforward. I clashed at interview with the director. We held opposing opinions and clearly were two different types of people, personally and professionally.

My role was home-based and, to be honest, it wasn't at

all taxing, but it was damaging to my health. I hadn't realised that the charity actually supported paedophiles and not their victims. Essentially, it was an anonymous helpline service; it was primarily used by paedophiles who had been arrested and charged, and to me it was clear that the vast majority saw it as a tool to show the courts their willingness to stop abusing children, so influencing the reduction of any punishment. When I asked for a statistic for reformed paedophiles, in other words how many stopped abusing, I was told that no such figure existed. It all seemed very amateur, and when I learned that the total number of calls received by the helpline included those from professionals working in the child sexual abuse prevention/reduction field, who would phone seeking information, it made me further question the benefits of the whole thing.

Within three months, I could see the charity was achieving nothing. The director was a small man with a big ego. He reminded me of Jack, since he viewed himself as always being in control and demanded respect because he was a self-proclaimed expert in the field of helping reduce child sexual abuse. I didn't respect him at all. We remained opposites. He had said at the outset that he was concerned about appointing me since he felt we had conflicting opinions about child sexual abuse. He was right too; there was no way I wanted to help paedophiles. I knew from experience that until they are caught they don't want help and don't seek it.

Thankfully, working from home, I didn't have to see the director every day. The people who worked for the charity – there were only six of us – were as disparate a group as they come. We were all based in different areas of the United Kingdom – England, Scotland, Ireland, Wales and London – and on the rare occasions we did meet up it was all very false.

It was never going to last. I switched off, and did what I had to do to get by. I was actually very ill, and I realised that I needed to resign from this organisation.

As usual, I parted company with my employer in an acrimonious manner. I mentioned at a meeting with the director that whenever I spoke to members of the public about the charity's aims they were repulsed that anyone, or any charity, would want to commit to helping paedophiles. I explained that I agreed with this perception, that there was therefore a need for a professional rebranding and that perhaps we should look at helping victims. I was shouted down and told I was talking 'bullshit' by the director. He reminded me that I was the monkey and not the organ grinder, so I should keep my stupid thoughts to myself. After a heated discussion, I reminded him that my opinions and beliefs were wholly contrary to his; in my mind, helping support paedophiles or helping them evade proper punishment was plain wrong.

He seemed confused by this statement. He shook his head and called me thick, and dismissed my opinion with a wave of his hand. I snapped. I very nearly took his head off, but instead I told him where to stick his charity, because it clearly achieved nothing for the thousands of children suffering abuse every day throughout the United Kingdom. Opportunities to put one's employers in their place are few and far between, so when he asked me to justify my outburst, I shocked myself when I told him, 'Actually, Mr Self-Proclaimed Expert, I know because I am a victim. I suffered abuse in every form as a child for several years. I was raped countless times by a paedophile ring. Virtually everything you claim as an expert is wide of the mark. It may look good in academic papers, but in the real world it's garbage, utter crap. Paedophiles have no conscience. The only remedy in my opinion is incarceration. A helpline staffed by one or sometimes two unqualified volunteers isn't going to stop paedophiles committing their crimes.'

He gasped in shock, as did I. For the first time in my life, I had admitted to an outsider what had happened to me as a child. There was a stony silence and then he said, 'Well, I'm going to have to report you to the trustees and seek guidance on what we do here. I'm not happy and cannot see a way forward between us.'

Emotionally, I was a wreck, unable to think straight or act normally. I was suffering a complete mental breakdown. A week or so passed with no contact from the charity, so I submitted my letter of resignation. It was over and I felt a sense of relief. I had no sympathy for the charity or for any of the people who worked there or for myself.

I had tried to prove to myself that I was a valid human being, someone who could hold down a regular job without any conflict or problems, even when confronted by corruption or improper practices. But I wasn't able to do it. The legacy of Jack was still with me, I couldn't accept or understand incompetence or sinister behaviour from anyone. I felt a need to speak out about it and to confront those committing it.

When I later discussed this with my daughter, she made a comment that resonated with me. 'It's a bit like you're fighting the bad people, sort of like Batman does. He fights the bad guys and uncovers corruption.' As ridiculous as it sounded, she was right. Batman had helped me when I was locked in the cupboard under the stairs. He had been my imaginary companion. When I was being raped and suffering abuse, I would force myself into another world. There, I became Batman and played out in my mind the consequences of the baddies' actions and how Batman would one day put everything right. Then, as an adult, I had become a protector of my own family and of society, through being a policeman with day-to-day responsibilities that included crime-fighting and dealing with bad people. Later, without the police uniform, I had simply become a crusader, without a mask and cape, but still very much in the tradition of Batman. I still laugh nervously when I consider this.

The mask is a very important aspect of my true self; it hides and protects me and allows me to become invisible. Although I don't physically wear a mask, the fact that for many years I could never be my true self, mainly because I didn't know who I was, was something I hid behind. I didn't allow anyone into my personal world. Nobody other than my children knew who I really was. It's difficult to explain, but because of the abuse I suffered as a child there is a huge void in my emotional life, massive gaps that can never be filled. It feels like my life has been one huge lie because I couldn't discover my true self. That was taken from me when I was first abused and raped. Since that time, I have become what others have made me: Jack, his teacher friend, countless police officers, the weird collection at the model-railway club, RAF officers, Freemasons – in fact, all those who participated in the vile and disgusting behaviour of raping and abusing me as a child. It was each and every one of these people who destroyed my once innocent personality and forced upon me a life of torment. They created in me a complete mistrust of the human race, all to satisfy their own depraved sexual appetites.

Whether society wants to accept or believe it, paedophilia is very much alive and present in all walks of life. Since I was a child, paedophiles and paedophilia have become more virulent and widespread, so much so that it only now makes the news when it involves a well-known personality or when yet another paedophile ring has been identified and arrests made. The other point I am trying to make here is that paedophiles come in all shapes and sizes. They are masters of deception and are excellent at blending into the background and waiting for the opportunity to strike at their prey. Like most criminals, they are manipulative and cunning, and they tell lies to distract attention or to disguise their actions.

I appreciate that this is a worrying picture, but I possess more experience of their manner and conduct than most. I know how they operate. I recognise the signs, the coded language they use, the methods of grooming, the excuses they make and the guilt trips they force upon their victims, the modus operandi. Believe me when I tell you a paedophile looks no different from your next-door neighbour or the man or woman who lives across the road. The paedophile who preys on children he doesn't know is far less common than the media would have anyone believe. The vast majority of paedophilia is intra-familial; the offender is related to the victim.

I am a member of and voluntarily work with survivor groups nationally and internationally. I therefore know a lot of victims. Recently, I carried out an anonymous survey amongst these victims, and one of the questions I asked was about sexual thoughts and perversions about children. Of one hundred and thirty victims surveyed, just three had such thoughts; I hasten to add that they had never acted upon these. This basic piece of research completely destroys the belief that 'the abused very often becomes the abuser'.

The only real way we will have any positive impact in addressing child sexual abuse is to educate the public, get into schools and make it easier to report such crimes without the protracted trauma that can ensue when the authorities are more concerned about protecting their own reputations than helping and supporting the victim. There is a desperate need for vastly improved support networks specifically for victims of this sort of crime.

Chapter 24

To hell and back

I finally tried to release myself from the chains that had so restricted my entire life and had left me doubting myself and everything around me. My whole life had been one continuous trauma. Getting through each day had been difficult. And now, having kept my past locked away and secure for so long, I was beginning to doubt myself, blame myself for having allowed it to happen and for not speaking up more loudly about it all those years ago. I had told the family doctor and he had called me a liar and told me to never mention it again to a living soul. Now, as an adult, I questioned why I had accepted his advice and never told anyone else. The problem I had was having a voice that could be heard. I was only six years old and it's difficult enough for a child to be listened to and understood by adults without having to tell them something distasteful that they won't want to hear.

Maybe Jack was right after all, maybe it was all my fault for being a naughty little boy. My actions throughout my childhood and as an adult – lacking respect for authority and speaking out against Establishment corruption – had dictated that I was angry and ill at ease with my life. Since leaving the police, I had gone through jobs like confetti and knew I was not without problems. Not all were of my own making, but no one seemed interested or bothered by that. My professional career record read more like a list of failures. For me, it was over.

The easiest option I had was to end it all. My two children were doing well. I loved them unconditionally, and my grandchildren too. Other than my partner, there was not another living soul who I felt genuinely cared or showed any support for me. I love her very much and I know she loves and cares for me. She is the last person I would ever doubt on any matter; I refer to her on everything and rely on her. We are extremely close and she guides me through my life, making decisions and keeping me straight. I thought she deserved better than me.

I felt I had arrived at the final crossroads in my life. Behind me was the darkness from which I had continually fled. It had finally caught me and was now enveloping me; I was ready to succumb. Over a period of days, no matter how much I searched, I could find no purpose to my life. I was bringing nothing but pain to all those involved with me. It must have been dreadful for my children to see their father falling apart and losing control. I began to distance myself from my everyday life and organise my affairs so there would be little needing any attention when I had gone. I found myself in a place where it seemed easier to let life go than to continue to fight against the Establishment. It was a terrible situation and I wasn't certain whether I had put myself there or had been forced there by others who had failed me and heaped more turmoil on my tortured soul.

I decided how I would kill myself. I prepared everything, tablets and a couple of bottles of Australian wine. I opted to take one final look at images of my partner, children and family. I wanted my last thoughts to be about the meaningful part of my life that I'd enjoyed and loved. I turned on my computer and opened the folder where the images were stored. As I scanned through them, I was drawn to one particular picture: it was the Batman logo, just as John had drawn it for me in the cupboard under the stairs. As childish as it seemed, I wondered what Batman would have done in my situation. It dawned on me that, according to his story, Bruce Wayne had lost both of his parents in a shooting incident when he was a child. The incident changed him. He lost trust in everything and it made him different, yet he survived and went on to achieve a great deal. Although he was a fictional comic-book hero, I could still relate to the fundamentals of the story. We were similar in many ways, although I wasn't a superhero and nor did I want to be. In truth, I didn't want to be Batman; I wanted to be me.

To say that it was a light-bulb moment would be an understatement. I actually felt the inner strength growing within me. Seeing the Batman logo when I was at rock bottom aroused the desire to fight on. The fact that I had a life, no matter how bad it was or seemed to be, and that I had a few people who genuinely loved me, suddenly became clear. If I killed myself, I would be hurting them all: my partner, my two children, two gorgeous grandchildren and two dogs, who very much rely on me. I would miss them and they would miss me too. I put away the pills, returned the wine to the rack and contemplated the good things in my life.

OK, I was without work, and realistically I knew I could never work for anyone else again. I was living in a place I hated. My life was far from perfect. But it was my life and I had a right to live it. Yes, it had in the main been shit, but there had been highs and positive experiences that most people can only dream of. If I wanted to change my future and my mindset, then that was my responsibility, not anyone else's.

Within 24 hours, I had arranged counselling sessions

to help me deal with the legacy Jack had forced upon me. I had made an appointment to see my doctor and told him about the abuse. The experienced counsellor I spoke to showed a level of empathy I had never imagined possible. He listened to me, never judged me and was open in his thoughts and opinions about the abuse I had suffered. In one session, he told me that my father had the morals of Fred West or Ian Brady. That level of brutal honesty shook me. Up to that point only I had viewed Jack as genuinely evil; now here was someone agreeing with me. I had opened up to a professional for the first time since I was a child. The difference now was that I had someone believing what I told them without chastising or punishing me for speaking out.

Although it was difficult revealing such awful details, I felt sure that I was doing the right thing. After about a year of counselling, he told me I should consider reporting everything to the police. The reason was not one I had previously considered: to prevent other children being hurt by Jack and his cohorts. When I explained my concerns that the police wouldn't believe me, he assured me that there was an entire structure of support for victims of child sexual abuse and that help would be implemented from the moment I reported it. The decision didn't take long. I agreed that my counsellor should tell the police I wished to speak to them.

I was surprised to be told that because of the severity of what had occurred to me as a child he had already alerted the police and they were aware of some basic details. I attended a video interview locally. Five hours and several breaks later I resurfaced, mentally and physically exhausted. I had gone through the basics of the abuse I had suffered with them, but it was just the tip of the iceberg. The police officer who interviewed me was first class in every way, attentive, caring and non-judgemental.

He was one officer who did his job professionally and properly and provided the duty of care I had hoped for. He has remained something of a rock for me. I rarely contact him, but just knowing he is available provides some comfort.

One of the most difficult things I have had to come to terms with throughout the police investigation is not knowing what's happening. Contact between myself and the Cumbria force was rare, not helped by the 300-mile distance between us. However, when contact was made, it was sincere and meaningful. One of the first things the investigating officers did was visit the house at Crindledyke Estate and look at the cupboard under the stairs. Quite incredibly, 46 years after the event, the drawings and words etched on the wood beneath the stairs by my brother remained visible. The red Batman logo was his legacy, his contribution towards making sure that justice would eventually be achieved. I was thrilled, even a little overwhelmed, when the police rang to say they had found it precisely where I had said it would be. It confirmed what I was saying and was clearly positive evidence.

Suddenly, from feeling my life was in the doldrums, I now felt I was taking massive steps forward. It wasn't that my problems had suddenly disappeared; they were still there. The major difference was that I was now confronting and addressing them.

According to the authorities, there is much in the way of support networks for survivors of child sexual abuse, yet the reality is somewhat different. There are few that actively achieve anything. One survivor service I called told me I was one of the lucky ones, as many victims kill themselves before reaching my age. I was so shocked by the comment that I hung up. A different service provider promised to call me back and didn't, and yet another told me to seek help through victim support and talked incessantly about how I should try to get compensation. This lack of real support and help seriously undermines the challenge of getting more victims to come forward.

With this in mind, I wanted to do something about the quality of service provision for victims. Helplines offered very little and most simply signposted other organisations. Without any doubt in my mind, the best service in terms of offering understanding and guidance is the Samaritans, and I would strongly recommend that anyone who wants a non-judgemental ear calls them.

My own quest to help started by my writing to local authorities, primarily identifying what services they offered in their respective areas. It is with a heavy heart that I have to say that the vast majority of local authorities failed to respond, some ignoring as many as half a dozen professionally worded requests over a period of a few months. Local Safeguarding Children boards were my next port of call; these aspire to consistently deliver best practice, yet few realise that aim. There are claims about specialist training programmes and continuing staff development. Sadly, what I could find consisted mainly of in-house training. Bespoke partnership training for those working in the field often commands fees of around £500 per candidate. For this sum, one would expect a comprehensive training programme, but this isn't always the case. While it could be said that it is good that training does take place, the basic understanding of the effects of the crime is flawed, which damages the ability to provide proper, focused help. An accurate victim perspective is not always provided and the victim's needs and support requirements aren't always taken into account.

Having received such training while in employment with a local authority and with a charity working in the area of child sexual abuse prevention, I am perhaps more qualified than most to state that the current standard of training does not deal with victim needs. It does, however, address the vital performance indicators required for attaining top comprehensive assessment scores and for meeting the Home Office criteria. Essentially, it looks good on paper but is ineffective in its outcomes.

While I confess to being cynical about the overarching quality of the formal boards and partnerships working in this area, I have no doubt that a reasonable percentage of the people working in the child abuse profession, volunteers or otherwise, are dedicated, focused and genuinely want to make a difference by delivering a high-quality service and helping victims.

I too wanted to make a difference, change attitudes and create a proactive training programme that was victim-focused but still delivered outcomes and achieved regional and national targets. I wanted to explain to practitioners what it meant to suffer abuse, not only as a child but also as an adult living with its legacy. Over a period of years, I developed a generic training package to supplement that already being delivered; every aspect of the content was checked and amended by people who I respected and who understood the subject.

With everything in place, I contacted each Safeguarding Children Board and offered my services, initially as a guest speaker and later, once they saw my competence level and thorough knowledge of the subject, as a trainer. Once again, there was a depressingly negative response, with less than a handful bothering to respond. Finally, I was given an opportunity to speak at a regional practitioner event. It went well and by the time my presentation was over there wasn't a dry eye in the house. I was overwhelmed with requests for further information.

In 2009, I was nominated for and presented with the prestigious Una Padel Outstanding Individual award from the Centre for Crime and Justice Studies, London. The award panel comprised many eminent figures in the field of criminal justice, including Lord Woolf, the former Lord Chief Justice of England and Wales. It remains one of the proudest achievements of my life, since it was given for unpaid voluntary work that had emerged from my own suffering. I had changed the overwhelming negativity of my situation into a positive and saw that I was actually making a difference to victims and enhancing the perspective and knowledge base of those working with and providing victim-support networks.

As I wrote these final few words in November 2011, I received the decision from the CPS as to whether Jack was to be charged with any offences. He had been on police bail since February, a brief time when compared with the lifetime of punishment I and countless others have endured as a result of his actions. Because of his age, the historical basis of the case and the fact that so many abusers have died, the CPS opted not to proceed.

It was a pathetic and wholly wrong decision and I was devastated by the news. I can only wonder if Jack's influence in the police service and the Masonic world outweighed justice. If Jack had been charged, what might he have come out with? Whom might he have named as his fellow conspirators? I have no doubt that many respected and now mainly retired senior police officers, senior officers in the RAF, local politicians, solicitors and influential people from the Carlisle region who were involved in my abuse breathed a sigh of relief, knowing that criminal prosecution was not going to occur. I have no proof of pressure being exerted, obviously, but my experience makes me fear the overpowering influence of bodies and people in authority and their power to undermine even the law.

I know that I was the victim of satanic abuse. There

were no rituals as such, but there were countless indications of allegiance to the Devil and the dark arts. The authorities and many academics state that such things don't exist and are simply down to the misguided perception of the child victim. I am one such victim and I know how wrong these people are.

For what it's worth, I don't believe in God or organised religion; my only faith is that in my partner, two children, grandchildren, two dogs and Leeds United. Batman will always be there, along with John, Mam and all of her family.

Society is deliberately deceiving itself because it's too difficult to comprehend (or admit) that police officers, Freemasons, lawyers, political figures, senior officials in HM services, teachers and influential businesspeople could ever involve themselves in such vile and abhorrent activity. In writing this book, I simply want to spread the word that, no matter how much the Establishment or society in general dislikes or objects to cases like this being written about, the truth must be told if we are to help other children.

Epilogue

Having been devastated by the negative response from the Crown Prosecution Service, the decision that Jack wouldn't be charged or punished for his crimes, my trust and belief in the system and in mechanisms of support for victims of crime understandably collapsed. The police and the Government make all the right noises about asking victims of historical child sex abuse to come forward, yet, from my own experience, when I was strong enough to speak out I was given only lip service and altogether abandoned from the moment I reported the abuse. I can still recall the day in October 2011 when Cumbria Police advised me that Jack wouldn't be prosecuted. In a fit of angst-filled emotion, I told the investigating officer that I would find Jack and kill him. For this outburst, I was threatened with arrest and prosecution and told to leave well alone. He was old and most unwell, I was told, ready to die even, and anything I said against him would be taken seriously by the police.

It wasn't easy coming forward and revealing my childhood trauma to complete strangers. However, I felt sure the system would be there to support and help me. I was wrong. With the decision of the Crown Prosecution Service confirmed, no official body contacted me again;

no one offered any form of post-investigation support. To the system, I was nothing but a statistic. This is something that any victim of such a crime should think about before reporting it: the authorities may make promises that they don't deliver on. From everything I know and endured, support is for the victim to find and not for the investigating bodies to provide. It's such a dreadful and dirty crime that no one knows how to deal with it and the so-called professional support services don't base their efforts on general experience but on academic research. Ultimately, it boils down to money and how much public funding they receive. In England, the support infrastructure for victims is extremely poor. The Samaritans are the sole body I could recommend, as they will direct victims to the best local service provider.

It is with some pain that I admit that shortly after I received the news from the Crown Prosecution Service my life all but fell apart. Relationships with my nearest and dearest were tested to the very limit as my mood altered like the changing wind. I could sense that I was in a state of mental exhaustion and collapse. I couldn't think about anything in a rational manner. I constantly felt embarrassed, humiliated and, worst of all, guilty about what had happened to me as a child. I wished I had never reported it, and that was wholly the system's fault. It felt like nobody believed me. Realising my failing state, I did what came so naturally to me as a child when locked in the cupboard under the stairs: I retreated into my shell, enveloped my very being in a cocoon that felt safe for me and blocked the outside world from access.

I contemplated ending my life and in doing so ridding myself of the guilt and pain I felt and putting a stop to the daily hurt I was clearly causing to others by being so weak. Every fibre of my being, my self-worth, my pride had been destroyed, principally by Jack. But now the system I had put my faith in had left me feeling worthless and alone. My life was in tatters. The guilt and shame of being abused as a child somehow felt worse than it had at any other point in my adult life. Being dumped by the Crown Prosecution Service in favour of Jack and his health issues made me feel like I was being further punished for sins that were not mine. I found myself calling the Samaritans and telling them what had happened and how I felt. They listened; they never judged. They would never be able to understand, yet they always did their best to try to help and guide me. They are good, reliable people who I would trust well beyond any other service.

I now know and understand how alarming the almost vegetative state I withdrew into was for those closest to me. They too suffered as a result of Jack and the system. I felt suffocated by life itself. It was as though I was drowning in my own pit of depravity and pain. No matter how hard I tried, I couldn't extract myself from the doom and gloom of my life. Nothing about it seemed good or decent. One of the legacies of childhood sexual abuse is that one always feels tainted, guilty and dirty. The burden abuse adds to a life damaged by it never dissipates or decreases; all that can happen is that the memories are better managed.

It was while I was out walking along a beach that I realised I had again hit the bottom of the well of despair. I was alone with my dogs and saw them revelling in the sea and sand, chasing sticks and a ball. They were full of life and unconditional love and affection for me. They relied on me to be there for them; I was responsible for them. I then thought of those closest to me, my own children and immediate family. I had a responsibility to them too. It was an epiphany. I wished the important ones were there with me right then, so I could hug them and tell them that everything would be OK. In that moment, I knew I had taken the first steps to recovery, if recovery from such trauma is ever possible. Each day is a challenge. The memories don't ever go away. I just think about better, more important things. It's not only about surviving, it is about achieving things, small steps that slowly make a positive difference, not only to my life but to the lives of those around me. In my own mind, I know I did the right thing in reporting Jack. Everything I said was accurate and true. It was the system that failed me. It is the system that is flawed because the system was created by humans, and humans have emotions and feelings and desires.

Perverts and abusers exist in all areas of society. They are in all kinds of occupations and at all levels of power and authority. Most haven't been and won't be caught because they have created a safety net around them, and, as can be seen in my own case, when exposed they won't be brought to justice.

With public and media attention recently focused on the vile crimes allegedly committed by the late Jimmy Savile and others, historical child sex abuse is being publicly recognised and discussed to a greater extent – not that it makes it any easier to deal with or understand. However, there is talk that positive steps will be taken and real support to help victims developed. Politicians have seized upon the issue as an opportunity to win votes, and they spout propaganda about how such matters are to be dealt with and the need for transparency and openness in the investigations being carried out as part of Operation Yewtree. I doubt very much whether such transparency will occur. The system will tell the public what it needs them to know and no more. I also feel sure that a few individuals will be made scapegoats as part of the Yewtree investigations. It takes the pressure off other issues if some individuals are publicly maligned and punished for their illicit and seedy acts with innocent children.

The media coverage of the alleged crimes of Jimmy Savile and others makes for harrowing reading. Many people will deliberately ignore such news stories because they don't want to know about them or believe them.

The authorities must take a stand and make the reporting of such crimes much easier and less traumatic. Victims suffer not only the trauma of the past but also the trauma of speaking to other people about it – police officers, social workers or health officials who are sceptical and self-centred and don't know how to deal with such matters. For a start, victims should be listened to, and care and support should be based on individual cases, not on academic reports and surveys. The mechanisms of support must improve throughout, from reporting to post-investigation matters.

In my case, the health service provided an inappropriate counsellor, who was dismissed for unprofessional conduct and who had most serious allegations of a sexual nature made against him by victims of child sexual abuse! He was quietly dismissed and suffered no prosecution because the support system would be viewed as flawed if such a matter ever became public and got to court. Meanwhile, those he was counselling, such as myself, were left in the dark about how and why this situation could have happened, why vulnerable people who felt exposed were allowed to be alone with him in a private room for over an hour at a time when the system knew about and had already received complaints about his predilections.

With the support of my family, many letters were penned to various organisations who could make a positive difference to the lives of victims, explaining the reality of proper support. The police, the NHS, local authorities, the Government were all contacted. Not one reply has ever been received, this despite there being named individual recipients of the letters. I now realise that not one of these public bodies actually wants to know or listen; it is only when such an organisation's own reputation is threatened that it will react – solely to protect itself.

On Saturday, 15 December 2012, I was at home when a woman I had never seen before presented herself at the front door. She asked for me, I introduced myself and she told me that she was a locum doctor. I invited her inside. There, she told me the news that for 48 long years I had waited to hear: 'Your father has passed away.'

I didn't know how to feel. The ecstatic euphoria I expected to flow through my body never came. Immediately, I went into denial, believing it to be another of Jack's deceitful acts.

I looked at the woman and asked her outright, 'Are you saying the bogeyman is dead?'

'Yes. I am aware of your past and I'm certain he is,' she replied.

The doctor went on to tell me that I was the only next of kin, that he had died earlier that morning in the Cumberland Infirmary, Carlisle, and that I was to call them soon. She had been sent by the police, who had located me as a result of the crimes I had reported against Jack. They had asked her to break the news to me. There followed a catalogue of emotions. I was happy and relieved, yet angry that he had escaped justice and made me suffer further. I rang the hospital out of curiosity. I so wanted him to have suffered. I was given no detail that confirmed to me that it was my lifelong tormentor who was laid in their mortuary.

Then, out of the blue, I was contacted by the manager of the sheltered housing where he had spent his last years. She confirmed to me that I was the next of kin, that there was a will and that I was named as executor and sole beneficiary (of what turned out to be his debts). I asked how she knew this and she went on to tell me: 'Jack was like a father to me. I really was close to him. He used to buy me gifts and presents. I even knew the PIN number on his bank account, he trusted me so much. I was the only one in his life, really. As I say, he was just like a father. I know he could at times be really nasty, terrible in what he said and what he did, inappropriate and crude, but I think I understood him better than anyone else. He drank a lot, but that was to help him forget, he said. I think he had lots of pain in his life, bless him. He loved children. He was always buying them things when they came to see him. In his last years, he was a recluse in his flat. As his next of kin, you'll have to clear it out. There's not a lot, but what there is was personal to him and meant a lot.'

I was disappointed by her insensitivity, but withheld my thoughts and opinions from her other than to remind her that he had never acted like a father to his own children and that none of us had wanted anything else from him, just that he be a real father, and he couldn't ever do it. Her response sent a chill coursing through my veins: 'Yes, but he didn't like little boys at all, or men come to that. He loved girls and women. He was really good with them. He's happy and in heaven with his beloved Mary now, so hopefully he can rest in peace.'

Thankfully, he had a funeral plan in place, so I didn't have to make the arrangements. He wanted cremation; I was pleased about that. Flippantly, I asked the undertaker if his ashes could be dumped in a skip. I received a resounding no to that request. Some associated matters were not so straightforward. For instance, the hospital didn't have the death certificate signed for 16 days, meaning that the coroner was involved and I couldn't register his death in Carlisle, which was some 500 miles from my home. This in turn meant that no funeral could take place and he was held (almost forgotten about by all) in the Cumberland Infirmary mortuary over Christmas and New Year. Eventually, with the kind assistance of the senior registrar in Carlisle, matters were resolved. Jack's death remains uncertified. However, with special dispensation, the funeral arrangements were allowed to go ahead. By the time this happened, Jack had been dead almost a month. Although I despised him for what he had done to me, I find this fact of great concern: that the system can fail a human being in death as well as in life.

A huge part of me still didn't believe he was dead. I needed conclusive proof in my own mind that it was him, and the only way that could be achieved was by my physically viewing the remains. That in itself caused many personal issues for me. I didn't know how I would react to seeing him dead, or what I might say. I spent several sleepless nights weighing up all I wanted to say to his corpse. Part of me wanted to tell him how much I despised him for what he had done to me and our family. Yet when it came down to it, I was respectful. I simply bent over him and quietly whispered, 'Jack, you are the bogeyman, but you can't hurt me or anyone else any more. I guess that means I win. I truly hope you are happier in death than you were in life.' It was difficult seeing the man who had given me life and then destroyed it laid out looking so weak before me. I felt mostly indifference, although a tinge of sadness existed deep within the lower reaches of my heart.

My son and daughter were with me in Carlisle, which is a depressing and grey city. They helped me clear the flat where Jack spent his last years. The stench of whisky and stale cigarettes was everywhere. The windows evidently hadn't been opened for a long long time, and the once white walls and ceiling were now yellow and brown, stained by nicotine. I felt some consolation that the place where he lived was like purgatory. It was a tiny, squalid flat located on one of Carlisle's most illustrious council housing estates. A place once regarded as a police no-go area, it clearly still had social issues, as drug abusers sat in a nearby park and needles were scattered in abundance on the streets outside the flats, streets where young children played. How he must have detested being among the kind of people he so loathed as a policeman.

The views from his windows were non-existent. Just a few feet away were the rear gardens and backs of council houses. Abandoned washing machines and fireplaces stood where, many decades past, flowers and manicured grass were to be found. My son looked at the view and offered some words of wisdom: 'To be fair, it looks as though they [the local council] have tried to spruce up the estate, but you can't polish a turd, Dad, can you?' We laughed. Any view from the kitchen window was obstructed by the presence of a large, industrial-looking CCTV camera that was attached to an outer wall. How ironic, given Jack's passion for cameras and photography, that this monstrosity should sit there blocking out the daylight.

It was a dreadful place for anyone to spend their last years, yet I found some satisfaction in this fact. In hindsight, he had suffered. Spending all those years cooped up in a place like that must have been the equivalent of a living hell to him. No wonder he allowed relatively few people access into that seedy, filthy place. We found bedbugs and lice on his bedding and mouldy food in his cupboards. He had daily carers, apparently, though they could only loosely be termed as such, I think.

In his flat there was not one photograph to be found of

my brothers and me. I believe that our images would have served as a painful reminder of his crimes and that he had chosen to obliterate us from his memory. On display there were several of my mother in her youth and some of their pet dog, Roy. More mysterious were other photographs of children I did not know or recognise. I also found letters from young children who weren't relatives. I confess that the implications of young children writing to him deeply concern me. However, that is a matter for the authorities, who should have investigated his crimes thoroughly while he was alive.

Three days later, after unsuccessfully trying to trace other relatives in the city, I had Jack cremated at Carlisle Crematorium. Just four people were in attendance: me, my two children and the manager of the sheltered housing. Such a waste of a life. He had spent his entire life in the city of Carlisle, yet he had not one friend or person who cared sufficiently about him to attend his cremation. I ensured that the lives of my deceased sister and two long since passed away brothers and mother were remembered during the brief service. As the curtains closed on Jack's coffin, a collective sigh of relief could be heard from the family members. We stood clasping one another's hands and held our heads high as we walked out of the chapel. Outside, my son turned to me and said, 'Dad, the bogeyman is dead. That means you are the head of the family. That's some responsibility. I love you, Dad.'

The three of us had a group hug and reaffirmed our care and love for each other as I vowed never to let another human being hurt or bring harm to the family again. Above everything else, the one thing I have learned from my life and from the catastrophic episode since I reported my abuse to the authorities is that family love is to be cherished. Without my own immediate family (particularly my brother John, as my childhood protector),

The Cupboard Under the Stairs

I could never have survived and would not be here to tell my story. It is my desire to make sure that I am always there for them. They have my unconditional love and care for always.

The bogeyman is dead!

Paul Mason
April 2013